THE DUNLOP STORY

THE DUNLOP STORY

The life, death and re-birth of a multi-national

JAMES McMILLAN

Weidenfeld and Nicolson
London

Published in Great Britain by
George Weidenfeld & Nicolson Limited
91 Clapham High Street
London SW4 7TA

ISBN 0 297 79429 9

Printed in Great Britain by
The Bath Press
Avon

CONTENTS

ACKNOWLEDGMENTS

I am immensely grateful to a host of people who have given of their time and knowledge to make this book possible. As is to be expected they are, in the main, former executives or employees of the Dunlop organization. It would be impractical to mention all their names but I am particularly indebted to the following: Sir J. Campbell Fraser, Sir Reay Geddes, Sir Maurice Hodgson, Sir Michael Edwardes, Sir Maurice Coop, Messrs David Beharrell, Tony Bullfield, David Clutterbuck, David Collett, Peter Darvall, (Dr) Keith Grieves, Alan Lord, John McLean (of Dunlop Pacific), Roy Marsh, Findlay Picken, Eric Root, Peter Rossiter, Brian Rudd, John D. Simon and Dane Sinclair. I am also particularly grateful to Sir Owen Green (chairman of BTR), Mr Kyohei Yokose (chairman of Sumitomo Rubber) and Dr Leopoldo Pirelli (President of Pirelli).

Unless specifically quoted, I alone am responsible for any opinions put forward.

James McMillan

ILLUSTRATION ACKNOWLEDGMENTS

The illustrations can only represent a series of snapshots of Dunlop through the years, but this function I hope they perform.

They have been culled from a wide variety of sources and unless otherwise attributed they are credited to Dunlop Archives/Darvall. Grateful thanks are specially due to Tom Grover and Brian Ashmore, Dunlop's own photographers; Ron Salt of SP Tyres; Bob Haines of Slazengers, and to Stephen Harrison of BTR, and also to many others.

Peter Darvall

CHAPTER I

IN THE BEGINNING...

Numerous substitutes can be suggested for the automobile, but none for the pneumatic tyre.

Maurice Olley, design engineer of General Motors,
the world's largest car manufacturer

When John Boyd Dunlop, a Scottish-born veterinary surgeon invented (or, strictly speaking, re-invented) the pneumatic tyre in Belfast in February 1888 he had no such grand ideas in his mind. He simply wanted to make cycling more comfortable for his ten-year-old son Johnnie.

The streets of Belfast, like those in most British and Irish cities, were laid with granite setts, causeway or cobble stones, and crisscrossed with tramlines. Equipped with solid tyres, cycles were an extremely uncomfortable means of travel, shaking and jarring the unfortunate cyclist.

There is no evidence that Johnnie Dunlop was a particularly delicate boy, but as his father was obsessed with health ('I have always been handicapped by an extremely delicate constitution,' he averred in 1892) he may well have imagined his offspring was similarly afflicted, a belief on which any sensible child would capitalize.

So it proved. Little Johnnie must be cushioned against the harsh realities of Belfast streets, in so far as it was in his parent's powers. And these powers were formidable.

John Boyd Dunlop may have been a hypochondriac (he lived to the ripe old age of eighty-one), but he was also a man of many talents and quick perceptions. 'Cushioning Johnnie' is precisely what he did. As he recorded, 'it dawned on me that the problem [of freeing Johnnie

1

from a sore bottom] might be solved by means of a triple tube of rubber, canvas and rubber distended with compressed air.'

Thus was the problem solved. Thus was an industry born. And the names pneumatic and Dunlop entered into the commercial lore and language of the world.

Briefly, what John Boyd Dunlop did was, in the words of his patent specification of 31 October 1888, to

> employ a hollow tube tyre of india-rubber surrounded with cloth, canvas or other suitable material adapted to withstand the pressure of air introduced and contained within the tube tyre. The canvas or cloth being covered with rubber to protect it from wear on the road. Said hollow tube tyres secured to the wheel felloes – say by a suitable cement or by other efficient means – and is inflated with air or gas under pressure, being introduced to the interior of the hollow tube tyre through a small duct formed in the rim of the wheel and provided with a non-return valve.

Nothing so complicated was used to try out the first pneumatic tricycle tyre wheel, which John Boyd bowled along in the Dunlop backyard to test its springiness. It worked. It had the resilience of a rubber ball compared with the deadly solidity of the old-style tyre.

There are many descriptions of a pneumatic tyre :

> In essence, $2\frac{1}{2}$ ounces of a compressible, deformable material, in the form of air, contained within a rubberised, flexible envelope. The combination of these two parts, and their individual characteristics working separately or in unison, enable the pneumatic tyre to perform the functions expected of it by a vehicle.[1]

Or :

> a hollow tube inflated with air under pressure attached to the periphery of a wheel so as to present a cushion of air to the ground . . . the canvas pocket containing the rubber tube protected from wet by outer rubber strips, thickened on the running surface, the whole forming a 'D' section tyre with the rim to which it was taped and stuck by rubber solution with the aid of flaps formed for the purpose of the inner canvas jacket. A simple non-return valve for inflation (but not deflation) and swathing the tyre onto the rim.[2]

The first description is of a modern tyre ; the second of J.B.Dunlop's rough-and-ready model for Johnnie, a pioneer of cycle technology, but *not* the first pneumatic tyre in the world.

Credit for that goes to another Scotsman. Robert William Thomson,

2

born at Stonehouse, Kincardineshire, in 1822, patented the first pneumatic tyre (No. 10,980) in June 1846.

Scotland's contribution to wheeled travel is quite extraordinary, for another Scot, Kirkpatrick Macmillan of Courthill, Dumfriesshire, invented the bicycle in 1839 and yet another Scot, Thomas MacAdam from Ayr, perfected the road surfaces (macadamized) that made cycling possible.

Unfortunately for Thomson, cycling was in its infancy when he brought out his pneumatic tyre, or 'aerial wheel' as it was called, in 1846, and so the invention was confined to horse-drawn vehicles (though he recommended them for steam-driven ones and even for railway carriages).

Thomson's specification naturally bore a close resemblance to Dunlop's. It proposed

> employing a hollow belt composed of some air and watertight material, such as caoutchouc [from the American Indian word for weeping wood] or guttapercha, and inflating it with air, whereby the wheels in every part of their revolution present a cushion of air to the ground or trail or track on which they run. The belt may be made of a single thickness of india rubber or guttapercha in a sheet state and then enclosed in a canvas cover....

When Thomson produced his practical idea, the process of vulcanizing rubber – hardening by sulphur the sticky substance which is tapped from trees – was a mere seven years old. A rubber industry in a true, structured form did not exist.

Until 1876 the rubber tree was indigenous to Brazil, and the crude rubber that was extracted was often of abysmal quality and uncertain supply. In that year Sir Henry Wickham – an Englishman this time! – secretly conveyed 70,000 seeds of the *Hevea* rubber tree from Brazil to Kew Gardens where many of the seeds germinated. Then they were despatched to the natural humidity of Ceylon and Malaya, thereby founding the rich rubber industries of these British Colonies – which fact tends to puncture the claim, made by some Malaysian politicians, that the British 'exploited the natural rubber of Malaya'.

Anyway, in 1846 cycling was in its infancy, as was vulcanized rubber. So Thomson faced formidable obstacles. Even so, his invention was successfully tested in Regent's Park. The *Mechanics Magazine* of 1849 reported that when Thomson's 'aerial wheels' were employed on a horse-drawn brougham, there was a 38 per cent reduction on the pull required on macadamized surfaces and 68 per cent reduction on broken flints.

3

Moreover Thomson envisaged a whole range of improvements, suggesting that the new tyre might be filled with 'various solid substances of an elastic quality ... horse-hair or sponge. If the elastic part were first stuffed with horse-hair or sponge and then inflated by blowing in air to a high degree of tension, the belt would be less likely to be cut by concussion between the tyre of the wheel and the roadway.' Thomson thus foretold, by some 120 years, a process developed in the USA in the 1960s. He sought to diminish the effects of punctures by having multiple tubes inside the tyre run at differential pressures, fixing the tubes sausage-fashion to restrict damage from puncture.

He saw his invention as having almost limitless possibilities – for example, bringing ease and comfort to bath-chair users. Yet the young engineer, still only in his twenties at the time of the Regent's Park experiment, could interest no one of consequence. He went abroad to work, returned to Edinburgh in 1862 and died, aged fifty-one, in 1873, fifteen years before John Boyd Dunlop re-invented the pneumatic tyre.

Inevitably the question arises: why did Dunlop not know about Robert William Thomson's patent?

There is no evidence that he employed chartered patent agents to conduct a search and no easy way, in those pre-computer days, for a cross-checking system to reveal the existence of the Thomson patent.

Dunlop was penitent when the fact of the Thomson aerial wheel was revealed to him in September 1890, via Mr Redfern, London patent agent. He admitted that 'doubtless very many engineers and scientists in England must have been aware of Thomson's invention and through the articles [in the *Mechanics Magazine*] thousands must have known of it, but I never heard of it until 1890 and consequently have not been influenced by it.' He wrote, 'it is doubtful if my first patent is valid.'[3]

Almost certainly Dunlop was ignorant of the existence of the Thomson tyre. He was a veterinary surgeon, well off enough not to need to concern himself with additional sources of revenue. He was not a big spender; not obsessed with money.

Sheer chance must be the verdict on the similarities between the Thomson and Dunlop patent specifications. In contrast to Thomson's fate, sheer good fortune attended the Dunlop venture.

Cycling and Dunlop went together like bacon and eggs. His tyre appeared at the precise moment when cycling was enjoying unexampled popularity, as urban populations sought the beauty of the countryside on a mode of travel that was well within the reach of young artisans.

Music halls resounded to the chorus of 'Daisy, Daisy . . .'

> It won't by a stylish marriage
> For I can't afford a carriage,
> But you'll look sweet
> Upon the seat
> Of a bicycle made for two.

Cycling clubs covered the land – covered Western Europe, for that matter. Junior members of Mr Gladstone's administration such as Charles Hobhouse, thought nothing of cycling fifty miles or more in a day. 'Biked [from London] to Wells.' 'Bicycled from Abergavenny to Caerleon and from Patchway to Westbury-on-Trym.' His editor remarks that these extended cycling tours 'appear quite remarkable by the sedentary standards of the second half of the 20th Century.' But quite appropriate to another sample of later Victorian energy, described in this entry: 'Went to Studley Royal [Lord Ripon's house] for grouse shooting. Lord Granby, De Grey, C.V.Harcourt, F.St.Quintin and self shot 1,194 grouse and 750 next day. The best two days they have yet recorded.'[4]

Bicycling crossed the class barriers and the sex barriers. H.G.Wells's 'New Woman', exemplified by Ann Veronica, was a keen cyclist. So was a daring young Dublin lady of the early 1890s who astonished the city by appearing on the street riding a man's bicycle and wearing a man's clothes to match. Her name is unrecorded, but she could well have been a Fabian socialist by persuasion, for in some quarters cycling was looked upon much as 'demos' were in the 1960s. It was the 'advanced' thing to do.

Not that cycling was an innovation of the 1880s. It simply soared to its popularity peak then and maintained that position until the Great War and Mr Henry Ford replaced leg power with mechanical horse power.

Kirkpatrick Macmillan pioneered the pedal-drive bike, although the 'Dandy Horse', as its precursor was called, had a pedigree going back to the eighteenth century. According to the *English Mechanic* of 1868:

> The Dandy Horse was propelled by the feet upon the ground and, after a good speed had been obtained, the feet were temporarily rested upon a small projection at each end of the front axle until the horse required further propulsion. Fox, Sheridan, Pitt and other notabilities of the period, patronised the Velocipede in St James's Park, taking their constitutional daily on the Dandy Horse, after a hard night spent in the House of Commons or around the gaming tables.

Nearly a century spans the aristocratic jogging of the Dandy Horse

5

to the safety bicycle of the Dunlop era. One of the most bizarre developments was the penny-farthing which reached a peak, literally, of 8ft in 1875 and weighed in at over 80lbs.

Ten years later the average safety bicycle had appeared with equal-sized wheels, ball bearings, diamond frame and an all-up weight of less than 20lbs.

By 1889 Dunlop had established a tiny organization for manufacturing bicycles equipped with his tyres. They were produced by a cycle shop owned by Mr Edlin, and he was assisted by Mr Sinclair, who received verbal instructions to make twelve bicycles and six tricycles a year, later extended to fifty bicycles and twelve tricycles.

Cycle racing in the 1880s was near the top of the popular entertainments, and it was through cycle racing that Dunlop's pneumatic tyre was brought to the attention of the public and John Boyd Dunlop brought into contact with the real creators of the Dunlop Rubber Company : the du Cros family of Dublin.

Two of the du Cros brothers – there were six in all – raced against a Willie Hume of Belfast in May 1889. Mr Hume, a modest rider, chose to use Dunlop tyres. His opponents, including the du Cros boys, stuck with the solid tyres.

The appearance of the balloon-like pneumatic tyres produced roars of derision from the spectators. But the jeers turned to cheers when Hume whizzed past the pack to take the winner's trophy.

It would be nice to say that there and then the pneumatic tyre came into its own. It would be nice – but wrong.

Arthur du Cros (of whom a great deal later) avenged his brothers' defeat by beating Hume, once more mounted on a set of pneumatic tyres, although du Cros was on the solid variety. Clearly young Arthur, aged eighteen, was a far better performer than his brothers. When he, and those with similar talent, were persuaded to adopt the pneumatic tyre, success then, and only then, was assured.

Victory in Ireland did not, however, ensure acceptance in England. Arthur du Cros described the hilarity with which Londoners greeted him when he rode his pneumatic-tyred bicycle for the first time in the streets of the capital :

Omnibus and hansom drivers, making the most of a heaven-sent opportunity, had the time of their lives ; messenger boys guffawed at the sausage tyres, factory ladies simply squirmed with merriment, while even sober citizens were sadly moved to mirth of a comicality which was obviously designed solely to lighten the gloom of their daily routine. There are many forgotten heroes in history, not the least of whom was the man who wore the first silk hat. His name and that of the first stalwart who carried an umbrella should be commemorated with my own for we all deserve immortality.[5]

Immortality is what Arthur wanted for himself, his father and his brothers. When it came to family pride and personal conceit, Arthur would brook no master. It informs all his writings, reminiscences, diary entries and his book *Wheels of Fortune*.

The meeting between Arthur's father William Harvey du Cros and John Boyd Dunlop marked the start of one of the most outstanding partnerships in the history of transport.

William Harvey du Cros was forty-three when he met Dunlop in 1889. Unlike the big, shambling, black-bearded inventor, du Cros was a small (5ft 5in.) dapper man with aquiline features and a splendid twirly moustache about eight inches from end to end which more than made up for his receding hair-line. He was a bundle of energy, a devoted family man, a gregarious fellow (assistant secretary of the Irish Commerical Travellers Association) and a considerable wheeler-dealer.

Harvey du Cros was also combative, perhaps by nature, certainly by upbringing. Child of a broken home, he was educated at the Blue-coat School, Dublin, and struck out on his own at fifteen. Even at school he had to fight. As the son of 'decayed gentlefolk' his social status, which was easily recognizable from the obligatory long blue coat he was required to wear, was constantly being questioned and he himself attacked. The assailants were particularly venomous because the Bluecoats were Protestants and their street attackers were Catholic.

Decayed gentlefolk the du Cros' may have been, but they still belonged to the Protestant ascendancy which had dominated Ireland from the days of Queen Elizabeth I.

The du Cros', as the name implies, were French Huguenots. Captain Jean Pierre du Cros fled to Britain to escape religious persecution, finding his way to Dublin at about the same time as Catholic refugees were fleeing from Ireland to France to avoid persecution at the hands of the vengeful partisans of England's Protestant champion, William of Orange.

Jean Pierre served in the wars of William and later Anne, under the Duke of Marlborough. One of his descendants, William Harvey's grandfather, was initiated into the Royal Orange Association, thereby formalizing his acceptance into the Praetorian Guard of the Protestant ascendancy.

William Harvey was intensely proud of his Huguenot background, as was his son Arthur. They had every right to be; with the possible exception of the Jews no single immigrant group has done so much for their host country than the sober, intelligent, hard-working, civic-conscious Huguenots.

William Harvey was resolved to expand the breed and continue the tradition. He and his Scottish-born wife Annie Jane Roy, produced seven sons (one died in babyhood), who grew to strapping adulthood.

Harvey insisted that they strive for success in everything they did. He himself was a fitness fanatic, having been advised by his doctor to take up athletics. Well into his thirties, he won the all-Ireland fencing and middle-weight boxing championships and urged his sons to try to emulate his feats. He taught them to box and hit them hard if they could not bob or weave away from his fists. They became practised gymnasts, hard-playing rugby footballers, sailors, swimmers and finally cyclists.

Harvey bore a strong resemblance to another Irishman, Joe Kennedy, father of President Jack Kennedy, who demanded the same incessant will-to-win from his large brood.

The du Cros will-to-win, allied to superb physical fitness, came to be concentrated on the bicycle. Harvey took Arthur, aged thirteen, on a cycle ride from Dublin to Belfast and back. They covered 103 miles in a single day on solid tyres. Fourteen years later it took a motor car twice as long to cover the same journey.

Although William Harvey advanced to considerable business eminence – owning a paper-bag-making enterprise in Dublin – it was his position as President of the Irish Cyclists' Association which proved decisive in the establishment of the Pneumatic Tyre Company. As the Association commented : 'Had he not been a keen sportsman, he would never have seen, or, having seen, appreciated the potentialities of the pneumatic tyre.'

Harvey du Cros made it clear to Dunlop's Dublin agent, William Bowden, that he, Harvey, would come into association with Dunlop, Bowden and a newspaper-owner J.M.Gillies on one condition only : that he, du Cros, would assume complete control, appoint the directors, write the prospectus and take the stock issue to the public.

Which is just what he did, and on 18 November 1889 the Dunlop Rubber Company was born.

CHAPTER II

FLAIR AND FORTUNE

It was not called that at first. Its title was the 'Pneumatic Tyre and Booth's Cycle Agency' of 65 Upper Stephen Street, Dublin. (Later this became the 'Pneumatic Tyre Company', then the 'Dunlop Pneumatic Tyre Company' and eventually, by 1900, the 'Dunlop Rubber Company'.) The 'agency' represented various leading makes of English cycles in Ireland and could provide a fall-back position if the pneumatic tyre failed to take off.

Dunlop himself was gloomy at the prospect of any lasting success for his invention. Letters he wrote at the time make it clear that he thought the tyre had only very limited application. Even on cycles it was advertised simply for its ease of propulsion and as 'indispensable for ladies and persons of delicate nerves', rather than for speed and reliability. Anti-vibration and ease of propulsion were its principal claims. Certainly John Boyd Dunlop didn't imagine he was going to make his fortune out of the thing.

Along with other men – Frederick Woods, Richard McCredy, J.M. Gillies and Richard Booth – Dunlop sat on the board under the direction of William Harvey du Cros.

The capital of the infant company was fixed at £25,000. But even the first tranche of £15,000 was not forthcoming from the canny folk of Dublin.

Didn't the tyre puncture easily? It did. Each time it suffered a puncture the casing had to be soaked apart with naphtha to reach the tube inside. After the repair the tube had to be replaced and the outer casing built up again with solution and refixed on the wheel. The operation was a small construction job in itself and a disaster area for those unblessed with do-it-yourself deftness.

When, a mere ten months after the company's foundation, the Thomson patent, pre-dating Dunlop's by some forty-three years, was

9

unveiled to the world, the bottom dropped out of the market. The firm was fortunate to have got off the ground at all. During its first ten months it held the world monopoly in pneumatic tyre production. In this euphoric period Harvey du Cros wrote: 'A cycle fitted with pneumatic tyres runs over rough surfaces with extreme ease. . . . This, taken in conjunction with the absence of nervous exhaustion [!] and the conservation of power will, it is believed, place the pneumatic-tyred machine beyond the reach of competition.'

With the disclosure of the Thomson patent it was made obvious that anyone could manufacture a pneumatic tyre without a yea or nay from Dunlop. As was proved when the French refused to accept Dunlop's patent as valid.

Yet the tiny Dublin enterprise still had much going for it. The intrepid du Cros youngsters were winning cycle races on the Dunlop tyre all over the place, culminating in the world cycling speed record.

Dunlop was in the business of making and selling pneumatic tyres and no one else was.

What was needed now was to make the tyre commercially attractive: to modify the construction of the tyre and wheel so that they were independent parts of the whole, so that tyres could be sold over the counter and could be fitted by owners with but a modicum of engineering skill.

Enter another little genius, this time from Tottenham: Charles Kingston Welch. According to Sir Arthur du Cros, Welch was the 'father' of the detachable tyre which revolutionized the transport industry. Welch, twenty-nine in 1890, was smaller than Harvey du Cros: a mere 5ft of chubby, smiling, good-tempered humanity. His wife was tinier still, and du Cros claims that the well-known lines of 'Daisy, Daisy', already quoted, referred to them, except that the last line of the chorus ought to have been rendered, 'of a *tricycle* made for two', Welch having actually designed and built a tandem tricycle for his wife and himself.

Working in his father's small engineering plant, Kingston Welch in two or three days produced the perfect detachable wheel.

The process is best described by Eric Tompkins:

Welch began with the notion of putting wires into the edges of a horse-shoe-shaped tyre and seating these inextensible edges of a rim with ledges or seats for them to locate upon. The first idea was a wire with its two ends joined by a screw-connector which could be undone for fitting and then reconnected when the tyre was in position on the rim. This was soon discarded in favour of a continuous circle of wire together with a pin with a 'well' in the centre of its section. The 'mummy' (layers of rubbered sailcloth) was replaced with a simple separate cover and tube and they were fitted to a similarly simple one-piece rim. The process of fitting the mixed-edge cover to the well-based rim consisted of merely pushing part of the cover edge over the rim flange and then working the rest of the edge over the rim flange. This process was reversed, with the help of small levers, when the cover came to be removed.[1]

The invention was patented on 16 September 1890 – just five days after Dunlop had heard about the Thomson patent. Straightaway the rights to the Welch patent were bought up by the Pneumatic Tyre Co. for £5,000. Welch himself joined the firm as technical adviser and the wired-edged cycle tyres were sold under the Dunlop-Welch trademark.

At almost the same moment, an American inventor living in Edinburgh, William Erskine Bartlett, aged sixty, developed another, perfectly practicable, means of detaching a pneumatic tyre. As Bartlett was managing director of the US-owned North British Rubber Company, this was a distinct threat to the Dunlop-du Cros organization. Du Cros met it with characteristic aplomb. He bought the *English* rights for £200,000, the inventor retaining the right to manufacture tyres in *Scotland*, paying a royalty of 2s 6d (12½p) per tyre to the Pneumatic Tyre Co.

An interesting sidelight to this episode is its connection with Charles Goodyear, the American whose discovery – but not sole discovery – of the process of vulcanizing rubber (converting a useless sticky product into material of unbelievable hardihood) transformed the rubber trade. An Englishman, Thomas Hancock, had been working on the same process in the 1840s and Hancock anticipated Goodyear in lodging a patent. The Americans discovered that Hancock had omitted to take out the necessary patent registration in Scotland, so they established a plant in Edinburgh in 1855 for manufacturing rubber products (principally over-shoes). And why 'North British'? Because in the nineteenth century it was fashionable to refer to Scotland as 'North Britain', partly as a way of distancing the country from the unfortunate Stuart rebellion of 1745 and partly for commercial purposes: encouraging English tourists, for one thing. Two of the most impressive hotels in Glasgow and Edinburgh were titled 'North British'.

With Welch and Bartlett under its belt, the Pneumatic Tyre Co. completed the treble by purchasing the rights to a valve invented by Charles Wood, brother of one of the company's directors.

John Boyd Dunlop's valve was an advance on its predecessors but it suffered from one overwhelming fault : it could not be used to deflate the tyre. Wood's valve – an ingenious device, which combined one-way air suction for inflation with a simple plug removed for deflation – solved the problem.

Favoured by extraordinary good fortune (Welch, for instance, initially approached another rubber manufacturer who turned him down) and borne forward by swift, superb commercial judgement (Harvey du Cros signed up Welch in five minutes flat), the Pneumatic Tyre Co. climbed out of the Slough of Despond on to the Highway of Prosperity – as the Victorians might have put it.

Not that there weren't plenty of pot-holes on the way. There were scores of actions to be defended in the courts on allegations of patent infringements. The Pneumatic Tyre Co. won them all.

John Boyd Dunlop told the board that he had been offered £5,000 for the use of his name by an English firm. Straightaway the company's name was altered to the Dunlop Pneumatic Tyre Co. Ltd.

But now the minutes, which had been concerned with such mundane matters as 'resolved by the Board that a typewriter be procured and the services of a stenographer engaged', started to reflect graver issues.

One such, dated November 1894, recorded that Dunlop was aggrieved that other inventions he had in mind were not being tested. His ruffled feathers were smoothed on that occasion and he was assured by his fellow board members – minute of December 1894 – that he was free to order whatever materials he chose to continue his experiments.

Yet three months later he resigned. It has never been adequately explained why he quit; least of all by Dunlop himself. He was deeply hurt that the French had rejected his patent claim, doing so in language that was intended to bruise : 'Your patent never had the smallest claim to novelty ... under the circumstances [of the Thomson invention forty years previously] your patent is null and void.' Perhaps he wanted nothing more to do with the harsh world of business.

Arthur du Cros advanced another possible reason for Dunlop's resignation – his jealousy of Charles Welch, whose detachable discovery had rendered the Dunlop tyre commercially successful and invulnerable to litigation. Indeed du Cros went further and said that John Boyd Dunlop was excessively fortunate in having his name given worldwide prominence when he really didn't deserve any such accolade. 'Thomson had the patent and no business, while Dunlop had the business and no patent.'

But *did* Dunlop have much of the business or was he, like so many inventors before him, robbed of the fruits of his work by less creative and more acquisitive souls ?

Well, Dunlop received £500 and 3,000 shares for his patent. Initially they went to a discount but recovered when the Welch and other inventions rescued the tyre from patent oblivion. By 1896 the capital was valued at £1,400,000 on the Stock Exchange. Following a cash sale and re-capitalization Dunlop *could* have sold his 3,000 shares for £380,000 (multiply by about 30 for late twentieth century values) provided he had re-invested the dividends – which in its first six years paid 75 per cent per annum!

Dunlop had, however, generously donated half his holding to Gillies and Bowden for promoting the business side of his invention and so denied himself 50 per cent of his prospective reward. As it was, he ended up with £100,000 profit : no mean achievement considering that the Patent Act of 1902 would have rendered his patent claim in the UK totally invalid.

Not only did the Dunlop name survive and thrive ; so did the Dunlop features. His bearded face became the company's trademark. It proved highly profitable in certain markets, notably in Nigeria and other West African areas, where it was taken to be the features of Jesus Christ ; an endorsement which could not be surpassed.

John Boyd Dunlop took his leave of the company at the moment when it was about to become a power on the international stage.

As a first move, Harvey du Cros transferred the headquarters of the company's operations from Dublin to Coventry. The ostensible reason for this was the complaint by Dublin Corporation against the smell of naphtha and rubber and its threat to institute an action for unsocial conduct. Du Cros riposted that the smell of the River Liffey was more intolerable and took himself and his company off to the English Midlands.

He was, in truth, happy to be quit of the Irish capital. For while he loved its soft clime and easy ways, he found the Irishman's constant search for a grievance unbearable. He told a shareholder who assured him of a 'a hundred thousand welcomes' if he would hold the company's Annual General Meeting in Dublin : 'I have been promised that before and the 100,000 welcomes materialised in 100,000 abusive epithets ... if any meeting of this company is held in Dublin it will be without me.'

At any rate, the Dunlop Company had, by 1895, outgrown the provincialism of Dublin. It had established selling companies in France and Germany. It had begun manufacturing in Australia and North America. The restless drive and acquisitiveness of the du Cros family could only be satisfied by operating internationally from the home base of the biggest empire the world had ever seen.

Harvey and his son Arthur (the rest of the young brood were pushing business in the United States and Canada) applied themselves to expansion at home: first in Coventry and later in Birmingham, where in 1896 Arthur purchased Byrne Brothers' Rubber Manufacturing Mills. Dunlop was on its way.

Financially too the company was becoming too big for its capital. And now came the firm's first contact with that intuitive speculator of genius, Ernest Terah Hooley.

Mr Hooley was one of those Victorian entrepreneurs who provided the infant socialist movement with a useful ogre. Like the lilies of the field he neither toiled nor span, yet he accumulated a vast fortune. He was, in the words of *The Clarion*, 'a parasite grown huge on unearned largesse'. In short, he was a fixer, a wheeler-dealer.

In his long book *Wheels of Fortune* Sir Arthur du Cros makes a single brief reference to Ernest Terah Hooley. In Sir Arthur's privately published *Recollections*, Mr Hooley is again mentioned only once. Yet he bought Dunlop, in 1896!

Sir Arthur had a most selective memory and Hooley's stained reputation as a buccaneer, or money-mad ogre, put him in the best-say-naught-about-him category.

Yet Hooley was an essential lubricant in the capitalist system. Unscrupulous, he undoubtedly was; criminal he may have been – a century later and he would almost certainly have been prosecuted. But in the last quarter of the nineteenth century he fulfilled a role in the free market.

Born in 1859 in Derbyshire, son of a lace-mill owner, Hooley had become a half-millionaire by the age of twenty-five, largely through land speculation. He then turned his attention to company promotion, or share-pushing. He was the quintessential contact man, with a genius for public relations. In short order he reorganized and sold off twenty-six companies to a value of £30 million, including such nationally famous names as Raleigh Cycles, Bovril, Schweppes and, of course, Dunlop. When Boots the Chemist was in formation difficulties, Hooley came to its rescue with a large cash injection. In all some £100 million passed through his hands – and a great deal of it, in personal terms, stuck there.

He made, and spent, money with a passion worthy of a finer cause. When he couldn't make money any more he still spent it. As a result he died penniless in 1947 at the age of eighty-eight.

As a larger-than-life character Hooley deserved far greater recognition for the advancement of Dunlop than Sir Arthur du Cros accorded him. He didn't get it because he was not respectable, even though he furnished the du Cros family with a sizeable fortune.

14

So far as the Dunlop Company was concerned, Hooley moved in his traditional fashion : setting the financial world by the ears in organizing a syndicate of wealthy and greedy individuals and offering £3 million for the company.

On 2 April 1896 the directors of the Dunlop Company summoned a special meeting of shareholders to consider the offer ; nine days later they agreed to the purchase.

Hooley, of course, had no intention of keeping the company. He and his fellow speculators were intent on selling it and making as much on 'the turn' as possible. Which is exactly what they proceeded to do.

On 6 May the Dunlop Pneumatic Tyre Company Ltd was registered in London with a capital of £4 million plus a debenture issue of £1 million. The flotation was a success, netting the promoting syndicate – so it was reported – some £1.7 million.

Thus in seven years the Dunlop organization had grown from a capital of £25,000 (of which only £15,010 was subscribed in cash) to £5 million, yielding the original shareholders £3,545,623 12s. 3d. from the transaction.

For the flotation Hooley, again true to tradition, 'dressed' Dunlop with a fine crop of aristocrats. He openly admitted that he had a price tariff for prospective directors to inspire confidence in a company's prospectus. A duke collected £25,000, an earl received £15,000 and a simple baronet pocketed £5,000.

On the Dunlop board of directors in the prospectus of May 1896 were the Duke of Somerset, Earl de la Warr and the Earl of Albermarle. They were reaping the benefit of being born to the purple. Others who aspired to glory were, at this period, paying their chosen Party similar sums to be promoted to the peerage. The 'beerage', as the brewing chiefs were called, were the first to be enobled. Lord Salisbury set the pattern with a barony for Henry Allsop ; William Ewart Gladstone replied for the Liberals by creating the rival Burton brewer, Michael Bass, Lord Burton.

Thick and fast the honours came. Banking got a look in with a coronet for John Hubberd, governor of the Bank of England (still a private concern). Stout followed with a Guinness peerage. Textiles donned the ermine : Lord Cheylesmore for silk and Lord Masham for wool. Engineering advanced through Lord Armstrong and bookselling was acknowledged via Mr W.H.Smith. Between 1886 and 1914, 246 new titles were conferred, more than one quarter of them going to representatives of industry, the money providers and magnates in the new power structures.

Mr Hooley was simply 'playing the honours game'. A Mr Maundy Gregory thought he was too when, with the knowledge of honours short lists, he went around hawking peerages, baronetcies or knighthoods for £10,000 to £35,000. While Mr Hooley went on to fortune, Mr Maundy went to jail. That, however, was forty years later.

In the jolly nineties (the term actually was 'gay' but that later took on a wholly different connotation) the aristocracy was very happy to lend names to letter-heads in exchange for a considerable down-payment and £1,000 a year. It helped to make up for income lost during the agricultural depression.

One of the conditions of sale of Dunlop shares was that shareholders had the prior right of taking up shares in the new company. Harvey du Cros and Arthur du Cros became joint managing directors in the new enterprise.

The launch coincided with a tidal wave of development. Companies tumbled over themselves to get a share of the cycling boom and inventors hastened to offer them the improvements that would put their particular product ahead of the field.

Brisk little Harvey du Cros revelled in the competition. He became a master of patent law and successfully defended the Welch innovation. He campaigned vigorously to uphold his company's patents against infringement, especially in overseas markets (a pretty forlorn undertaking as the unconscionable time taken to reach a verdict in the courts – six years, frequently – rendered favourable judgement costly and futile), but his biggest achievement was to tie the best technical brains to Dunlop. He had already won Welch who, in the years between 1890 and 1894, added a cord casing section, a well-based rim and a non-skid principle to the triumph of his detachable tyre. He had the Wood valve and the Frederick Westwood tubular edges, and finally he embraced the American inventor, William Erskine Bartlett.

Bartlett, of Springfield, Mass., was only thirty-six days later than Welch in lodging his patent. This embodied the principle of the beaded edge tyre secured to the wheel by means of a hooked pin under which the edges of the cover were held and kept in place by air compression. As Fletcher Moulton, a noted patent lawyer of the day remarked, 'he made the pneumatic tube act as its own gaoler'.

Harvey du Cros finally won Bartlett's co-operation in a complicated deal which gave Dunlop the technical supremacy which was to be its hallmark for decade after decade.

It was as well that Harvey du Cros had such foresight, for in 1896 the company was short of cash, just as the capital re-organization demanded more resources and more and more firms competed in the market place.

To generate additional funds the company decided to realize some of its overseas interests. With this aim in view William Proctor of Melbourne, general manager for Australasia and Richard Garland of Toronto, general manager for Canada, were given the option of exercising a management buy-out through local capital. They did so and the concerns thrived.

Dunlop's US company was sold off in 1898. The reason for Dunlop's early – and, as it turned out, premature – expansion overseas was to overcome tariff protection of domestic markets and to secure a presence for the defence of patents.

The initial development of the pneumatic tyre was largely British, and wholly Anglo-Saxon. And there is a price to pay in being first. Dunlop in the late 1890s had to pay the price by recoiling from its multinational advance.

England was then the champion of free trade, while Germany and the USA were building formidable industrial economies behind tariff walls, and had indeed surpassed the UK in manufacturing output.

Harvey du Cros's instinct was absolutely right to vault his company over these walls and in addition to push production and sales in the Empire lands of Australia and Canada (where no prohibitions were placed on British goods). Where du Cros's aim exceeded his grasp was in the resources to make Dunlop into a multinational at that juncture. The cycling boom, by itself, was simply not sufficient, financially, to sustain that role.

Then, as Dunlop fell back, the greatest revolution of modern times, the internal combustion engine, came along to alter everyone's perspectives.

The motor car and the pneumatic tyre were made for each other. As Henry Ford remarked – on a plaque at the Ford Motor Corporation HQ in Dearborn, commemorating the achievement of John Boyd Dunlop: 'The inventor of the pneumatic tyre made the automobile possible.'

CHAPTER III

'SUCH EXCESSIVE SPEED'

If the pneumatic tyre was an Anglo-Saxon venture, the petrol-driven motorcar was a Franco-German phenomenon.

Three names stand out: Carl Benz and Gottlieb Daimler in Germany and Émile Levassor in France. Naturally, they built on the work and experiments of others, going back more than a hundred years. But practical motoring only became a reality in the 1890s due the work of these three – plus two others, whose names were to haunt Dunlop down the years: André and Edouard Michelin, whose pneumatic tyres had an enormous impact on motoring.

In the very earliest days it would have been hard to imagine tyres having any function for the curious contraption known as the horseless carriage.

Indeed, in the Constatt-Daimler of 1885, studs were added so that a horse's harness could be attached. This was no gesture to tradition. The studs had sound, practical value. They were to hold the harness in place when the horse returned to rescue the car and its hapless occupants when, as usually happened, the engine failed!

Ten years later matters had much improved as light vehicles were delivered from the workshops, designed like real cars with the driver placed in the centre of the wheel base. By this date the French had emerged as clear leaders with 200 different vehicle makers, against twenty-nine in Britain and, incredibly, a mere four in America. Cars ran on solid tyres or steel rims. Speeds above 12 mph led to such vibration that the vehicle shook itself to pieces. Emile Levassor took eighteen months of constant trial and error to achieve a journey of 6 miles non-stop.

Clearly the way was wide open for the use of pneumatic tyres. It was the Michelin brothers who took it – to Dunlop's and Britain's shame.

André and Edouard announced they would have pneumatic tyres ready for the 1895 Paris–Bordeaux race, a journey of 754 miles. However, they could get no takers. Not a single one of the 200 manufacturers wanted to add to the risk of motoring by trying out the Michelin tyres. So the brothers bought a 4-horse-power Daimler engine and built their own car to run on the first pneumatic tyres ever designed for a car.

Michelin's first car to be designed around the tyres did not come in first. The brothers were, however, among the nine to complete the course. They had proved the staying power of the pneumatic tyre and in tribute to this (according to Arthur du Cros's *Recollections*) motor tyres in Britain were, for years, measured in millimetres.

France continued to forge ahead while Dunlop involved itself in fruitless efforts to contest the French right to adapt Bartlett's invention to the motor car.

The experience and knowledge gained in bicycle tyre development was largely ignored in the application of pneumaticism to motoring. The British let their lead slither away, not only in tyre design but in the motor industry as a whole, to such an extent that a headline in the *Daily Express* in 1902 recorded : 'Car Market in Foreign Hands'. Some time later motor manufacturers and traders met at The Ritz Hotel, London, to consider the peril of 'excessive' importation of cheap American cars. One participant remarked that on his journey from Carlisle to London two cars out of every three were 'cheap American ones'.

There was certainly nothing cheap about the British-made products. An advertisement for the first Motor Show at Olympia proclaimed :

> Luxurious interiors are of the utmost importance in these days, as the motoring woman is becoming an expert in the art of being comfortable, and all sorts of new refinements will be seen in this direction in Olympia.
>
> Soft footstools shaped like great cushions will be a popular novelty and Venetian blinds made of polished wood is another new idea. They enable the occupants of the car to see out without being seen.

Britain was still building horseless carriages for the gentry, while across the Channel motor racing was becoming a popular pastime and across the Atlantic Henry Ford was about to launch mass standardized production. ('They can have any colour as long as it's black.') Venetian blinds, forsooth !

Moreover at this Edwardian period a pneumatic tyre in the UK cost £12 – almost as much as the *annual* earnings of a tweeny maidservant – and its life expectancy was a mere three months.

Motoring in Britain had simply not caught up with that on the Continent and in the USA. Despite the inventiveness of British engineers, and the commercial drive and unusual far-sightedness of people like the du Cros family, there was a curious reluctance to grasp the enormous implications of the motorcar.

Strangely, British war correspondents had foreseen the need for a military version of the motor vehicle. One commented as far back as the South African war in October 1900:

> The fact that nigh on 100,000 horses have perished in the campaign so far [it had then lasted exactly one year] is enough to make one pause and ponder seriously over any possible escape from so appalling a waste of substance.
>
> The petrol car can be here, there, and everywhere; so long as there is a road to travel by, it can bridge distances with a swallow-like flight.

Yet despite such prescient comments and despite the British horror at the sacrifice of magnificent horseflesh, the cavalary and supply animals continued to bear the whole brunt of the war. Cars, such as were there, were reserved for the Staff!

For decades British road transport was dominated by the 'Red Flag' Act of 1865, under which mechanical vehicles – presumably steam-driven – were accompanied by two men, preceded by another with a red flag and limited to a speed of 4 mph. For the nation which had invented the railway engine, pioneered iron ships, and made cycling possible, this was a retrograde step of quite exceptional severity.

No doubt the railway companies were delighted to see possible competitors virtually eliminated, but there was also a deep national repugnance to speed on the roads.

Kirkpatrick Macmillan had been fined in the Gorbals for speeding and knocking over a child as far back as 1842. By the 1890s, while cycling was wholly accepted, the Red Flag law still applied to mechanical, and therefore petrol-driven, vehicles.

Road safety lobbies were opposed by the Self-Propelled Traffic Association under the Presidency of Sir David Solomons. They had an uphill struggle. In 1895 – ten years after the appearance of the first horseless carriage – a Mr Harry Hewetson had the temerity to drive his car in London in broad daylight. Scotland Yard warned him not to do it again. A Mr H. J. Lawson had a summons taken out against him for driving a car in the Lord Mayor's procession without permission and without being preceded by a man with a red flag.

These prohibitions were, however, the last gasp of a lost cause.

In 1896 the Conservative government accepted a measure sponsored

20

by Henry Chaplin MP, to scrap the Red Flag, and royal approval of the motor car was signalled when, in the same year, the Prince of Wales, later King Edward VII, was taken for a ride in a car driven by the Hon. Evelyn Ellis.

Arthur du Cros reviled in *Wheels of Fortune* 'that instinctive distrust . . . of anything new which so frequently hampers British progress and placed the petrol driven motor car at the mercy of Bumbledom.' He went on: 'England lagged behind in motor tyres partly because she failed to take motor cars seriously in their earliest years, partly through public prejudice, the hostility of county councils and the strictness of her speed laws.'

Samples of public prejudice, local opposition and the impact of speed restrictions abound in the journals of the early days.

A Mr Brett of the London Cab Drivers Union (horse-drawn, of course) claimed that there would be no future for motor taxis in the capital's streets as 'the vibration and nauseous smell would tell upon the system' – presumably of the fare and the driver.

Public prejudice and council hostility to motorists were whipped up to fine rage by drunk-driving or 'scorching', as speeding was known in those days.

At Marlborough Street Arthur Howe, 39, taxicab driver, was sent to prison for 21 days for being intoxicated while driving.

At Acton, Henry Martin aged 40, of Riverview Grove, Chiswick, was sentenced to one month's imprisonment for being intoxicated while driving a motor car.

To many, 'scorching' was even worse than drunk-driving. The Church militant gave voice, as reported in the *Daily Express*:

Canon Greenwall of Durham, who on Wednesday warmly denounced scorching motorists, was asked whether or not he wished to amplify his views.

'No,' was the reply. 'I do not think I can say anything more. I am not like the Marquis of Queensbury (of boxing rules fame) in saying that these people should be shot, but at the same time I think it would do good if some of them were shot.

'I should like to see them horsewhipped and brought to wreck and ruin,' he added.

Authority resolutely sided with the anti-motoring lobby – royal endorsement or not. A Mr Leycester Barwell of Ascot who was fined £3 (say £80 by late twentieth-century values) for speeding complained:

'I emphatically state that it is impossible to go through a police trap at 17 or 18 mph without being summoned for driving at 27 or 28 mph.'

Surrey police took delight in enforcing the 10 mph limit in towns and regarded motorist-trapping as a kind of sport, sometimes – according to a Godalming resident – 'hiding in the top window of a house ready to pounce on an unsuspecting victim'.

But if the Surrey County Council and constabulary were quick to catch the motoring miscreants, the newly formed Automobile Association, the AA, was resolved to cheat them of their prey.

From October 1905 comes this report :

> The campaign organised by the Automobile Association against police traps began in earnest yesterday when a large party of well-known motorists and their guests travelled down to Guildford to test the methods adopted by the association.
>
> The result of the day's run was a complete rout of the police, and it was evident that when the association is generally supported every road in the country will be so patrolled that police traps will become a thing of the past.
>
> At Cobham breathless association scouts had scented a police trap, and the AA members and their guests cheered two cold and disgusted policemen who were seen moving their trap further up the road.
>
> Between Ripley and Guildford ... one astute policeman, thinly disguised as a working man, made an attempt to get rid of one of the AA scouts by telling him he was wanted by a gentleman down the road.
>
> This manoeuvre of the police is to be defeated by giving button badges to all members of the Automobile Association and scouts will, in future, be instructed to take their orders only from those wearing such badges. Among those who watched the sport yesterday with keen interest, was Colonel Bosworth, the chairman of the Automobile Association.

Thus was born the famous AA badge. Later the 'salute' from AA patrolmen to members sporting the car badge was used to warn members of an impending police trap. In time it became a courtesy until it vanished altogether in the era of mass motoring in the 1960s.

Heaven knows what the police would have done with motorists in Australia.[1] One such, and a leading one, was Henry Barton James, advertising manager of Dunlop Australia.

In 1901 James rode a $2\frac{3}{4}$ hp de Dion 'Quad' from Warrnambool to Melbourne, a distance of 165 miles, to see whether or not this type of vehicle could beat the train. The run was later reduced to 100 miles due to the state of the roads. Even so, James completed the trip in 4 hours 40 minutes against the train's 5 hours. The car consumed 3 gallons of petrol at a cost of 6 shillings, averaging under one halfpenny per mile.

One incident in that memorable race, when James's car broke up a funeral, would have put him behind bars had it occurred in over-regulated England. As he related :

> In those days horses became frantic at the sight of a motor, and the position was worse because of the excessive noise my engine was making. Near Colac I saw a funeral approaching.
>
> I steered over as close as possible to the fence and slowed down the engine, but the horses pulling the hearse shied and tried to climb the opposite bank. As I chugged slowly along I could see horses rearing and the mourners – men and women – jumping down from abbot buggies and jinkers while the drivers tried to control the animals. As I passed down the line I could see the commotion extending far ahead. The abuse shouted at me all along the way makes me shudder to this day.

Du Cros was correct in identifying public prejudice and establishment hostility as major causes of the slow progress in motoring in the UK. He could also have mentioned the fact that, throughout its history, Dunlop has tended to mirror national moods. Instead du Cros contented himself with excusing Dunlop's far from inspired reaction to early motoring by explaining that 'the company possessed neither the motoring experience nor the rubber mills . . . to offer competition to foreign successes.'

In truth, Dunlop was still a pedal-cycle tyre company, forever defending its patents.

It was the end of these patents, notably the Welch patent, plus the Gordon Bennett car races and rallies, which revitalized Dunlop and set the company once more on the track of worldwide growth and expansion.

James Gordon Bennett was an extraordinary combination of reckless daring, bordering on effrontery, with a nice calculation of what was in it for Gordon Bennett. Son of a Scottish journalist who had emigrated to America to found and edit a newspaper, Bennett was a man of unending enterprise and lavish risk-taking. He was debonair, eccentric, publicity-conscious – and a millionaire to boot. Proprietor of the *New York Tribune*, he financed Stanley's search for Dr Livingstone. He came to live in Europe to escape a society scandal in New York (he was threatened with a horse-whipping for his behaviour) and established himself in European society quite smoothly. Indeed in England he became so popular that the expression 'Gordon Bennett' uttered with jaunty awe established itself as a polite substitute for 'cor blimey'. In the US the term was 'Oh, my hat and Gordon Bennett' – Bennett having introduced a dashing form of headgear.

Bennett's flair for the unusual, the exciting and the challenging led him naturally to the newest and fastest form of transport – the motorcar. He founded and financed the Paris–Vienna race and later extended the circuits. It was the victory of S.F.Edge in a Napier on Dunlop tyres in 1902 which won belated laurels for the British motor and tyre industries. The laurels were somewhat withered by the fact that the race-leader, a Dutchman, had to retire with a broken suspension, 20 miles from the finish.

Nonetheless, Edge, Napier and the Dunlop tyre had shown what the British could do: they had beaten the Continentals on their own ground, at their own game. At long last, the country's sporting instinct had been aroused and there soon appeared a host of engineering pioneers – Austin, Morris, Frederic Royce, Charles Rolls – to follow in the footsteps of Montague Napier.

Success in the Gordon Bennett race gave Dunlop a taste for motor racing which it never lost. Winning endowed the company with a marvellous advertising asset and the experience gained aided technical improvement. In a sense the early days of motor racing were more relevant to the actual road conditions experienced by ordinary car drivers, rather than the specially prepared race tracks of later days. But the heavy loss of life suffered among spectators and road users in the Paris–Madrid race of 1903 ended a practice which had become hazardous in the extreme.

Charles Jarrott, a fearless English rider, recounted in his *Ten Years of Motors and Motor Racing* how 'drivers in company could see little but the enshrouding dust although other vehicles, cattle, closed railway gates and unexpected corners could be encountered at any moment... in bad weather the muddy, swimming roads led to cars slipping and sliding so that they frequently turned completely round.'

Despite these dangers, or perhaps because of them, Sir Arthur du Cros endorsed his brother's claim that motor racing was 'better than steeplechasing' and warmly congratulated the French government for its farsightedness in sanctioning racing 'which was of inestimable value in the rapid development of the automobile and tyre industries'.

Quite so. The hair-raising exploits of rally drivers could be, and were, equalled on the roads by ordinary car drivers in the pre-First World War period. Most tyres in these days had completely smooth treads. Even Rolls Royce were obliged to remind their customers: 'Always remember that when a car is being braked it occupies twice

24

as much road as when travelling normally !' Tompkins, who recounts this in his *History of the Pneumatic Tyre*, comments that 'this instruction conjures up visions of cars with no front wheel brakes still proceeding forward, but with the rear wheels locked and with the line of the vehicle at 45° to the direction of travel.'

Lanchester Brothers had exact advice in their motoring manual of 1902 :

> The swing-round stop. The speed should be 9–11 mph. The car is braked and at the same time steered. The tail comes round and the car describes a U-turn, ready to return to the other side of the road. It should on no account be attempted in the presence of other traffic as it is a performance thoroughly disconcerting to other users of the road. Remember that, whatever the state of the road, it is bad driving to navigate the car sideways.

The technical challenge, as has been said, brought out the best in Dunlop and led, in 1906, to the world's first non-skid tyre.

Before then, however, Dunlop had bade a fond farewell to the Welch patent. It had become a millstone round the comany's neck, absorbing a disproportionate amount of time and money to defend it against copiers or to try to get royalties.

Now it was time to consign the Welch patent to the flames, literally. At a wake to which 400 guests were invited Harvey du Cros cremated the specification, giving the following address (reported in the newspapers) :

> Here lies Welch ; he was saddle or arch-shaped ; he rested on a median convexity ; his boundaries are inextensible ; he dies and yet lives no longer for the few, but for the use of all. According to Irish custom this is his wake, these are his ashes. But according to another Irish monumental legend there arises from these ashes a phoenix. That Phoenix is Dunlop, the manufacturer. Welch is dead. Dunlop lives. He too is saddle or arch-shaped ; his median convexity is the world, his boundaries are extensible – may they extend.

So they did. Even before the obsequies for Welch – the patent, not the man who remained with the company and enjoyed the whole mock proceedings – Dunlop was on the move.

Harvey du Cros had excused Dunlop's lack of manufacturing capacity and its own rubber stocks by telling shareholders that buying ready-made materials in the open market safeguarded Dunlop from the vagaries of poor quality. In the son's view it was 'all my eye and Betty Martin'. The absence of manufacturing capacity meant that

Dunlop had to pay top prices and take its place in the queue whenever there was a shortage of rubber or cotton.

Arthur opted for self-sufficiency and, as his brothers were developing the company's fortunes abroad, Arthur's influence on his father was paramount. As he recounted in *Wheels of Fortune* :

> The programme which was to be completed over a series of years was no less than to establish ourselves as manufacturers of rubber, an art of which we were totally ignorant, to search the world for raw rubber and obtain a *preferential position if possible* [du Cros's italics], to study the cotton manufacturing industry, of which we knew nothing, with a view to becoming cotton spinners, and to manufacture for ourselves the rims, wheels, wires, pumps and valves required for our business. Simultaneously our task of creating a world-wide selling organisation was to proceed : and by these comprehensive methods alone could we secure our place in the sun.

Such was Dunlop's 'Declaration of Independence'. It was implemented through the fortuitous combination of sport and kinship.

There was in Birmingham a family of six brothers of Irish descent, the Byrnes. Like the du Cros', the Byrnes were prominent athletes (rugby, cricket and hockey). Again, like the du Cros', they were in the rubber business. Following investment portfolio connections, the two groups came together in 1900 when Arthur persuaded the Dunlop board to buy the Byrnes's Manor Mills, Birmingham, to start rubber manufacture. Two years later a factory at Aston Cross, Birmingham, was acquired for the production of all types of tyre.

The method used was an American one, the invention of J. Doughty. It consisted of an automatic collapsible metal mould, upon which covers could be vulcanized under high steam pressure and, by the addition of certain ingredients, finished, ready for use, in three minutes against two hours for the other process.

Arthur du Cros likened it to 'shelling peas'.

So the company moves its hand-made tyre process from Coventry to the new set-up in Birmingham. The Birmingham–Dunlop connection was well and truly cemented.

CHAPTER IV

EMPIRE MADE

Arthur du Cros was to christen the main Dunlop plant, custom-built and covering 400 acres in Birmingham, Fort Dunlop[1]. The title was appropriate to wartime England (1916) but, in a sense, Fort Dunlop was the bastion of a very British company which had 'conquered' in worldwide markets. The name was an expression and promotion of a philosophy.

The du Cros family, especially father Harvey and son Arthur, were in the business of making money and then of buying estates in the country as generations of British merchants had done before them. Arthur purchased Craigweil House and estate together with other important lands in Sussex (he invited King George v and Queen Mary to occupy Craigweil during the King's convalescence in 1929 and claimed to have persuaded the monarch to raise nearby Bognor to Bognor Regis) and went on to buy Newberries Mansion and estate, Radlett, in 1934. He explained this land hunger by recalling how his Huguenot forebears had been oppressed and robbed for their Protestantism. In his *Recollections* he clearly felt the need to justify his acquisitiveness, for Arthur du Cros was no mere businessman-on-the-make, he was a fervent nationalist, Tory imperialist and a staunch supporter of Tariff Reform.

Dunlop's connection with Birmingham may have been fortuitous – anywhere in the Midlands heartland of the cycle and infant motor industry would have sufficed – but Birmingham had a special appeal: it was the home town of Joseph Chamberlain, the arch exponent of imperial expansion and later, in 1903, of Tariff Reform.

Dunlop's history had paralleled national economic attitudes: the du Cros family with Tariff Reform, the Geddes family with first Empire Free Trade and then the European Economic Community.

As the 1890s drew to a close, the Conservative government of Lord

27

Salisbury became more and more concerned about national and imperial security. The glorious days of splendid isolation from Europe ('Fog in the Channel, Continent Isolated') were clearly coming to an end.

Germany's spectacular industrial growth and her mounting political and territorial ambitions posed a threat. So, in a different fashion, did American economic expansion. Both these states had built up their industrial sinews behind tariff walls. They had protected infant industries against foreign competition and were now able to launch their products on the world market.

Britain however remained true to free trade. This policy had served her well when she was the 'workshop of the world'. With Germany and the USA exceeding her in industrial output she was now in danger of becoming the workhouse of the world.

Joseph Chamberlain, Colonial Secretary in the Salisbury administration, argued that Britain could no longer afford to be the sole major free trade nation in the world. Other countries could, and did, subsidize exports, thereby undercutting British sales at home and overseas. The resultant unemployment, contested Chamberlain, was a direct result of free trade and could be countered only by protecting domestic *and Empire* markets through tariffs on foreign produce : hence 'Tariff Reform', a more appealing title than 'Protection' and one designed to tempt radical-minded folk to support a Tory administration.

Chamberlain himself was of a radical disposition. Indeed he had been a radical MP well to the 'left' of his Liberal Party. His appearance – immaculate dress, aristocratic mien, haughty stare made haughtier still by a monocle – belied his background and beliefs.

A Londoner, he had made a fortune with his partner Nettlefold in Birmingham's engineering components industry. Birmingham in the nineteenth century was the enterprise culture writ large. Thousands of small firms vied with on another to create and satisfy public demand. A number rose to giant status (one such is the amalgamated concern of Guest, Keen and Nettlefold) but they, in turn, were served by sub-contractors, so sustaining a huge number of smaller concerns.

Jo Chamberlain was a triumphant product of the capitalist system : a self-made captain of industry imbued with and driven by the Protestant work ethic. He was also a capitalist with a social conscience. On embarking on a political career, he swiftly became mayor of Birmingham and then one of its MPs. (The city was a Chamberlain fiefdom. So secure did he make it that it remained true to the Tory tradition, Mr Chamberlain having switched allegiance in 1886, until the Party's rout in 1945.)

By the late 1870s Chamberlain was advancing the causes of munici-

28

pal management of housing, universal free state education and the compulsory purchase of land from landowners to provide allotments for all who wished to work the land. He was accused by members of his own Liberal Party of being a closet socialist – this in the days when the public image of a socialist was that of a bearded anarchist twirling a smoking bomb.

Then came Mr Gladstone's bill of 1885 to give Home Rule to Ireland. Chamberlain, a dedicated Non-Conformist, could not stomach the idea of an Ireland separated from England and under the dominion of the Roman Catholic Church. He split with Gladstone and took his fellow Liberal–Unionists – the union being with Ireland – into coalition with the Conservatives, thereby effectively denying the Liberals power for almost twenty years.

On holding office in the Board of Trade and then in the Colonial Office, Chamberlain studied the patterns of commerce and came to the conclusion that Britain and the Empire should put up a tariff barrier on industrial goods to protect native industry against dumping of artificially cheap foreign products. This would help British industry and British jobs. The colonies, however, demanded, and deserved, reciprocity. They wanted a secure market for their food and raw materials. If they were to give preference to British industrial goods – admitting them free of duty while imposing taxes on non-British products – the motherland, in turn, ought to tax foreign food and raw materials to provide a guaranteed haven for Empire products.

This food issue split the Tory Party asunder. It was one – though only one – of the reasons for Winston Churchill deserting the Conservatives and joining the Liberals.

The spectre of 'dear food for the workers' was grist to the Liberal mill. They harvested millions of votes and drove the Tories from office in a landslide election in 1906.

Despite that tremendous setback, Tariff Reform was now at the centre of British politics and was to remain so for sixty years, with Jo Chamberlain's sons, Austen and Neville, realizing much of their father's programme.

Chamberlain viewed the British scene in 1894–1906 as a practical industrialist, a nationalist and an imperialist. The du Cros family took precisely the same attitude from the same Protestant–capitalist roots.

Harvey du Cros, a passionate Tariff Reformer, won Hastings for the Tories in the disaster election of 1906, one of the only two gains the Conservatives enjoyed in that contest. His son, Arthur, helped to found and was elected first chairman of the Junior Imperialist League, an organization which, after 1945, became the Young Conservatives. Arthur too was a fervent Tariff Reformer and got himself elected MP in 1908. Politically the du Cros' shared Chamberlain's convictions, and as fellow Midlands industrialists they agreed with his prescription for Britain's economic ills, with its shrinking sphere of world trade and a growing toll of unemployment.

Anticipating the expansion of tariffs worldwide, Dunlop, by 1900 (the year incidentally, in which the company officially adopted the title 'Dunlop Rubber Company') was established on the Continent, in Australia and North America.

The political impact of Tariff Reform, and the almost religious hold it took on its disciples, should not be underestimated in determining Dunlop's policy and in turning the firm into a mighty multinational corporation.

Allied to this was a resolve to share markets, to 'divi up' selling areas in order to eliminate, or certainly diminish, costly competition. An early example of Dunlop's keenness to come to such understandings is furnished by the Reciprocity Agreement with the Australian arm of Dunlop.

On 30 March 1899 the Australian company was capitalized by the issue of 110,000 shares of £1 each, effectively giving financial control of the Australian company to Australians. This development was dictated by domestic financial considerations but Dunlop of England was resolved to give nothing for nothing and Dunlop Australia, literally a branch of the same family tree, was an 'Australian Firster'.

What was eventually agreed was a carve-up of territories: The English company promised not to manufacture or export tyres to Australia and New Zealand, with the exception of tyres fitted to cars exported to Australia and New Zealand (Australia did not start mass assembly of cars in her own territory until 1929). In return the Australian company engaged not to sell, export or compete directly with the English company in any territory outside Australia and New Zealand.

The English firm pledged itself to give the benefit of all patents, trademarks and inventions relating to tyres taken out in the past in the Australasia area to the Australian company; the Australians would reciprocate on any Australian patents taken out in Europe. The English company guaranteed to provide technical knowledge to the Australians for which the Australians were to pay royalties, which were later commuted to an outright payment of £35,000.

This agreement lasted in substantial form for some forty years. It was considerably amended by one in 1942 which, in deference to advancing US interest in Australia, modified the partnership considerably – making it clear, for example, that information in the possession of either consequential upon an agreement with a third party, could not be made available. In other words, the Australians were not to pass on to the UK company information gleaned from, say, a US rubber concern. At that time, the amendment suited the Australian firm more than the British. Thirty years on, in the early 1970s, it was the British who were reminding the Australians that they, the Aussies, couldn't expect details given in confidence by Pirelli to Dunlop UK.

So Dunlop's relations, not only with its Australian connection, but with others, mirrored changes in national economic policy and international relations.

Personal relations also played their part in the Australian enterprise. The two young men originally despatched from Britain to establish Dunlop's presence in the southern hemisphere were nephews of Harvey du Cros.

William John Proctor was a mere nineteen years old when he arrived in the colony of Victoria in 1893 to take charge of Dunlop operations. He was a true sprig of the du Cros' tree. No sooner was he in possession of a factory in Tattersall's Lane, Melbourne, than he was writing an article for the *Australian Cyclist* entitled: 'The Dunlop Record – Published For The Good of Humanity'. He had a flair for selling – himself as well as Dunlop products – that seems to have been bred in the du Cros bone.

At one o'clock every day a crowd would gather outside his office in Flinder Street to watch Proctor and his friends drive off in his de Dion Phaeton.

Proctor and his de Dion were to make local history. For it was in this car that he so frightened a race horse that it collided with the car's iron step and broke its leg.

The owner of the horse sued Proctor and Dunlop, and this was the first case in a Victoria court on whether a motor vehicle had any right to be on the road.

Proctor lost. The judge ruled that motorcars must be stopped in the presence of horses.

William was not at all pleased. But his younger brother Charles, who had arrived to be assistant general manager to William's general manager, doubtless calmed him down.

Charles had the hot Irish–Huguenot blood too, but Uncle Harvey saw in Charles the qualities needed to provide a stabilizing influence. Both Charles and William served Dunlop, Australia, until 1928.

A family atmosphere pervaded Dunlop and was to remain for generations; it was at one time the company's strength, at another, its weakness, as changing economic challenges demanded differing responses.

Yet without the du Cros clan – including the inevitable nepotism – Dunlop Rubber would not have got off the ground and, having done so, would not have spread itself throughout the British Empire and beyond.

Sheer greed played its part. In his *Recollections* Sir Arthur demonstrated an other-worldly approach to business ethics, at least so far as the family was concerned. Thus, he listed two items which would certainly be open to other intepretations. In 1907 he recorded,

> My brother Harvey as director of a newly formed limited company in Dublin was, with his colleagues, defeated in an action taken by a shareholder upon an unimportant technical omission, by a solicitor, from the prospectus. Harvey's share of the capital restitution ordered by the Court was £30,000, this sum being provided jointly by my father and myself (on the family principle that 'united we stand, divided we fall').

Harvey's share of the fine being close on £1 million by late twentieth-century values surely prompts the Churchillian riposte, 'Some omission! Some technicality!'

Another entry, two years later, recorded one of Arthur's money-making schemes far removed from tyre manufacturing and an augury of that restless yearning for easy fortune which was to bring Dunlop close to disaster. This time it was property speculation.

> Purchased Covent Garden Market with its surrounding property and also the Founding Hospital and Estate in Bloomsbury for the purpose of modernising and transferring the market to the Bloomsbury site and relieving congestion in the Strand area. [There's that altruism again!] Introduced a private member's bill in Parliament, but did not proceed, owing to organised opposition by the residents in the Bloomsbury area – supported by their local authority – and to objections voiced by stall-holders in Covent Garden.

Yet that same self-regarding conceit which disguised his purely money-making motives from himself also prompted Arthur du Cros to schemes of a genuinely visionary nature.

Motoring demanded a far vaster Dunlop development than that required for cycling.

In quick succession Dunlop went into the business of manufacturing rims and wheels in Coventry, launched studies of rubber-growing and cotton-spinning and established the first Dunlop subsidiary in the Far East, outside the British Empire, at Kobe in Japan.

In all these events family ties exerted a strong influence, not least in Dunlop's foundation of its rubber plantations.

As previously related, the Byrne family, like the du Cros', were Irish Protestants who had developed rubber goods for the British market. Also like the du Cros', there were six sons and one of them, E.J.Byrne, offered to proceed on a voyage of discovery to find where best to secure supplies of rubber for the joint du Cros–Byrne ventures.

Brazil had already proved a disappointing starter after an earlier Dunlop pioneer, B.J.Ebbsworth, reported in 1902 that the Amazon Basin was too intimidating to justify purchase of plantations. The intimidation came from the rough and violent elements who were scampering and shoving to get at natural rubber to feed the soaring demands of the new car industry.

CHAPTER V

EXPANSION – AND WAR

Thomas Hancock and Charles Macintosh were to rubber what Robert William Thomson and John Boyd Dunlop were to the pneumatic tyre.

Hancock, working in his Stoke Newington laboratory, took caoutchouc, or india rubber, and transformed it by a vulcanizing process into a material with a mass of applications. The term owes its derivation to the Vulcan of mythology 'as in some degree representing the employment of sulphur and heat with which that theological personage was supposed to be familiar'.[1]

French explorers had discovered caoutchouc in Spanish South America in the early eighteenth century. The resinous, milky liquid with gum-like qualities had few uses: one, involving the erasure of pencil marks, was 'rubber'.

Hancock began his experiments in 1820 with a view to improving the elasticity of india rubber and applying it to the wrists of gloves, to waistcoat backs and waist bands; to pockets, to prevent their being picked, to trouser and gaiter straps, to braces, to stockings and garters, to riding belts, to stays; to boots, shoes, clogs and pattens, 'when the object is to put them on and take them off without lacing or tying . . . .'

He also applied rubber to the soles of shoes and boots to render them waterproof, and with the invention of his 'masticator' machine the rubber industry may fairly be said to be launched – although the method by which the masticator worked was kept a secret for twelve years, until 1833.

In Glasgow, at roughly the same period, Charles Macintosh had perfected a waterproofing process for textiles, to be universally known as 'Mackintoshs'. They reached a pitch of fame when in 1827 Captain Parry in his *Narrative of the Attempt to reach the North Pole in His Majesty's Ship Hecla* reported:

Just before halting on July 5, the ice at the margin of the floe broke when the men were handing the provisions out of the boats ; we narrowly escaped the loss of a bag of cocoa, which fell overboard, but fortunately rested on a tongue. This bag, being made of Macintoshes waterproof canvas, did not suffer the slightest injury. Of this invaluable manufacture which consists, I believe, in applying a solution of elastic gum or caout-chouc between two parts of canvas, it is impossible to speak too highly. I know of no material which with an equal weight is equally durable and watertight – in the latter quality, indeed it is altogether perfect.'

With such a recommendation Macintosh could hardly fail. Steadily he and Hancock worked together more and more closely in Manchester until Macintosh's death. Year after year the uses to which rubber could be put multiplied.

Such a one was air-filled rubber and canvas pontoons for military purposes. These flat-bottomed boats had previously been made of metal, and because they were heavy and awkward and were carried on timber wagons, they fell far behind the van of the army so that when the troops reached a river they perforce had to wait until the twenty or thirty pontoons needed to ford the obstacle were forthcoming.

Inflatable pontoons of canvas and rubber, however, could be carried quite easily : light and portable enough to be carried on one horse. Each pontoon was furnished with several openings having a screw nozzle attached with a proper valve to close it ; to these nozzles a kind of cylindrical bellows was screwed on and with one man acting on each pair of bellows the pontoon filled in 5 to 6 seconds.

The timber superstructure was of conventional design. The old Duke of Wellington personally inspected the structure and, with the aid of forty foot guards, satisfied himself as to the efficacy of this important piece of military craftsmanship.

Unfortunately his open-minded attitude towards scientific progress was not shared by his successors. After his death the Crimean War broke out and was conducted in an unbelievably incompetent fashion by feeble-minded politicians at home and mentally impaired generals at the front. The Commander-in-Chief Lord Raglan invariably referred to the enemy (the Russians) as 'Those Frenchies' – who were our allies.

The military application of rubber products was forgotten until someone at the War Office had the bright idea that rubber might stop bullets !

Hancock had experimented with a compound structure of metal and vulcanized rubber to serve as a kind of shield for troops in the trenches. Sadly, he commented : 'I gave it to some officers, but heard nothing further of it. I am inclined to think it should have had attention as from trials on my models the results were promising.'

Instead of being guided by a brilliant chemist, designer and innovator, the military wiseacres convined themselves that rubber itself could resist bullets. They came to this conclusion because they had fired at a piece of paper with a thickened rubber backing. There was a hole in the paper, but none in the rubber. Ergo: rubber was bullet proof! When Hancock told them that the rubber had simply closed up they wouldn't believe him. They were about to exhibit their 'discovery' to the Duke of York. To save them from embarrassment, or worse, Hancock conducted an experiment in his garden. He fixed a breast of mutton to the wall protected by thickened rubber. He then took a rifle and sent a ball through the rubber and mutton and halfway through the wall itself.

This little foray into the byways of military history is relevant to the Dunlop story in that it exhibits the effect military open-mindedness and closed-mindedness can have on industrial concerns. In World War I the latter tended to prevail; in World War II the former, so that Dunlop would render unparalleled service by utilizing rubber to the maximum advantage.

As far back as 1838 Hancock had warned of the need to cultivate rubber trees in areas other than Latin America, in order to ensure supplies of a raw material swiftly growing in demand. As previously mentioned the Brazilian rubber tree had been successfully transplanted to the Far East. Nonetheless, South America remained the prime production area and it was to this that the Dunlop leaders addressed themselves.

For quite some time Harvey du Cros had been telling the shareholders that Dunlop got the best results by buying their rubber from whatever seller could offer the best deal. Son Arthur privately confided to his diary that both father and he knew that was hogwash. Whenever a shortage arose – either through owner-manipulation or political crisis or natural disasters – those who possessed no plantations of their own would be hopelessly placed. Brazil having proved a grievous disappointment, an expedition under E. J. Byrne was mounted to test the market in Portuguese Angola on the west coast of Africa, where flourished a wild bush containing a resinous gum that could give a 20 per cent yield of first class rubber.

Having negotiated a concession area, about the size of Ireland, Byrne and his party set off for Angola in 1906.

The expedition was a minor catastrophe. The area was a trackless wilderness. The labourers whom he 'hired' were in fact slaves. Byrne collected samples and shipped them home. But before he could return himself, he succumbed to enteric fever. He was so ill that his head man asked him what he'd like done with his body after he had expired. This tactlessness so enraged Byrne that he resolved to live, come what may. He survived – and insisted that nothing on earth should persuade Dunlop to establish its plantations in Angola.

The Empire beckoned. Two countries which had benefitted from Sir Henry Wickham's foresight – Ceylon and Malaya – were surveyed by Arthur du Cros and E. J. Byrne. They chose Malaya as the place which would yield the finest crop. In 1910 Dunlop's flag was planted there. Within ten years, spurred by the claims of war, the plantations of rubber plants covered 50,000 acres.

Paralleling the entry into rubber growing, the company moved into textiles to secure the second raw, or semi-manufactured, material for tyre-making. After some experience with a small weaving mill and an association with an old-established doubling concern, Dunlop bought cotton mills at Rochdale in Lancashire.

The 'all-up' company was complete: from raw rubber via cord to the finished tyre: manufactured worldwide and sold worldwide.

Dunlop Rubber was now a multinational, perhaps the first of its kind on the face of the globe. Yet, somehow, it maintained the family atmosphere.

Credit for this belonged to the du Cros family and especially to its head, Harvey. The old man revelled in encouraging his work-force to take part in sports as once he had spurred his sons to the same endeavours.

Rugby football remained a passion with the du Cros' and each factory had its own team. Arthur's interest in the Territorial Army found expression in the recruitment of a company of volunteers (commanded by his brother, William) of the Royal Warwickshire Regiment from employees at Coventry. This formation saw service in the Boer War. Another company was formed in Birmingham and men from both took part in two rifle-shooting competitions at Bisley.

A volunteer fire brigade was founded in the Midlands and Dunlop employees were encouraged to take part in local charity activities.

In sensible fashion, charity began at home. When the company was recapitalized, bonus payments amounting to £85,000 were paid to the staff. When new issues of shares were made, directors took up blocks to ensure that in the months to come, employees should have the opportunity of buying them on easy terms. Group endowment insurance schemes were laid on and worker participation schemes led to a two-way flow of ideas between management and employees.

The *Motor Trader* was moved to comment in 1909 :

> Now and then one comes across a business concern of which the members seem to be a happy and united family. That is one of the characteristics of the Dunlop Co.
>
> Many of those who started in the business as boys are now holding responsible positions, helping to guide its destinies. In the loyalty to 'the Governor' is an article of faith from which they would never dream of swerving by a hair's breadth. They know he is true as steel to his friends of his earlier days. In these facts we have at least some of the causes of affection with which he is regarded by every member of the staff.

Occasionally the tributes to Harvey du Cros became a trifle cloying. When, in 1909, a grand banquet was held to commemorate the twenty-first birthday of the pneumatic tyre, hyperbole was piled on hyperbole. Finlay Sinclair, one of the originals, leading a delegation of employees, spoke of his surpassing generalship 'in not only creating a great and thriving British industry, but with amazing rapidity having established kindred industries in the four quarters of the world.' And of his 'genial courteous manner which has endeared him to us and made our work a pleasure'. The *Globe* newspaper referred to him as 'The Napoleon of the tyre industry'. The *Irish Cyclist*, not to be outdone, especially as Harvey du Cros was a son of Erin, commented that while J.B.Dunlop was 'the man who had enabled the world to ride on air, Mr Harvey du Cros was the driving power behind this great invention and to his marvellous skill and unique abilities for organisation and administration belongs the honour of making the tyre a household word in partically every civilised country in the world.'

'The history of the Dunlop tyre', said the *Standard*, 'will go down to posterity as one of the greatest romances of all time.'

Testifying to that fact was his enrolment in the Légion d'Honneur, and the presentation to Harvey du Cros of a casket and address signed by over 1,000 representatives of the car and cycle industries worldwide. The address declared in part :

> It must be a source of never-failing satisfaction to you that the child you so bravely nurtured has reached so vigorous a manhood. It must also add greatly to your pleasure to feel that in founding a new industry no other trade has been crushed out of existence, but, on the contrary, new sources of wealth and new occupations for countless workmen have been found.

Here was a key phrase. For by the second decade of the twentieth century labour relations bulked larger than they had ever done before in the consciousness of the employing class.

This was a period of mounting strife at factory and mill. Mild inflation with static pay – or even wage cuts – combined to drive down living standards. Jobs were threatened, were being lost, as new industries rendered old ones superfluous. Industrial unrest in the UK was reaching a peak not to be equalled until the General Strike of 1926.

Dunlop's contented, almost deferential, work-force, well-paid at an average of £2 10s (£2.50p) a week with insurance, sports facilities and a paternal management, contrasted startlingly with conditions elsewhere in Britain.

Mrs Thorogood of Lambeth, aged sixty-three, was paid one penny an hour by a contractor for finishing trousers at a factory in Tooley Street. Her midday meal consisted of bread and water. Mrs Thorogood's case was raised in Parliament. An employee of Mr Quinn's farm at Santry near Dublin was not to fortunate. He was instantly dismissed for demanding a half-day's holiday a week. He had worked twenty-six years for Mr Quinn.

Safety precautions were drilled into the Dunlop workers. Their fellow toilers in other trades were less well protected. From 1900 to 1910 an average of 1,000 people a year died in workshops. In one year alone, 1904, 1200 miners died in the pits and 400 railway servants lost their lives on the line (compared with 4 a year after World War II). The men were often as much to blame as the masters, for while employers may have been slow to introduce safeguards, their employees frequently ignored them when they did, refusing to put safety before custom and convenience.

If a somewhat cavalier attitude existed on both sides to safety at work, a hard, unyielding puritan work ethic persisted in other aspects. Insubordination brought instant punishment.

Cottagers who refused to operate Lord Penrhyn's quarries at Bethesda in Wales were evicted from their homes.

When striking coal miners in West Yorkshire failed to pay their rents to the coal masters they suffered the same fate.

Coal-mining, the least protected against foreign competition and most vulnerable to slumps and booms, produced the most violent reaction to dismissals prompted by market conditions. Nowhere were these conditions more prevalent than in South Wales, which was heavily dependent on the coal export trade.

When the coal owners, in August 1911, sought to cut miners' and railwaymen's earnings as a result of diminished overseas demand for coal, the men struck, and a madness gripped the valleys. Towns such as Tredegar, Brynmawr, Ebbw Vale, Bergoed, Giltash and Llanelli erupted. Llanelli was the worst affected.

A mob broke into the Great Western Railway's goods shed and stole a large quantity of whisky. Having extracted and drunk the liquor, they set fire to the warehouse and shortly afterwards turned their attention to trucks standing in a siding. They were set ablaze. Unhappily one of them contained petrol. It exploded. Portions of the blazing truck were hurled into the air. The mob scattered, but four men and a woman lost their lives.

Eventually, 500 men of the Essex Regiment arrived and marched through the town with fixed bayonets. A further detachment of the Worcestershire Regiment charged the rioters near the railway station. The Home Office reported briskly: 'Order has been restored at Llanelli.' Military officers reported the railwaymen themselves were not responsible for the rioting.

Evidence in this respect was furnished by the fact that one of the fatalities, Leonard Worsell, had come to Llanelli from London, presumably to aggravate local unrest.

Jewish shops were the target for particular spleen, doubtless because the rioters owed them money and the proprietors were not prepared to extend them credit for an unlimited period.

Three months before these events, striking coal miners had demonstrated in Tonypandy, where the hooligan element – some of it imported – added its own brand of destructiveness.

The local police could not cope and the Chief Constable asked the Home Office for troops to aid the civil powers. The Home Secretary of the day was Winston Churchill, then in his Liberal Party phase. He refused to sanction the use of troops, preferring instead to reinforce the police with London bobbies. They could not cope either and when the rioting persisted, and worsened, Churchill reluctantly endorsed the despatch of two squadrons of cavalry and two companies of infantry.

Churchill was assailed for his timidity. Those on the spot, including the correspondent of the *Western Mail*, observed: 'Had firm action been taken at once . . . many thousands of pounds worth of property would have been saved.'

In later years, however, a black myth about Tonypandy came to be propagated by Churchill's enemies on the Left. It was said that Churchill had ordered troops to gun down the miners of Tonypandy. In truth, there were no fatalities at Tonypandy and Churchill *restrained* the troops. Those who died – at Llanelli – did so by their own actions. Yet the 'massacre at Tonypandy' took its place in the martyrs' parade alongside Peterloo Fields and Tolpuddle. For millions of loyal trade unionists, Winston Churchill was marked down as the enemy of the workers, and this belief persisted into the 1950s, unquestionably influencing Churchill's attitude to labour relations. 'We must not offend the trade unionists,' he was heard (by the author) to mutter on one occasion.

His policy of perpetual appeasement was followed by successive Conservative − and naturally, Labour − administrations so that, by the 1970s, rampant industrial ill-discipline and union bossmanship was inflicting near-fatal injury on the economy. Dunlop, as will be seen, suffered gravely the consequences of false memories and mythology.

In 1910, however, Dunlop could congratulate itself on model relations, in a modern industry free from the inheritance of past bitterness and with a future of unlimited expansion.

It was in this year Dunlop produced the first tyre for an aeroplane − and the first Dunlop golf ball rolled off the assembly line in Birmingham. No stoppages clouded this sunrise industry. In contrast, by 1912 half the trade unionists in Britain were on strike and it seemed that revolution was in the air. Tom Mayfield, editor of the Militant Socialist paper *The Dawn* uttered this blood-curdling proclamation:

> A worker pays 6 pence a week to his union. Why not save threepence a week for a revolver? The time will surely come, if it is not already here, when you will need it.
>
> Meet the soldiers and police on more equal terms ... shoot low, not too low, just low enough ....
>
> If blood has to be shed, I do not see why it should always be the workers' blood. Let us see how the master class like the operation of blood-letting. If it would take too long to get a shooter saving threepence a week, let the unions get them for you. It would be money well spent. Or join the Territorials; here you would get guns and instruction ....

How different, how very different was Dunlop's world of joint service by employers and employees in the Territorial forces for the national interest. When the time came in 1914, the ideals of Dunlop prevailed over those of Comrade Mayfield and his kind. World War I found the Dunlop Company ready and willing both in morale and manufacturing capacity for a nation at arms.

However, while the Dunlop Company was ready and willing, the War Office was not. A senior officer there pointed out to Arthur du Cros that Dunlop tyres were too highly priced. Du Cros gently explained that true pricing depended on mileage and, on that basis, Dunlop's products were a good buy. Sir Arthur righteously recorded: 'The company promptly received all the orders with which it could cope.' Which were colossal.

The Great War of 1914–18 was the first conflict in which wheels came into their own. The first modern war was the Civil War in America (where the total American casualties, North and South, exceeded those in all the other wars in which America has been involved, including World Wars I and II). In that war railways were the vital transport, enabling the North to be 'fastest with the mostest' most of the time.

Railways were of enormous importance too in the Great War, which, in its initial stages, was war by railway timetable as the German offensive in the West was predicated on precise military build-up. But as the war progressed the role of road transport, tanks and aircraft swiftly advanced.

Indeed as early as October 1914 the first flickering idea of the tank (originally a code word to disguise the reality of an armoured fighting vehicle) crossed the minds of British military planners. Viewing the trenches which bisected France from the Channel to the Swiss frontier, a Colonel Swinton of GHQ broached the project of an armoured caterpillar tractor to cross the trenches, destroying the barbed wire in its path and wholly immune to rifle or machine-gun fire. He passed on his ideas to Col. Maurice Hankey, Secretary to the War Council, or inner cabinet.

Winston Churchill too envisioned a 'land cruiser'. As First Lord of the Admiralty he asked Admiral Bacon, the general manager of the Coventry Ordnance Works, near neighbours of Dunlop's wheel and rim plant, to draw up plans for a tractor carrying men and guns capable of breaching trenches. Bacon came up with a design for a caterpillar tractor which would cross a trench by means of a portable bridge which it laid down before itself and hauled up after passing over. Churchill ordered thirty of these machines to be constructed. They were tested in May 1915 and rejected by the War Office because they could not descend a 4ft bank and go through 3ft of water. Arthur du Cros, who knew of the developments, was much disappointed.

Churchill observed to Prime Minister Asquith:

Forty or fifty of these [armoured fighting vehicles] prepared secretly and brought into position at nightfall could advance into the enemy trenches, smashing away all obstructions and sweeping the trenches with their machine-gun fire and with grenades thrown from the top. They would then make so many *points d'appui* for the British supporting

42

infantry to rush forward and rally on them. They can then move forward
to attack the second line of trenches.[2]

Churchill was so entranced with the conception that, despite cold
water from the War Office, he sanctioned expenditure on building
such machines, although he had no authority to do so. The man placed
in charge of the project was Sir Eustace Tennyson-d'Eyncourt, chief
constructor of the navy. Churchill gave him and the engineers Sir
William Tritton and Major Wilson the prime credit for getting the
idea of the tank off the ground.

Ten years previously H. G. Wells had foreseen such a development,
and, of course, since earliest recorded history armoured devices for
the reduction of fortifications had appeared on the battlefield. By 1914
the combination of hardened armour, the internal combustion engine
and rubber-tracked vehicles had created the conditions for the tank.
They could, and should, have been in action in 1915. Seventy of
them were ready then, capable in Churchill's words of 'traversing
any obstacle, ditch, breastwork or trench, fitted with 2 or 3 Maxims
and possibly with flame throwers. Nothing but a direct hit from a
field gun will stop them.'

He recommended to Sir Douglas Haig that they should be used
en masse. Instead nothing was done until July 1916 and then they
were used in penny numbers at the disastrous battle of the Somme.
It was not until November 1917 that British tanks triumphantly broke
the German front at Cambrai and provoked the only ringing of bells
on the home front during the hostilities. Unfortunately there was no
follow-up at Cambrai and the tanks' glory day had to wait till 8 August
1918 when 400 of them smashed the Hindenberg Line in what General
Ludendorff called 'the black day of the German Army'.

Had some of the brightest and best in the British motor and rubber
industries been involved from Day One, the story of the tank and
its contribution to victory might have been happily different.

A further example of War Office myopia was provided by an
exchange between Eric Geddes, who would become chairman of Dunlop, and the Secretary of State for War, the legendary Field Marshal
Lord Kitchener.

Geddes, then (1915) at the Ministry of Munitions, had the temerity
to inquire of Kitchener how many machine guns he would need in
1916. Kitchener exploded: 'Do you think I am God Almighty that
I can tell you what is wanted nine months ahead?'

Finally, relenting, he laid down two machine guns per battalion
minimum and four maximum; 'anything above four is a luxury'. When

Geddes's Minister of Munitions, Lloyd George, saw Kitchener's figures he exploded : 'Multiply that by four, double that for luck and double that again for contingencies. The sum of four multiplied by four, multiplied by two and doubled equals 64. Provide that per battalion.'[3] The figure of 64 did, however, only apply to special units of the Machine Gun Corps.[4]

No such War Office myopia afflicted Arthur du Cros. He had shown considerable vision in organizing a flying demonstration for his fellow MPs as far back as 1911 and in that same year aeroplane tyres and wheels, of motorcycle proportions, started appearing in the Dunlop catalogue.

Tank tyres and wheels presented a fresh challenge to the rubber companies. As with other heavy duty tyres for lorries and trucks, they were made of solid rubber, and were liable to over-heating and shredding at speeds above 20 mph.

In its original form the tank travelled on long caterpillar tracks running completely round the edges of its box-like shape. The tracks were pressed against the ground by a series of solid-tyred wheels along the whole length of the ground contact, and rose high at each end to cover the exigencies of dropping down into trenches, or shell holes, and climbing out again. The free portion of the tracks, running over the top of the machine, was guided by solid-tyred 'idler' wheels.

The rubber industry solved the problem of producing cool-running solid tyre compounds, and the knowledge thus gained was successfully applied by Dunlop to the pneumatic tyre in the post-war world.

National tank production and the opening of the aptly named Fort Dunlop ('stronghold of the British tyre industry') appropriately coincided in 1916. The Dunlop Company was now a vital part of the war effort controlled by one of the ten departments of the Ministry of Munitions. It was nowhere near as big as it would be in World War II, but it was advancing as the terrible technology of war progressed. Wheels meant mobility. Wheels meant tyres, and tyres meant Dunlop.

Sir Arthur and the entire du Cros clan were in their element. The company was prospering and they were giving full vent to their genuine and generous patriotism. Sir Arthur's *Recollections* are filled with accounts of what he and the company were doing for the war effort and with a little self-congratulation.

> Item. Raised and presented to the Army for the duration of the war a motor ambulance column, being the first all-motorised column to be employed in the British Army. Officered, among others,

by brothers William and George du Cros, both over military age. William never fully recovered his health, serving more than three years in France.

Item. Captain George du Cros mentioned in despatches for 'gallant and distinguished service in the field'.

Item. William du Cros mentioned in despatches 'for gallant and distinguished service in the field'.

Item. Together with Gideon Murray and an Indian Committee offered the Secretary of State for India, who accepted, a fully equipped ambulance convoy of 66 vehicles for the India Expeditionary Force [in France] and to maintain the same for the duration.

Item. Appointed to committee to select and withdraw skilled munition workers from the ranks. An unpopular job ... Mr Lloyd George [Min. of Munitions] wrote : 'The success of the scheme has been largely due to the valuable co-operation and assistance rendered by gentlemen like yourself.'

Item. My proposal to film Cabinet Ministers entering the Cabinet Room, made with the object of raising funds for disabled soldiers, was rejected as 'not being dignified'!

Mention of David Lloyd George draws attention to that minister's unique contribution to the mobilization of industry. Both as Minister of Munitions and later as Prime Minister, he brought into government outstanding administrators from the world of business : Sir Arthur du Cros, marginally, and the man who figures larger than any other in the Dunlop story, Sir Eric Geddes.

David Lloyd George said this about Eric Geddes :

Sir Douglas Haig [C-in-C of the British Army in France 1915–1918] strongly urged upon me the appointment of Sir Eric Geddes to the post of First Lord of the Admiralty. The power, and especially the punch, which Sir Eric had displayed in the reorganisation of transport to and in France had made a considerable impression on Haig's mind. Geddes was then [summer of 1917] engaged in putting fresh life into the construction of ships to fill up the gaps made by the enemy in our mercantile marine....

As First Lord, Geddes's over-riding vitality was soon felt in every branch of activity. Difficulties and hesitancies disappeared in every direction. There was a quickening in action all round. The convoy system at last had a fair chance. The naval officers who were wholeheartedly for it were encouraged. The attack on the submarine was developed. The Nash invention of the fish hydrophone [to listen in on U-boats] was attached without delay to patrolling vessels. Many other new and ingenious experiments were resolved for breaking down and destroying the enemies' submarines.[5]

The scale of the U-boat threat to Britain's sea-lanes, and hence to the entire combat capacity of the Allies, was to be measured by the losses suffered by the Merchant Navy in 1917.

On 1 February Berlin announced unrestricted submarine warfare. By April the UK and her allies were losing 423 ships of a gross dead weight of 849,000 tons *a month*. The German High Command reckoned that if British shipping could be sunk at the rate of 600,000 tons a month, Britain would be finished within five months.

Sir Edward Carson, the Ulster Unionist leader, was First Lord during the desperate days when one in four merchant ships leaving British ports never returned. Logic seemed to dictate that a convoy system would simply concentrate the victims and make them easier prey for the U-boats. The official policy of the Admiralty, endorsed by the head of the Royal Navy, Admiral Sir John Jellicoe, the First Sea Lord, stated flatly :

> A system of several ships sailing in company as a convoy is not recommended in any area where submarine attack is a possibility. It is evident that the larger the number of ships forming a convoy, the greater the chance of a submarine being able to attack successfully and the greater the difficulty of the escort in preventing such an attack.'

But, as Churchill was to observe :

> The size of the sea is so vast that the difference between the size of a convoy and the size of a single ship shrinks in comparison almost to insignificance. There was in fact very nearly as good a chance of a convoy of 40 ships slipping unperceived between the patrolling U-boats as there was for a single ship ; and each time this happened 40 ships escaped instead of one.

Regular convoys were instituted and swiftly proved effective. But it was left to Eric Geddes to implement the most sweeping changes in naval command that were to consolidate the convoy success and take the war to the enemy.

Geddes sacked Jellicoe. This virtually unknown businessman, who was hurriedly found a seat in Parliament – he took the Tory Whip – dismissed the most illustrious figure in the British navy.

Geddes, according to his own account[6], had tried to work with Jellicoe, but the admiral was probably set in his ways, and possibly too tired. A major policy difference between the two concerned the

Dover patrol which under existing (early-1917) practice had totally failed to prevent the passage of German submarines through the arrows to the sea-lanes. In replacing Admiral Jellicoe with Admiral Wemyss, Geddes also opened the door to the comparatively young (45) Roger Keyes. This admiral, in Churchill's words, 'revolutionised the situation. He redoubled the patrols and by night the barrage across the Straits was lit up from end to end as bright as Piccadilly.' In addition, Keyes launched a brilliant attack on the U-boat base at Zeebrugge, completing the rout of the German submarine arm : 'The finest feat of arms in the Great War, . . . an episode unsurpassed in the history of the Royal Navy,' said Churchill again. To quote Lloyd George : 'The real decision of the war, for the sea front, turned out to be the decisive flank in the gigantic battlefield.'

Admiral Jellicoe's entry in the single volume *Dictionary of National Biography* describes his dismissal by Geddes as 'unjust'. That must, of course, be a matter of opinion. In his single volume *World Crisis* Churchill makes no mention of Geddes. Maybe the two did not get on. But the fact remains that Geddes chose the right men at the right time to do the right job.

This ability was to prove invaluable for the Dunlop Company in the harsh economic climate of the twenties. And his selection by Lloyd George for the highest administrative offices – he followed his stint at the Admiralty by being appointed Minister of Munitions and, after hostilities had ended, the first-ever Minister of Transport – emphasized the close connection between the able businessman and the state which was to be a hallmark of the Dunlop ethos for sixty years.

Lloyd George was a fervent exponent of the government partnership with progressive and 'pushy' industrialists. Although labelled a radical he was a really a supreme pragmatist, not too worried about the course the ship of state took so long as he was at the wheel.

His experience as President of the Board of Trade and then as Chancellor of the Exchequer had given him insight into the workings of business and the capacity of businessmen to conceive correct policies, implement them and impose their will on colleagues and rivals.

Eric Geddes exactly fitted Mr Lloyd George's ideal. As long ago as 1904 Geddes had impressed Lord Kitchener, then C-in-C of the Indian Army, with his logistics mastery when, as the young general manager of a small Indian railway system, he had helped transport troops and material for a mock mobilization. Twelve years later his expertise, much extended by his work as general manager of the British North-Eastern Railway (later LNER), led to his appointment as

supremo of British transport behind the lines in France and Flanders
with the rank of major-general (his brother, Auckland, was a surgeon
brigadier-general of the same period). His achievements prompted
the taciturn Field Marshal Douglas Haig to commend unstintingly
his 'broad views, quick intuition and powers of drive and energy'.

Sir Eric Geddes – the knighthood came in 1916 – was throughout
much of his business and all of his state service life accompanied by
an extraordinarily able statistician, George Beharrell. Together these
two men and their sons, Reay Geddes and Edward Beharrell, were
to succeed the du Cros dynasty and dominate Dunlop for some fifty
years.

The years 1918–19 mark the end of the du Cros era in the Dunlop
story and illustrate the activities of the new men who would lead the
company in its second stage.

Just before Christmas Eve 1918, Harvey du Cros, founder of the
Pneumatic Tyre Company and the real architect of the fortunes of
Dunlop Rubber, died at his country house, Inniscorrig, County Dub-
lin.

He had ceased to play a major role in the firm some years previously
and enjoyed the fine-sounding but empty title of president. Nonetheless his very presence kept Arthur on the straight and narrow and
ensured decent behaviour.

His death coincided with the end of World War I, and an immediate
lessening of the patriotic imperative, as well as the disappearance of
the profitable military contracts.

It is impossible to resist the conclusion that without the ballast
of 'the Governor', 'the Napoleon of the tyre industry', to quote *The
Motor* magazine, the company lost its way.

Even before hostilities ceased the shadow of Jimmy White had fallen
over the company, as will be seen in the next chapter.

Harvey du Cros had been able to control the activities of the scally-
wag financier Ernest Terah Hooley in the 1890s, while advancing the
family fortunes through these self-same activities. Son Arthur had
no such good fortune. He simply let White and his cronies take over
Dunlop, while blocking his mind to the consequences. Jimmy White
does not rate a mention either in Arthur's semi-autobiographical
Wheels of Fortune or in his privately circulated *Recollections*. In the
latter he merely records

1919 : retired from active business . . . sailed from Southampton, 22nd
November for a voyage round the world in the 900-ton yacht Emerald.

48

1920 : Returned in June to be confronted with Dunlop Company losses
of £8m (actually £11m) due to a general national collapse, incompetence
and questionable direction, leading to a highly irregular gambling Derby
in raw materials.

Unscrupulous, determined, but unsuccessful efforts made to embroil
me in this disaster, notwithstanding my absence. . . .

If Arthur du Cros didn't know what was happening, he should
have done, but having assured himself and his family of a great deal
of money from the company founded by his father, he seems to have
slipped his business moorings and shrugged off his responsibility to
shareholders, workers and the company in general. So long as he
received lots of money to feed his land hunger, Arthur du Cros couldn't
have cared less what happened elsewhere.

In contrast, Eric Geddes joyfully grasped responsibility to his
bosom. Wearing two hats during the war — those of major-general
and admiral — he launched his post-war career in transport.

The North Eastern Railway paid him off with a golden handshake
of £50,000 and his entry in *The Dictionary of Business Biography*
makes it clear that his colleagues, or some of them anyway, were not
sorry to see him go. Perhaps they feared they would suffer the same
fate as Lord Jellicoe.

As it was, Geddes left the railway system at just the right moment.
The great days of the steam train were ending ; road transport — cars,
lorries, trucks, buses, coaches — was about to take over.

Geddes and Beharrell, who accompanied him, were being unwitt-
ingly groomed for their jobs at Dunlop and indeed it was as Minister
of Transport that Eric Geddes was brought to the attention of Frederick Szarvasy, the banker, who was to play a vital part in the crisis
which brought Dunlop to the brink of bankruptcy. For the period
1919–20 saw the first attempt to create an integrated transport structure
for the country. War planning seemed to show the way forward.
Geddes had had intimate and testing experience of scheduling road
and rail transport behind the lines in France. Could this be applied
in peace ? In one sense it was.

Railway companies were in dire, nay desperate, need of rationalization. Even before 1914 they were facing financial problems. The war,
with its assured market for the transport of troops and munitions,
had provided a respite, but it also aggravated the problems beyond
solution. For four years the rail network had been starved of capital
expenditure. Tracks and stock had been neither repaired nor renewed.
Everything had been make-do and mend. Many of the 123 rail companies faced ruin in the aftermath of hostilities.

No one could have been better suited to dealing with this situation than the brisk, practical team of Geddes and Beharrell. Go-go Geddes and the quiet accountant Beharrell set about amalgamating the railway companies in record time and with a minimum of fuss. Within two years the number of operating concerns had been reduced from 123 to four: London, Midland and Scottish; London and North Eastern; Great Western; and Southern. As they were no longer in competition with one another the stage had actually been set for nationalization, which indeed happened after World War II.

That was not what Geddes and Beharrell intended. They were free enterprise industrialists. It was however what the conditions, and their conclusions, determined in the long run.

In the shorter term, Geddes and Beharrell exactly mirrored the national temper which was in favour of a sensible carve-up of the market: particularly for sectors like the railways facing destructive competition from rival services.

Geddes and Beharrell were simply responding to necessity. That fact, however, did not make their solution any more palatable to ideologies on either side of the political divide. The hot gospellers of the market economy deplored state-inspired amalgamation which eliminated competition, while the advocates of state socialism denounced a system which provided directors and shareholders with assured markets and dividends.

Still greater political controversy – and on this occasion not confined to the politically committed – concerned Geddes's role in chairing the committee on the economy which, by advocating reductions in wages, salaries and expenditure throughout the public service, raised an outcry and forever after associated the name with 'The Geddes Axe'.

Again Geddes was responding to reality. The public sector had grown to huge proportions during the war. It had to be reduced both to conform to peace requirements and to diminish its claim on scarce resources. Unfortunately the Geddes recommendations coincided, in 1921, with an unparalleled slump in world trade, as the boom created by repair of war damage and neglect and the satisfaction of deferred demand gave way to saturated markets. The Geddes proposals created tremendous bitterness because they fell on people who were already suffering hardship. Sixty years later men in retirement would recall how their pocket-money had been cut by fathers in the Civil Service or the Armed Forces, and that the diminished sum was known as 'Geddes money'.

Poor Sir Eric. For doing his duty as businessman, politician and disinterested administrator he was denounced as a hard-hearted, cheese-paring, uncaring bureaucrat. He was also saddled with the phrase 'Squeeze Germany till the pips squeak'. Actually he had said, in the last days of the war, 'We will get everything out of her [Germany] that you can squeeze out of a lemon – and a bit more.'

Such remarks were perfectly acceptable, even moderate, in 1918 when the general demand was for hanging the Kaiser, but by 1921 sentiment, at least among the intellectuals and like-minded folk, had swung towards sympathy with Germany, the defeated underdog, and comments like Sir Eric Geddes's were much deprecated.

It was doubtless with considerable relief that Geddes quit political life in March 1922, resigning his Cambridgeshire seat some seven months before the fall of the Lloyd George coalition signalled the return to all-out Party warfare.

Geddes had flowered and flourished in the atmosphere of national service induced by war. He had fulfilled superbly the tasks allotted him in transport, naval affairs and munitions supply. He had undertaken a mammoth and nationally acceptable duty in reorganizing the rail system. But the controversy surrounding his chairmanship of the committee on the economy and the delayed fury that erupted over his 'squeeze Germany' remark were not at all to his liking.

By 1922 he and his ever-loyal collaborator, George Beharrell, were ready for a new challenge.

Unbeknown to them it was being prepared for them by the events at the Dunlop Rubber Company.

CHAPTER VI

THE CRISIS OF 1921

The best side of Arthur du Cros was shown by his dedication to national service. As previously mentioned, he was an early and enthusiastic supporter of aviation and a pioneer of military preparedness in the air, establishing the Aerial Defence Committee of the Commons in 1909. He was painfully aware of the War Office's animosity towards the air arm, neatly, if cruelly, illustrated by the fate of one Colonel J.D. Fullerton.

The colonel intervened in a debate on strategy at the Royal United Services Institution in November 1906. In the course of his remarks he gave a remarkably prescient commentary on air power, declaring :

> In the next great war flying machines will be regularly employed. The aerial battles will practically settle the first period of the campaign, the victor gaining command of the air and all the advantages that will ensue therefrom. Against an enemy's sea forces, the flying machines will fire specially designed projectiles vertically downwards on the decks of ships. . . . The location and destruction of submarines will also be an important function of the aerial ships as their position high in the air will enable them to trace the course of vessels some 30 or 40 feet below the surface. [This foreshadowed aerial radar by about thirty years !]

The colonel's reward was to be retired from the active list, and three years later – a mere five before the outbreak of World War I – the War Office recommended cancellation of the £2,000 a year being spent on aviation research as 'a waste of money'.

It was to counteract this purblind attitude that Arthur du Cros applied his considerable energy and talents for persuasion. He adopted a high profile in this task of public education and one of the people to take note of him was a rising star in the business firmament, Mr James White.

James White was a roistering financial adventurer. Born in Rochdale in 1878 he started adult life as a bricklayer. When he was nineteen he concluded his first business transaction, which was to buy a share in a local circus for £100. He probably borrowed the £100, but he had a keen eye for a prospective winner. The circus flourished and he cleared a profit.

Spurred by his success, he gave up bricklaying and took himself off to London where he swiftly built himself a reputation for daring, and triumphant, speculation. *The Times* observed, 'He has a passion for deals on a large scale with corresponding risks.'

Clifford-Turner, the solicitor for the Dunlop Company, described White as 'a most likeable rascal.... I knew him very well and liked him. We had a lot of business with him.'[1] Turner records that he made £10,000 out of a deal concerning Dunlop, organized by White. 'Jimmy [he was always known as that] could make money for others as well as himself.'

It was probably this feature which attracted the notice of Arthur du Cros who had an insatiable desire for money and a splendid capacity for enjoying what money could buy.

White and he both had a gusto for life. White involved himself in boxing promotion – as much for the love of the sport as for the income it brought – and was also active as a racehorse owner. He was successful here too. He gave Gordon Richards, who was to become one of racing's all-time greats, his first professional ride, in 1920.

White and du Cros shared that jaunty, risk-taking, not-quite-the-done-thing attitude to life, so characteristic of the money-makers of the Edwardian age.

Their partnership was mutually rewarding: it was not so for the company in which they were involved.

According to the report by inspectors into Dunlop's affairs the business relationship between Jimmy White and Arthur du Cros began when a proposal from White and others to build and operate textile mills in Rochdale (White's home town) was received by the Dunlop board.

By 1912 motoring was fast expanding, as was demand for tyres. The company acquired 481 acres of land in Birmingham for a factory which later became Fort Dunlop. Similarly to secure raw material supplies the rubber estates in Ceylon and Malaya were extended. That left the other staple of tyre production, raw cotton, to be dealt with, and the White proposal met Dunlop's needs in this respect. The board approved the scheme in January 1914. A spinning company, Tyre Yarns Ltd, and a weaving company, Fabric Weavers, were erected. About the same time, James White discharged himself from bankruptcy on paying his creditors in full with interest. Most of the board, which then consisted of eight members headed by Arthur du Cros's father Harvey (with Arthur as managing director), appear to have paid little attention to Mr White's financial antecedents. Indeed the absence of disclosure by du Cros and the lack of elementary curiosity by the other board members was to prove a deadly combination.

As soon as the factories were built, Dunlop contracted to take the whole output of the mills on a cost-plus basis with profits limited to 3d (about 1p) a lb. Dunlop also had an option to purchase all the shares of Tyre Yarns and Fabric Weavers once Dunlop had bought 12 million lbs weight of cloth from the mills.

In March 1914 the payment of £5,000 was reported to the Dunlop board, being Mr White's underwriting and negotiating fee. Only the money went not to Mr White but to Arthur du Cros. This curious transaction was to set the pattern throughout the following six years for deals worth many times £5,000, provoking this statement in the independent inspectors report of 1923 :

> Very soon after the introduction of Mr White into Dunlop affairs an agreement, or understanding, was come to between him and Sir Arthur du Cros [he had been given a baronetcy for war work in 1916] by virtue of which Sir Arthur became entitled to divide with Mr White any profits which the latter might make out of his transactions with the Company, i.e. Dunlop.
>
> There was never disclosure by Sir Arthur du Cros to the other members of the Board of this generous agreement, or understanding.
>
> The existence of this agreement placed Sir Arthur in a position in which his personal interests were in conflict with the duties he owed to the Company.
>
> As a result, the interests of the Company in various important matters were adversely affected by his personal interests.

These deliberations were emphatically endorsed by two distinguished lawyers, Sir John Simon and James Wylie, who in an Opinion for Dunlop shareholders commented :

> Sir Arthur du Cros is, in the absence of proper disclosure, liable to account to the Dunlop Company for, and to pay to it, all sums received by him from Mr White out of profits made by Mr White or any of his companies in relation to any transaction between Mr White or his companies and the Dunlop Company. . . . A director cannot be allowed to have an interest against his duty. . . .

The sums exchanged amounted to well over £100,000, equivalent in monetary terms seventy years later to £3 million.

If Dunlop had not crashed into a near £10 million loss in 1921 the Mr White–du Cros saga would never have seen the light of day. If the company had continued to trade successfully, the shareholders may well have remained indifferent to such shadowy deals, though some must have wondered how an ex-bankrupt could become virtual controller of Dunlop.

Yet that is precisely what he had become by 1917. The Dunlop organization at that time was split in two: the Parent Tyre Company and the Dunlop Rubber Company with the same set of directors.

Jimmy White and Beecham Trust, with which he was associated, negotiated the purchase of Dunlop ordinary shares held by the Parent Tyre Company. Simultaneously a concern known as the Tyre Investment Trust, in which Mr White was the moving spirit, acquired Dunlop Canada and Dunlop Japan, as well as the Dunlop rights in the USA.

The upshot was that Mr White and associates became possessed of 780,000 out of Dunlop Rubber's 1,000,000 ordinary shares. They proceeded to offer these shares to selected individuals – about 300 – who formed a so-called 'pool'. The object of the pool was to sell the pooled shares advantageously until it liquidated itself. As World War I was raging, very large profits were guaranteed any company involved, as was Dunlop, in vital war work, so the shares were gilt-edged.

But so long as the pool existed Jimmy White and Co. were effectively in control. Sir Arthur du Cros was now the chairman. White demanded, and got, the resignation of four directors and their replacement by two of his nominees.

Compensation for loss of office caused another scandal. The sum of £8,000 paid to a Mr Hely was met by the Tyre Investment Trust (a White instrument), which, in turn, was freed from the need to pay £53,000 royalties to the Dunlop Rubber Company. The company in other words lost £45,000. Nothing of this transaction appeared in the company records or in the recorded minutes.

White now had the bit between his teeth and from merely helping himself and others, notably Sir Arthur, in profitable deals with Dunlop, he began to form policy for the company.

As soon as the war was over he insisted that dividends should be increased from 15 to $22\frac{1}{2}$ per cent. Du Cros persuaded him to compromise on $17\frac{1}{2}$. Then at a dinner party at the Criterion Restaurant on 2 December 1918 he demanded Sir Arthur du Cros's retirement from Dunlop. There was, however, to be one last glorious pay-off.

In sum, Sir Arthur was to vacate the chair and become life president without remuneration. That was the public information afforded the shareholders at the Annual General Meeting on 11 February 1919. The secret deal was rather different. Sir Arthur was to receive £150,000 (say, £4.5 million in close of twentieth-century terms) in consideration of giving up office. In addition he was to receive £12,000 a year (£300,000 a year in 1989 values) as 'advisory expert' – *free of tax* – for a period of nineteen years.

Not surprisingly, Sir Arthur took himself off on a world cruise on the 900-ton yacht, Emerald, laconically remarking in his privately circulated *Recollections* : 'Retired from active business. . . .'

It was now that Dunlop entered on courses of action which very nearly killed the company stone dead.

America had long exercised a fascination for the Dunlop Company. It was the world's biggest single market and the home of mass motoring. The right to the name 'Dunlop' (very important as the company was known everywhere as the developer of the pneumatic tyre) had been granted to a group of US manufacturers. That right was returned, on payment of 100,000 dollars, during the war.

On the conclusion of peace, plans were made to re-establish an enterprise in the USA and to finance factory construction. Once again Jimmy White was the key figure, straddling Dunlop and two finance-raising concerns, D.A. Trust Ltd and Beechams Trust Ltd. And once again certain directors were due to benefit through his activities.

The site was chosen, Buffalo in the north-east USA. A contract to build was placed. The stock of the Utica Spinning Company was acquired. On 2 January 1920 the Dunlop Rubber Company raised £8 million in ordinary shares, one eighth of which was allocated to the American enterprise.

Then everything started to go wrong. The cost of land, buildings and plant in the US soared far above Dunlop's estimate. The £ fell in relation to the dollar so that £1 million raised in sterling brought only three-quarters of the dollars that could have been brought in 1919. Within a twelve-month period the US company was facing bankruptcy. Because of personal involvement Dunlop directors rushed the British company to the rescue of its American subsidiary and so precipitated a crisis in Dunlop as a whole.

The financial crisis was compounded by a technical one.

Throughout its history tyres – their research, design, development, patents and rival products – bedevilled Dunlop at crucial moments. So it proved in 1919–20.

The Great War had made the motorcar a familiar sight in Western Europe as it had been for years in the USA. Henry Ford had brought

Right: Autographed photograph of John Boyd Dunlop, *c.* 1895.

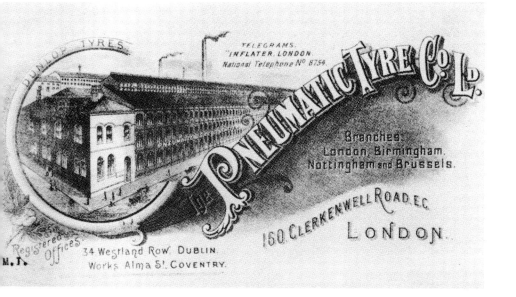

Dunlop Quint pacing solo rider, August 1897.

Harvey du Cros.

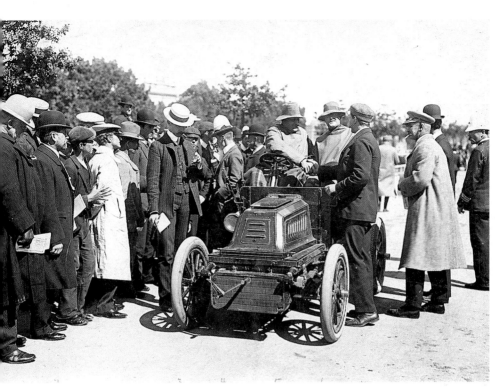

Start of Melbourne/Sydney/Melbourne
Dunlop Reliability Trials, 1904.

Sir Arthur du Cros.

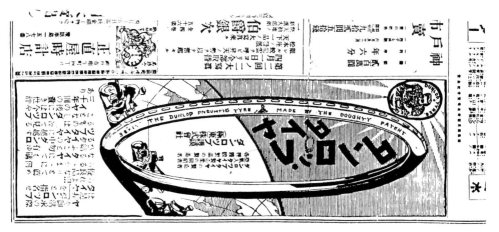

Dunlop Cycle Tyres – Doughty Patent – Japan, 1 April 1914.

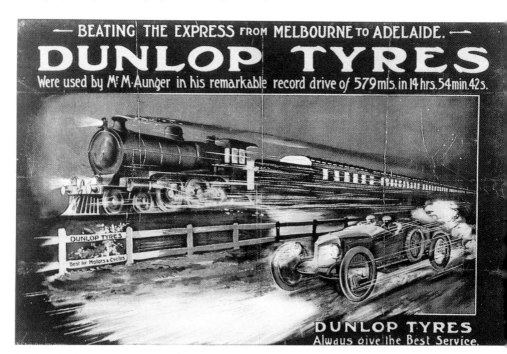

'Beating the Express', Melbourne/Adelaide, 1914.

Dunlop advertises at an early motor race, Eu,
Normandy, 1908.

Sir Eric Geddes, 1875–1937.

Fort Dunlop workers
arriving by barge at Fort
Dunlop, 1918.

Fort Dunlop from the
south. The base stores
were built in 1929
(before the M.G.
came!).

Left: Original cake mixer used in development of 'Dunlopillo', 1928.

Below: Dunlop's test fleet of vehicles, Fort Dunlop, 1928.

Bottom: Sir Malcolm Campbell and 'Bluebird' I, 1931.

First Dunlop latex bathing costumes, Fort
Dunlop, 1938.

Above: Dunlopillo mattress emerging from
mould, 1966.

Right: Kay on the largest, holding the smallest,
Fort Dunlop, 1938.

the benefits of mass production and conveyor belt techniques to car production. No longer was the motorcar a horseless carriage for the delight of the few. It was now the convenience of millions, and tyres fitted to machines for mass markets must be safe and cheap.

American tyre manufacturers, Goodyear, Firestone and others, had been free to experiment with means of meeting consumer needs while European industry had been devoted wholly to war production of existing models. As a result the Americans had developed a tyre with a rubber non-skid tread. Given their huge domestic market, there was every prospect of low-cost US tyres flooding the European market.

Even before the war's end, Dunlop engineers had started on experimental work to meet US competition. A tread pattern was devised known as 'Magnum'. Advancement, however, was slow, and board members – prompted by Jimmy White who zealously proclaimed the need for the swiftest possible growth – expressed themselves thoroughly dissatisfied with progress. On their behalf, Mr Bergin, the secretary, urged Mr Worthington, the technical superintendent in charge of output, to speed up the production of the Magnum tyre.

A harassed Mr Worthington pronounced himself 'satisfied' with the models prepared, and in September 1919 Magnum was offered to the motoring public.

As usual there were teething problems, but it wasn't until a year later that drivers started returning Magnum tyres in quantity because of defects. The tyre was turning into a disaster.

Blame for the failure was laid on the hapless Worthington, who had inefficiently tested the tyre, had failed to take cognizance of manufacturing faults (treatment of cotton and curing of rubber) revealed by such tests as did take place, and had submitted to the board's importunate hustling.

Mr Worthington's head was demanded. He resigned, but upon staggeringly generous terms: £20,000 compensation (current value, £600,000) plus the appointment as Advisory Expert (!) for five years at a salary of £5,000 (current value £150,000) per annum.

It is impossible to avoid the conclusion that Dunlop at this point was careering out of control with rewards *for failure* spiralling into the stratosphere ; with Jimmy White exercising power without responsibility – and calling for tyre production in the UK and USA to be pushed ahead by 100 per cent ; and with a board lacking expertise and commercial instinct, and common loyalty to the company.

Troubles in America merely precipitated a gathering crisis at the heart of Dunlop.

Board fallibility was demonstrated, to a striking degree, by the authority which it conferred on two committees, a finance committee and a development committee. These bodies were virtually autonomous and especially subject to the whims and policies of Jimmy White. Each committee was composed of three members, two of whom duplicated finance and development, and they were also excessively well rewarded. Thus Messrs Ormerod and Stephenson received £7,500 and £5,000 per annum respectively (current value more than £100,000) while Sir Harry McGowan, a new arrival on the Dunlop board and a member of the Development Committee, got £1,500 a year.

Sir Harry McGowan was later to march to fame and fortune as the first chairman of ICI, the Imperial Chemical Industries giant, formed to protect the British chemical manufacturers in the Empire against foreign, mainly US and German, competition. Sir Harry's own firm, Nobel Explosives, took the lead in bringing the consortium into being.

As a cartel-minded businessman, Sir Harry sounded a note of caution on the American operation: 'The big American tyre companies are somewhat afraid of Dunlop competition and would be willing to sacrifice something to arrange for that competition being of a friendly character. . . .'[2] This tendency towards 'friendly arrangements' with rivals was a characteristic of Dunlop policy throughout its life.

Sir Harry's caution did not, however, extend to limiting the purchase of rubber and cotton, nor to the extraordinary independence of the two committees.

Thus Mr Ormerod, the chairman – successor to Sir Arthur du Cros – on his own initiative and without consulting the board, authorized a loan of £525,000 from Dunlop to a subsidiary to purchase a small and badly-off textile firm, James Hoyle Ltd. The deal went through under 'any other business' and later the board merely acquiesced in their chairman's action (minute of 10 February, 1920).

Forward buying of rubber and cotton reached absurd heights, urged on by Dunlop's real boss, Jimmy White. Without expert knowledge, White insisted on forty weeks' stock of cotton being held, just before the cotton market sagged through the floor.

Rubber buying was even more frenetic. Jimmy White insisted early in 1919 that Dunlop was 'too parochial' and that if the severe post-war competition was to be conducted successfully, 50,000 tyres a week would have to be produced to gain the economies of scale. This was to be achieved at the same time as the ambitious penetration of the American market.

Dunlop's own estates in Malaya could supply only a proportion of the company's requirements so rubber buying on the open market was the normal practice.

What was abnormal was the extent of the buying on 'futures', contracting to purchase the commodity at the current price for future delivery.

Dunlop usually bought a margin of nine months ahead keeping three months in stock. Spurred by Jimmy White's conviction that a serious rubber shortage was going to develop, Dunlop in 1919 started buying two, three, even four, years ahead. Jimmy White, with Messrs Ormerod and Stephenson and other executives concurring, issued instructions to their export buyer, Mr Byrne, to buy, buy, buy. Between March and June 1920 contracts were placed for purchases in 1921, 1922, 1923 and 1924. Factory expansion plans were implemented in Britain and the US, all predicated on the belief that the country, and the world, was in for a prolonged period of prosperity and motoring expansion.

The reverse proved to be the case. With the world financial system wrecked by the consequencies of World War I (communist Russia repudiated her debts to the West, the Austrian and Turkish Empires expired in a welter of anarchy and the new German republic succumbed to hyper-inflation) trade moved from post-war replacement boom to grievous slump in late 1920.

Dunlop had been buying raw rubber at 2s 8d (13p) a lb for forward delivery. By August 1921 the price had fallen to 8d (3p) a lb. Dunlop purchased 22,494 tons of rubber for 1921 and only consumed 6,472 tons, adding to the 9,000 excess tons accumulated in 1920.

At the same time the American concern was costing far more than had been anticipated. There was a shortfall of £2 million after the issue of 3 million shares yielding £4.5 million. Messrs White and Ormerod, and Sir Arthur du Cros at a distance, were at pains to make sure that they were fully compensated, and more, for their involvement in Dunlop's international operations. The shareholders were left to carry the financial burden of £1 million diverted by directors to cover their own concerns from resources desperately needed to finance the American enterprise and the huge unsold and unusable stocks of rubber.

On 31 August 1921 the Dunlop board announced to the world a loss of £8,320,006 7s. (current value £250 million). At the Annual General Meeting the following February, the shareholders demanded a committee inquiry to investigate the running of the company. Under the Companies Act of 1908 four inspectors were appointed and their investigations and conclusions have formed the bulk of this chapter.

The inspectors – Sir Arthur Whinney, Sir Josiah Stamp, James

Thomson and Fred Sobey – interviewed fifteen past and present directors, including a Mr F.A. Szarvasy who had come to the company's
rescue by organizing a re-financing project; in the inspectors' words:
'The threatened appointment of a receiver [for Dunlop] in America
was avoided . . . and the English Dunlop was extricated from a position
of grave peril.' The inspectors examined books and accounts going
back to 1913 and board minutes back to 1896. They examined scores
of other witnesses including non-board executives. And they came
to the following conclusions:

> [the slump in world trade] undoubtedly contributed to the loss . . .
> although by no means the whole of the loss is attributable to this
> cause. . . .
>
> Throughout the period between 1912 and 1919 Sir Arthur du Cros
> dominated the affairs of the companies. He had an arrangement with
> Mr White under which he shared in the profits which the latter derived
> from the transactions he conducted. The existence of the arrangement
> placed Sir Arthur in a position in which his own interests were in conflict
> with the duty he owed the company. The interests of the company
> were materially affected by the personal interests of Sir Arthur.

The board as a whole

> failed to give sufficient consideration to important matters . . . arrived
> at decisions without calling for essential information . . . delegated to
> the Finance and Development Committees in vague terms powers which
> should have belonged to the Board . . . abstained from exercising proper
> supervision.

Executive directors (i.e. employees) were effectively 'Yes Men' to
the dominant personalities such as Sir Arthur du Cros and Jimmy
White. Or, in the more demure phraseology of the Inspectors: '. . .
were lacking those qualities which were needed if they were to be
useful to the Board when dealing with complicated matters outside
the scope of their duties as managers.'
Finally,

> Mr White's influence upon the company's affairs was of a unique charac-
> ter . . . his position as purporting to represent a majority of the ordinary
> shares enabled him to bring pressure to bear upon the Board and the
> Company's officials which was facilitated by the absence of disinterested
> criticism of, or opposition to, his views by the chairman, Sir Arthur
> du Cros. Mr White's views were equally effective through the new
> chairman, Mr Ormerod, whom Mr White had been instrumental in
> appointing.

The inspectors' report, issued in September 1923, was damning of the whole Dunlop set-up.

Counsel averred in an Opinon that 'there appears to be ample material to justify a claim for damages for conspiracy between Mr White, Sir Arthur du Cros and others of the directors and we think the damages awarded would be substantial.'

In short, the evidence appears overwhelming that Mr White, Sir Arthur and others were milking the company dry. And that those board members who were not in on 'the arrangement' and benefitting accordingly were guilty of crass stupidity or culpable negligence.

Sir Arthur himself dismissed the allegations, confiding in his *Recollections* : 'The inquiry before a specially selected and hostile committee (the inspectors) failed to make of me a convenient scapegoat. After months of persecution I accepted £31,250 on my retirement with my brothers, Alfred and George.'

Thus ended the era of the du Cros family in the affairs of Dunlop. Theirs had been a remarkable contribution to the company's prosperity and expansion in the first twenty-five years of its existence. Until the appearance of Jimmy White their service had been, if not without blemish, at least one that far excelled self-gain.

With Arthur du Cros in the chair there might have been a change even without the arrival of White. For Arthur was a man with a profound sense of his own importance, a property-hunger for himself and his family and a sublime conviction that he could do no wrong. This combination would have made him a wayward and greedy chieftain had White never appeared on the scene.

Du Cros's reminiscences are rich in a medley of land speculation . . .

Purchased large estates in England and Scotland, dividing them into lots and re-selling mainly to sitting tenants [presumably at considerable profit] . . . Joined the board of a Brazilian land company in low water. Visited Sâo Paulo and purchased city lands advantageously . . . purchased historic Canons, Edgware . . . purchased Covent Garden Market and also the Foundling Hospital and estate in Bloomsbury . . . Levestleigh, the Member's Home in Hastings [Arthur was MP for Hastings] burned down by suffragettes, leaving me free to live elsewhere. Subsequently purchased Craigweil House and estate as a residence *and for development*, together with other important lands in Sussex. Such are the oddities of life.

Other 'oddities' in this larger-than-life career included 'bagging' a gamekeeper and guest at a shoot, being elected chief of a Pacific island tribe at which he was presented with '20 complete costumes of 20 fat females who had danced them off, one garment at a time, commencing the show as 20 bulky women and ending it as 20 slim young maidens', and claiming credit for Bognor becoming Bognor Regis, which happened thus.

King George v fell grievously ill and Sir Arthur placed Craigweil house, Sussex, at royal disposal for his occupation. During his three-month convalescence the Archbishops of Canterbury and York were sworn in, and Sir Henry Segrave, the world land and sea speed record-holder, was knighted, all in the library of Craigweil. The future Queen Elizabeth II built her first sand-castle in the grounds. In gratitude King George v decreed that Bognor should be renamed Bognor Regis 'as perpetual memory [according to Sir Arthur] to His Majesty's recovery at Craigweil House'. Sir Arthur does not record – perhaps he never knew – that the king was reputed to have replied 'bugger Bognor' to a suggestion that he spend some time there during a later – and fatal – illness.

Yet the incident does illustrate how acceptable Sir Arthur du Cros was to the highest in the Empire.

Men of wealth do, of course, have an attraction simply because of their wealth.

With du Cros, however, there was much more than mere riches. The man was a devoted, far-seeing patriot, a bundle of high-spirited energy and manifold talents not least of which was the talent for making money. Properly reined in by a competent board of directors he might well have been a major asset to Dunlop instead of the co-author of its near demise.

The failure of the Dunlop board to do anything except rubber-stamp the decisions of the White–du Cros axis is an object lesson in how not to run a company. Some of the board were undoubtedly privy to the dubious transactions. Others were disgracefully ignorant. It is significant that when Mr Szarvasy introduced his restructuring plans he demanded the resignation of Messrs Ormerod (chairman), Dawson and White. In the end the following also resigned, in February 1921: The Earl of Albemarle, the Earl of Drogheda, Lord Hindlip and Messrs Stephenson and Craig. In Counsel's opinion other directors who could have been charged with negligence included Sir Harry McGowan.

Sir Harry was to prove himself a power in the land as chairman of ICI, but what is to be said of the Lords Albemarle, Drogheda, Hindlip and Dalziel?

Too often in these, and subsequent days, peers were put on boards to give company letterheads a distinguished (and reputable) appearance. Dunlop, however, had no need for any such embellishment.

There must, therefore, be a strong presumption that the peers were useful adornments in that they didn't question the acts of the two buccaneers, White and Sir Arthur. In other words, they had the jobs because they were passive peers.

That seems the only reasonable explanation for their silent acceptance of the pugilistically inclined ex-bricklayer and discharged bankrupt, Jimmy White, and his baleful influence on a fine organization.

Poor Jimmy. Within four years of the inspectors' report on the Dunlop Rubber Company he was dead – by his own hand. He committed suicide at his Wiltshire home on 29 June 1927. He was faced with paying a 'prodigious sum' on the next Stock Exchange settlement day and preferred to take a mixture of diluted prussic acid and chloroform instead. His death caused a slump in share prices and a mini-panic on the Exchange.

Shortly afterwards, the original Founder Pneumatic Tyre Company of 1889 went out of business, largely due to the frauds of another master-speculator, Clarence Hatry, who was sentenced to fourteen years' imprisonment for false conversion in the Founder's and other cases. Here too there was gross negligence by the board – the chairman of which was Sir Arthur du Cros! He had the gall to denounce the 'fatuous over-confidence and egotism' of his colleagues in undertaking speculative ventures while he, the chairman, was on holiday. To lose one company through absenteeism may be accorded unfortunate; to lose two. . . .

A sad little footnote to this time of troubles was provided by the man who had given his name to the company: John Boyd Dunlop. He sued the Dunlop Rubber Company for 'exposing him to ridicule' through advertising. For more than twenty years the company had used Dunlop's fine bearded face and his signature as its trademark. They had acquired the right to do this. What they had not acquired the right to do was to use a line drawing, full length, of this figure complete with top hat at a jaunty angle, morning coat, cane, spats and a monocle. This jolly old chap might, admittedly, have been mistaken for the 'Man Who Broke The Bank at Monte Carlo'. But it was a thoroughly cheerful cartoon and the directors were understandably dismayed when J.B. took out an action, claiming that it demeaned him and that the caricature was 'the antithesis of what he really was'. The dispute was settled; the advertisement was discontinued. Happily J.B. resisted the suggestion of a friend that he should shave off his whiskers and deprive the company of its trademark! Yet the incident, trivial in itself, added to the company's travails – it occurred in 1920 – and displayed J.B. himself in a far from flattering light.

He was, by then, an old man of eighty, but a year away from death. He somehow felt he had been robbed of the fruit to which his genius entitled him. His book on the pneumatic tyre, published posthumously, roused fierce criticism, provoking the *Irish Cyclist* (which had been closely associated with the venture) to condemn 'the manner in which it attempts to belittle everyone who had to do with improvements' and to sting Arthur du Cros to say that 'Thomson had the patent and no business, while Dunlop had the business and no patent'. Meanwhile the painting of Harvey du Cros was removed from the Dunlop boardroom.

These acrimonious exchanges marked the passing of the du Cros era.

Fortunately for the Dunlop Rubber Company a new era was about to dawn, dominated by men of outstanding capacity. Dunlop, as befitted its product, was about to bounce back, higher than ever.

CHAPTER VII

THE GEDDES MEDICINE

Little is known about the man who was instrumental in turning round Dunlop's fortunes. Frederick Szarvasy was an international banker, heading the British, Foreign and Colonial Corporation, who became interested in Dunlop both as an investor who wished to protect his investment and as someone genuinely concerned to rescue a vital segment of British industry.

It is never safe to underestimate altruism. Despite his name – which to many English people at that time suggested all kinds of Central European skulduggery – Frederick Szarvasy was an honest man at a period when Dunlop badly needed that quality. He was also exceedingly secretive. Sir Maurice Coop, for many years company legal adviser and director, recalls Szarvasy still serving on Dunlop's board in the early 1950s, keeping his counsel and rarely, if ever, reminiscing. When he died his executors found his safe empty of records.

His secretiveness extended to the approaches made to Eric Geddes. They were highly confidential. So were the financial considerations which induced Geddes and Beharrell to accept the challenge of salvaging a firm which had been milked dry. Rumour had it that they were tempted with attractive share options. Perhaps so. They certainly deserved payments if they could produce the results.

The Economist of 4 February 1922 observed: 'Dunlop's report and accounts are a candid admission of a state of affairs which result from bubble finances. The company is said to be in a position to meet all competition of a normal character, but there will have to be some drastic reduction of capital if the present loss is to be written off.'

So it proved. The first action of the new regime was to write down a debit of £7,731,000 to the profit and loss account of 1922 and write off £4,516,000 in depreciation in subsidiaries. By 1925 financial reconstruction had gone far enough to enable Dunlop to resume payment of dividends, although the £1 share had been written down to 6s 8d.

Whether the traumatic effect of the crisis of 1921 had longer term implications – notably on the City's perception of Dunlop as a worthwhile investment – is another matter. Certainly Dunlop was never a favourite with stockbrokers, even when it had, by 1930, become the eighth largest British firm in terms of market value.[1]

While Beharrell the accountant got on with the statistics of financial recovery, Geddes got busy with the practical side of expansion.

At Fort Dunlop tyre manufacture took a leap forward with the introduction of a wired-type fitted on a detachable flange rim which was made standard by 1924. This beat the opposition out of sight, for it meant that the car manufacturer might have a tyre and wheel unit of extreme simplicity. The racing driver, Paul Dutoit, carried out tests to prove that there was no danger of tyres coming off the wheel on deflation and with this reassurance the enormously successful Morris Cowley and Austin 7 cars took the market by storm on Dunlop tyres.

Geddes, however, was not content to rest on technical excellence in tyre manufacture. He sought to broaden the base of the company and reduce its dependence on the automotive industry.

Following a board decision in 1924, Dunlop acquired the Charles Macintosh group of companies the following year. This Manchester concern was one of the pioneers of the rubber industry making, among other items, footwear, cables, clothing (the word 'Mac' or 'Mackintosh' was internationally interchangeable with the word raincoat), hose and belting.

Dunlop's philosophy, however, dictated that cable and clothing were outside the company's field. First cable and then ultimately clothing were disposed of – probably mistakenly. It is, after all, difficult to understand why rubber footwear should be acceptable while rubber rainwear is not. Nor why hose should be welcome and cable rejected.

A too-narrow definition of 'core interests' was to haunt Dunlop policy down the years.

Nonetheless, the Macintosh products remaining were grouped into a highly successful industrial and consumer division.

Equally successful was the rapid expansion of sports goods. In 1923 golf and tennis ball manufacture was moved from Manor Mills to the Fort. Output was vastly expanded and shortly afterwards a racket factory was acquired at Waltham Abbey in Essex, which led to the formation of the Dunlop Sports Company Ltd: for generations the greatest name in the world of sport.

Paralleling these exciting non-tyre developments were some glamorous advances on the tyre front. In 1925 racing cars were added to the Dunlop's car fleet; the following year the world's first high speed test machine was installed and the year after the Major Henry Segrave took the world's land speed record of 203.8 mph on Dunlop tyres.

Then, in 1929, there emerged from the company's laboratories an invention which was to rank second only in importance to the pneumatic tyre in Dunlop's history. This was 'Dunlopillo' latex foam which was to revolutionize standards of comfort and hygiene in homes, hospitals, transport, cinemas and theatres ('Bottom, thou art transformed'). Dunlopillo also created a demand for a world rubber foam industry, thus providing a second main support for the rubber producing countries of South-East Asia.

Appropriately, the discovery of uses for latex bears a remarkable similarity to the humble experiments which John Boyd Dunlop conducted for his son's bicycle.

An equally humble domestic cake-whisk played a notable part in the industrial research which led to the invention of Dunlopillo. In the course of intense investigation into the possible use of latex – the milky-like substance which is the original raw material from the rubber trees – a cake-whisk was actually used to whip up the latex into a foam, exposing the problem of how to keep the millions of tiny air bubbles afloat so as to produce marvellous cushioning.

In his entertaining book *Dunlopera* (privately published by Dunlop in 1961), Paul Jennings describes the process:

A foam rubber factory looks like an enormous kitchen with large bath-like vessels and pipes and dials in a hotel for giants who are forever sending down huge orders for mousse, greyish-white mousse in all shapes and sizes. The only difference is that the place smells strongly of ammonia, which is added to the stirred latex as an anti-coagulant (we are not ready for the coagulant yet)... compressed air lines blow across the stirred latex to reduce the alkalinity caused by the ammonia. Then the latex goes to the mills where the 'dispersions' – sulphur and accelerators – are mixed in. Next comes the actual whisking of the mix by enormous 'cake-whisks'. The density of the foam is directly related to the height to which the mix rises – seats in a train will be heavier than that used for a pillow. (London Transport established that 1 lb off the weight of a bus saved them 33p a year.) After about 6 minutes the all-important gelling reaction takes place, and the bubbles are there forever. The great thing is, of course, that the bubbles are all inter-connected: you ventilate and freshen a foam rubber cushion every time you drive the air out by sitting on it and let new air into it by getting up again...

A few years later another rubberoid product of immense flexibility and instant appeal appeared in the form of Semtex flooring and wall tiling.

Presiding over this technical and commercial transformation of a once near-bankrupt concern was a true Titan of the age. Sir Eric Geddes had met his industrial destiny.

A picture of him at this time of total triumph comes from the pages of *Stars and Markets*,[2] an autobiographical work by Sir Charles Tennyson, grandson and biographer of the Victorian Poet Laureate. Tennyson joined Dunlop in 1928 as a personnel officer.

> Geddes, who was 45 when he accepted the chairmanship of the Company, was built on large lines – one indeed who could justly be described by that much-abused term, superman. He must have weighed well over 16 stone, with very little superfluous flesh. His huge physique, clear grey eyes and bulldog jaw gave his personality tremendous force. He was a mighty trencherman and a chain-smoker of strong cigars. His favourite drink was a Horse's Neck – brandy and dry ginger ale with a long curly strip of lemon peel protruding from the tumbler. He rode large horses and drove fast cars. He liked to drive himself in his great Daimler 'double six' between Hassocks on the Sussex Downs where he lived and the Dunlop Head Office in St James's Street, London. He covered the 45 miles at prodigious speed and his butler at Hassocks claimed that when the wind was in the North he always knew to the minute when Sir Eric would reach home as he could hear the Daimler coming over the ridge of the North Downs, 15 miles away.
>
> Geddes's mind was powerful – a bludgeon rather than a rapier – quick to seize the main point of a question but more impatient of detail. A rapid and tireless worker, relentless in his demands upon his staff, he was not a comfortable man to work for, nor was he always personally considerate. But he had inherited the high principles of his Scottish ancestry and insisted on complete integrity in personal relations and commercial dealings and on the best achievable conditions for the workers ... Geddes's great power, driving force and Scottish ruthlessness were invaluable in extricating the company from the difficulties into which it had fallen.

In contrast, Tennyson found Geddes's invariable No. 2, Sir George Beharrell, the ideal complement: the Sullivan to Geddes's Gilbert. 'He combined an unrivalled mastery of detail with an extraordinary shrewdness and sanity of judgement ... His geniality, patience and humanity were invaluable ...' And Tennyson concluded: 'Sir Eric Geddes and Sir George Beharrell were perhaps the most remarkable industrial leaders of their generation.'

Reay Geddes, Sir Eric's son and successor to the Dunlop chair, recalls his father telling him that when he (Sir Eric) decided to sack Admiral Jellicoe (see p. 46) he had checked with the Cabinet to ensure their support and when he *did* sack Jellicoe, the Cabinet did not want to know!

Geddes knew all about sacking. In his early days, while logging in America, he was sacked frequently. In an illuminating radio address on the BBC in 1932 he set out his philosophy of life, which he imprinted on Dunlop and on the industrial life of Britain; both he influenced mightily by example (in the chairs of Dunlop and Imperial Airways) and by his leadership of the Federation of British Industry.

The man who invited him to speak on the theme 'Rungs of the Ladder' was John Reith: like Eric Geddes, a towering Scot (Churchill called him Wuthering Height) of craggy mien and beetle brow. In their way the two men typified the best of British in an era suffering dreadfully from the loss of the nation's finest material in World War I. Reith stamped his image on the BBC for a generation or more. Geddes stamped his on Dunlop for even longer.

Unusual frankness was the surprise element in Geddes's broadcast. He didn't pretend he was the poor-boy-made-good, nor the earnest worker. He was a well-off impudent scamp, both as a schoolboy and a young man wandering about North America: expelled from schools – six in all – and dismissed from job after job. He learned the hard way that

> ... nobody I worked for cared very much whether I got on or not, and their only interest was how much I was worth to them ... no one was going to find me a job, I had to go and hustle for it myself. Unless I could 'sell' myself to a man so that he thought I would be of use to him, I would remain in that class which is indiscriminately employed ... We start by selling ourselves to our fellow-man and we go on selling ourselves till we retire. Some sell the goods they manufacture or buy, others sell their skills or their services. I sometimes wonder whether the art of salesmanship in this, its widest sense, is not a subject requiring more attention in youth than it gets.

Dunlop under Geddes's management was masterly in salesmanship. He used his contacts and high reputation to win the automotive industry to Dunlop, creating a web of personal ties and obligations which would make each section of the industry dependent on Dunlop. Thus, as son Reay told me, he phoned the chiefs of the car and motorcycle trade – Bill Lyons of Jaguar, William Morris, Herbert Austin – to tell them Dunlop was now in such a healthy position that there would be 'no cash-flow problems' should the car and motorcycle makers find it difficult to pay for wheels and tyres on the nose. Credit would be forthcoming and there would be time a-plenty to pay.

Such sympathetic generosity won golden opinions for Dunlop in the cash-strapped late twenties, and ensured customer loyalty in the decades to come. The car-makers' original equipment in tyres was invariably from Dunlop.

Geddes was the man for his time. In his BBC broadcast he referred scathingly to the power of 'influence' which in twenties' and thirties' terms meant inevitably the 'old school tie', that invisible linkage which ensured the supremacy of whom one knew over what one knew.

> The man who thinks he can get on by influence is of little use to himself or his employer. The firms that promote men for influence and not for merit will look after those men just so long as that influence lasts, or until someone with a stronger pull comes along. Then, if you have been relying on influence, you go the way you deserve to go, that is, out of the door. The man who looks to influence to help him on usually has little else to put in the shop window.

Geddes practised what he preached. He personally interviewed candidates for the most junior posts. David Collett, who was to become a main board director and who served forty-two years with Dunlop, recalls as an eighteen-year-old boy being cross-examined by the great man himself. 'An intimidating experience.' But it was thus that Geddes opened the road to talent in Dunlop. His son might have been permitted to accompany him on the occasional overseas trip as an unpaid acting secretary, but like everyone else in the company he had to prove himself and learn his trade : from the ground floor upwards.

Those on the ground floor, the thousands of Dunlop employees who had no managerial ambitions or pretensions, were Geddes's first concern.

On taking over the chairmanship he had propounded three aims. To make Dunlop 'a good place to sell to, to buy from, and to work for'. The firm had to be successful – purchasing the right materials and producing the goods customers wanted – or it would go out of business. But, equally, those who worked for Dunlop should enjoy fair wages and good conditions.

This was not by any stretch of imagination par for the course in the Britain of the 1920s and 1930s.

A continuing depression with an irreducible minimum of 1 million unemployed, rising to 3 million (20 per cent of the workforce), had given impetus to the 'treat 'em mean and keep 'em keen' philosophy.

In addition, the pure doctrine of free trade dictated that the way out of recession was to cheapen labour costs by cutting wages. To both attitudes Eric Geddes offered implacable opposition.

Having secured the services of one of the most imaginative and brilliant accountants of his period, Frederic de Paula, whose system of financial control enabled the fast-expanding Dunlop group to predict with remarkable exactness future costs and revenue, Geddes turned to labour relations.

No union for rubber workers existed, so a joint council of employees and managers was established. Geddes built a council chamber at Fort Dunlop for their deliberations. The council numbered thirty-six: twenty-four factory workers and twelve managers. They concerned themselves with all manner of topics, not least piece-work rates. Gradually the council absorbed wage negotiations, much to the chagrin of the Transport and General Workers Union and the General and Muncipal; these two taking the view that as rubber tyres enabled transport to move (and municipally owned buses were a principal means of transport) they should have charge of the workers' rights.

The workers didn't see it that way at all. They were perfectly content with the council and resented union interference. There is no evidence to suggest that Geddes and Beharrell encouraged them in this view. Rather the reverse. Charles Tennyson, who was involved with personnel at Dunlop for twenty years, recorded that they were quite willing to enter into a reasonable arrangement. They were not, however, prepared to coerce their employees. This was not at all to the liking of Ernest Bevin, general secretary of the Transport and General Workers Union and, in every sense, as big a man as Eric Geddes.

He contrived to persuade Labour-dominated local councils to boycott Dunlop products – no Dunlop tyres for municipal buses, for example. The ploy worked.

Dunlop management was obliged to tell its workers: 'Your jobs are at risk unless you join a union.' Most of them opted for TGWU. Ernie Bevin and Walter Citrine, boss of the TUC, were appeased and offered fruitful co-operation to a company they deemed thoroughly progressive: so progressive indeed that they accepted the closure of a Dunlop plant in the north when the craft workers there resolutely refused to have anything to do with mechanization. The work was transferred to the London suburbs to be performed by non-unionized women and unskilled men.

Dunlop *did* have training schemes for employees, but they were pretty basic. The normal system for big companies in the inter-war period was to recruit factory hands from local schools at age fourteen

– schooling was compulsory from five to fourteen – and to take on office staff from the same secondary schools, but with the expectation that they would have stayed on until sixteen. The only university graduates to be tempted into industry were from the science and engineering faculties.

Inside Dunlop however the road was made open to talent. The Geddes-Beharrell philosophy prevailed and the company thrived mightily.

For Dunlop, the social, political and economic climate of the twenties and thirties was exactly right.

Generally speaking, labour was docile and fairly deferential. High unemployment meant that a job in Dunlop was reckoned to provide a security topped only by such institutions as banks, town halls and the Co-operative Movement!

Security indeed was the 'buzz word' of the era. World War i had destroyed the delicate, interconnected financial world founded on free trade – stable money and steady exchange rates. Protection was increasingly in vogue: protection of one's own share of the market and of one's country's share of the world market. With the slump of 1929 – itself a delayed-action result of World War i – the need for Britain to shed the last illusions of a vanished age became palpable.

In June 1931 Sir Eric Geddes addressed the 1900 Club, an informal but politically significant group of individuals. His address was later printed under the title 'Mass Production. The revolution which changes everything'. Coming from the head of an expanding company, when almost everything else was *contracting* (unemployment trebled in two years, 1930–31), his words had an enormous effect. Lords Beaverbrook and Rothermere, proprietors of the dominant Express and Mail newspaper groups, gave 'Mass Production' mass publicity.

In essence, Geddes argued that without a secure home base, British industry could not embark on the huge capital costs required to transform the economy from craft production to mass production. He illustrated the change by contrasting the labour costs of one man drilling holes in a single plate individually with that of a machine drilling holes in 12 plates with jig and multiple drill. The direct labour costs fell by a ratio of 77 to 1. He observed:

> Craftsmanship of the old type is required only by the man who sets and adjusts the machine. The operative becomes a specialist and he justifies higher remuneration than even the fine old type of craftsman upon which our industry and export trade of the last century were built. The skilled craftsman in reproductive industry is passing as the bowman and knights in armour have passed in war.

72

Geddes pointed out that the importance of the mental worker, against the manual, was enhanced because of the need for advanced design technology.

His own firm gave practical examples of that. Dunlop's technical director W.H.Paull, who had joined Dunlop with the take-over of the Clipper Tyre Company, enrolled a brilliant research team headed by an outstanding rubber chemist, Dr D.F.Twiss, and a young graduate from Nottingham University, Albert Healey. Their work went far to integrate the pneumatic tyre with the suspension system of the motor car.

While a bright future beckoned the practitioners in science, engineering and design, their employment depended on the conversion of the car industry (and all other reproductive industries) from a craft to a mass production base. Geddes continued:

> The cost of research and development, of quality control, capital charges on machinery and equipment and their maintenance and depreciation do not directly vary as the volume of production varies. Its cost . . . overshadows productive labour in importance . . . If however the volume [of production] is uncertain, the risk is too great, the capital is not spent.

Geddes pointed out that a free trade Britain could not compete with protected nations, such as the USA, Germany and Japan, because without a secure protected home market (or, still better, Empire market) British industrialists would not risk the huge cost of capital conversion to mass production methods when unfair competition – below the cost of production – could deprive them of their domestic customers.

Geddes argued that *with* tariff protection modern industries, like the automotive industry, could expand dramatically and absorb much of the labour displaced by other declining industries. While the prices of motorcars fell by half between 1914 and 1930, the wages of those making cars doubled, in real terms, giving point to Henry Ford's dictum: 'Industry does not exist to find jobs for as many men as possible, but to find high-priced jobs for as many men as possible. Our working class must also become our leisured class, if our production is to be balanced by consumption.'

It followed, declared Geddes, that the government must provide fiscal protection to make home and imperial markets secure for British industry, so that it could apply mass production techniques.

Had he but known it, Geddes was pushing at an open door. Within months of his address a national government was implementing the very policy he had advocated. The Ottawa Agreements gave Britain and the Empire a stout tariff wall behind which the new industries, not least the automotive, prospered.

'Orderly marketing' became the accepted wisdom of the day – in agriculture as well as industry. The Milk Marketing Board was an early example. In this climate of opinion, Dunlop went from strength to strength.

Thanks to Geddes's administrative talents and personal contacts and the outstanding work of Dunlop engineers, the company assumed total leadership in tyre manufacturing. 'Check with Dunlop' became second nature to tyre firms from advertising to pricing policies.

Assured of domestic and imperial markets, Dunlop embarked on an unprecedented period of expansion :

1932 General Rubber Goods Division formed.

1933 First agricultural tyre manufactured.

1935 India Tyre and Rubber Company acquired in Scotland.

First factory opened in South Africa at Durban. (Dunlop produced tyres for Goodyear, the US company, at this plant – part of Geddes's 'share the global market' concept.)

Factory opened in Cork, Eire (largely because Premier De Valera threatened to open Southern Ireland to foreign competition unless Dunlop gave work to the unemployed).

1936 First factory opened in India, at Calcutta.

1937 Semtex Flooring Ltd formed.

In addition, the aviation and sports goods provided still more growth. Profits and dividends were not exciting, but then in the thirties they were not expected to be. In every other aspect Dunlop was *the* model company : orderly, visionary, yet hard-headed, aware of the national interest, caring for its work-force.

Dunlop really *did* care. When Alfred Rouse appealed against his conviction for murder in 1930, Dunlop directors offered £150 towards his legal costs. Rouse was at the time an employee of W.B.Martin, a Dunlop subsidiary. Rouse was a commercial traveller for elastic braces and garters. Like so many of his kind he was a compulsive chatterer. His counsel, Patrick Hastings K.C., remarked : 'If Alfred Arthur Rouse had only kept his mouth shut, he would never have been hanged.'[3]

Dunlop did their best to prevent him being hanged : not out of misplaced sympathy for Mr Rouse (whose extramarital activities plus gambling had led him to kill a tramp in the hope the body might be mistaken for himself) but because he was, however remotely, a 'Dunlop man'.

Pride, togetherness, dedication to the job: these were the hallmark qualities of the Dunlop Rubber Company. They had been planted during the reign of Harvey du Cros, had survived Arthur's unhappy spell and now blossomed splendidly under the Geddes–Beharrell banner. Utter reliability, mixed with brilliantly innovative technical talent, combined to give Dunlop an admirable international reputation.

Even the local Nazi *Gauleiter* of the district embracing Dunlop's German factory at Hanau had cause to remark that, although the concern was foreign-owned, Dunlop should be regarded by all good Germans as definitely a German company.

Wherever established, with whomsoever trading – capitalist or socialist, fascist or communist – Dunlop delivered. On time. Top quality. At the right price.

By 1938 Dunlop stood at the pinnacle of success. It was associated in the public mind with success. Wimbledon champion Fred Perry played with Dunlop tennis balls. Open Golf champion Sir Henry Cotton used Dunlop balls (the world-renowned 'Dunlop 65' recorded his record-breaking round when he achieved his first Open triumph.) The king of speed, Sir Malcolm Campbell, drove on Dunlop tyres, rims and wheels. Dunlop products, grouped in the Aviation Division, provided the technical sinews, in the form of tyres, brakes, hydraulic and pneumatic operating gear, which enabled the flying daredevils such as the Mollisons, Campbell and Black, to annihilate distance. No motor race or motorcycle race in the world was complete without huge Dunlop posters strung across the bridges which spanned the courses. Dunlop wellington boots shod mankind. Dunlopillo mattresses cossetted it, Dunlop rubber condoms did not limit it, because the board had decided, as a matter of moral policy, not to become involved in the manufacture of such products. (Many years later Dunlop decided as a matter of *pricing* policy, not to engage in condom production, owing to competition. The profit margin was too slim!)

But Dunlop did cover global floors with Semtex and always, always, there was the supreme position of its tyres. Thanks to Geddes's marketsharing methods, plus fiscal protection, the disastrous slump in prices (they fell 30 per cent per annum in the US in the twenties) had been halted and, while not madly profitable, provided the solid, dependable base upon which the company could build for the future.

How glowing that future appeared as summed up in the front page of the *Daily Mail*, which Dunlop took over in its entirety in 1938 to celebrate the fiftieth anniversary of the launching of the pneumatic tyre. The proclamation trumpeted :

> Exactly 50 years ago today occurred the most important event in the history of transport since the discovery of the wheel. It has touched and changed our lives, for today we and our goods are carried, quickly and smoothly wherever there are roads ; today a man has travelled on land at the incredible speed of 311 miles per hour ; today the air has been conquered. Exactly 50 years ago today was taken out the patent for the Dunlop pneumatic tyre.
>
> On that historic 23rd of July John Boyd Dunlop little dreamed that in half-a-century his invention would have revolutionised industrial and passenger transport throughout the world. Yet from his first crudely-constructed pneumatic tyre has grown the vast Dunlop industry. The Dunlop Fort tyre of the present day – the only tyre with TEETH to bite the road – is the culminating development of those 50 years of continuous research and experience.

Inside, the newspaper carried tributes from various worthies in the motor trade.

But immediately below these routine congratulations was an item which, alas, summed up the reality of life in 1938. The heading said simply 'Shadow Bomber' and the item stated : 'Sir Kingsley Wood, the Air Minister, yesterday visited the aircraft "shadow" factory of the Austin Motor Company at Birmingham and saw the launch of the first Fairey Battle Bomber plane produced under the Government's "shadow" factory scheme . . .'

Shadow factories were plants attached to well-known firms – some underground – for the production of weapons. Britain in 1938 was preparing for war. Dunlop, like its partner in the motor industry, Austin, would play a vital role in the coming struggle.

CHAPTER VIII

DUNLOP AT WAR

A few months before Dunlop celebrated the fiftieth birthday of the pneumatic tyre, Sir Eric Geddes died suddenly at the age of sixty-two.

In a sense the fifteen years of his life at Dunlop had been a preparation for the supreme test of war. He and George Beharrell (not forgetting Frederick Szarvasy) had rescued a bankrupt concern and, through drive and persistence, had created the conditions which allowed the boffins – the scientists, engineers, technicians – to flourish. They had built a machine, well-nigh perfectly suited to the demands of war.

It is not too much to say that, had Eric Geddes lived, he would have been the Churchill of industry (they were the same age). As it was, Max Aitken, Lord Beaverbrook, was put in charge of aircraft production and his daemonic energy and buccaneering methods ensured the aircraft were there when they were needed. Beaverbrook, however, was not a stayer. He hankered for the greater prize: the premiership itself, and quit the industrial scene after barely two years' service. Geddes would have remained to the end, and his administrative and technical gifts 'amounting to genius', according to *The Times*, would have given the British the same all-embracing industrial organization which Albert Speer afforded the Germans.

Fortunately for Dunlop, and for the UK war effort, Sir George Beharrell was in place to see company and country through the ordeal.

The quiet one of the Geddes–Beharrell axis was a year older than his great friend when he succeeded to the chair. John George Beharrell, son of a Yorkshire schoolmaster, was educated privately and at King James's School, Almondbury. He started his career as a £15-a-year fifteen-year-old clerk in the North Eastern Railway Company. Shortly afterwards he resumed full-time education, taking a degree at Leeds University. Because of his daunting flair for statistics, he was given a succession of quick promotions so that, by forty-one, he was assistant goods manager. His obituary notice in *The Times* observed: 'When the 1914 war broke out his brilliant work in the swift mobilisation and despatch of the men of Northern Command and his part in compiling a complicated railway service for purely military needs, such as the nation had not known before, brought him to the attention of the Government and particularly of Lloyd George who in 1915 got him into the Ministry of Munitions as Director of Statistics and Requirements.'

Beharrell had already established a rapport with Geddes in peacetime railway administration. The partnership now flourished in every department of war administration: munitions, transportation, Admiralty (especially anti-submarine measures). Back to transport in peacetime, including the inquiry into the excess cost of the public services, and finally Dunlop as managing director to chairman Geddes. For twenty-five years these two men worked as one. George Beharrell slipped into the boss's chair as easily as donning carpet slippers.

The two men shared the bulldog jaw, and the bulldog spirit was what the company needed when Britain went to war in September 1939.

An endearing touch was added to a grim process when Dunlop launched its own carrier pigeon service to secure communications between the company's new headquarters in a country house near Banbury, Oxon, and the various factories up and down the land. The idea was that if road and rail links were disrupted, contact could still be maintained. Happily the pigeons carried nothing more vital than inter-office gossip.

Long before the war started Dunlop technicians had made a survey for the Board of Trade of the likely effect of submarine attacks on Britain's rubber supply – a further dividend of the Geddes–Beharrell experiences in World War I – and of the loss of essential ingredients to tyre manufacture due to the exigencies of hostilities. Best quality French chalk, for example, used to prevent fabrics from sticking together during manufacture, was obtained from Italy, an ally of Germany (she declared war against Britain in June 1940), but Dunlop discovered excellent alternative supplies in India and Canada, both Empire countries in which Dunlop owned factories.[1]

First and foremost was the tyre. 'Keep The Wheels Rolling' was a slogan used equally by the Axis and Allied Powers. Dunlop's contribution to the British effort was crucial.

Between 1939 and 1945 the company produced the vast majority of the 32.7 million vehicle and 47 million cycle tyres manufactured in the UK. Dunlop also supplied : 2.5 million disc wheels, 600,000 aircraft wheels, 750,000 tank wheels (plus 1 million tank tyres to go with them), 15 million cycle and motorcycle rims, 3,000 *miles* of rubber tubing, 600,000 pairs of anti-gas gloves and 6 million pairs of rubber boots. This is just for starters.

But to return to the tyre. Dunlop were so successful with sand-tyre development that the German General Erwin Rommel issued the following order on 15 December 1941 during the British offensive in Libya : 'For every desert reconnaissance, only captured English trucks are to be used since German trucks stick in the sand too often.' These sand tyres were built from 4in models tested in trays of sand at Fort Dunlop after consultation with Miralai Hatton Bey of the Egyptian Camel Corps who suggested a tyre that 'would be to the car what its broad-spreading feet are to the camel'. The aim, triumphantly achieved as Rommel's tribute testifies, was to reduce pressure to a minimum so that the tyres glided over the sand.

Still more dramatic was the invention of the Run-Flat tyre. This enabled a vehicle to run at normal speed for 50 miles after being struck by bullets. A battlefield report stated :

> Cars equipped with RF tyres engaged in a raid on enemy communications. Subjected 3 hours concentrated air attack. Three cars set alight. One knocked out gunfire. Remaining 3 cars with all tyres punctured covered 70 miles by night to own lines. Commanding officer reports that but for RF tyres entire squadron would have been lost.

The general assembly of these tyres (with thick load-bearing rubber lining) was a consequence of safety measures to enable bidders for the peacetime land speed records to race at 300-plus mph. Thus were the fearsome risks undertaken by the likes of Messrs Segrave, Campbell and Cobb vindicated under yet more dangerous circumstances.

So effective were Dunlop tyres at withstanding bullets that, on one occasion at least, they rebounded to the disadvantage of the user. A Lysander pilot attempting to land an agent behind enemy lines in France shot at one of the plane's tyres to equalize its deflation with the other one which had been damaged by German anti-aircraft fire. He pumped bullet after bullet into the Dunlop tyre – and still landed lopsidedly !

When America entered the war in December 1941 the RF design was made freely available to Washington. The Americans modified the design somewhat – exchanging the heavy and expensive tread spacer for a spider device made of welded steel strip – called it a

Combat tyre, patented it and proceeded to try to *sell* the right to manufacture it to Dunlop ! This merry jape was not appreciated.

The Americans were also much taken with Dunlop's decoys. These remarkable dummies – guns, tanks, landing craft – bamboozled the enemy completely. On a tactical level they frequently led the Axis forces to give away their position by firing on these synthetic targets ; on a strategic level they played no small part in convincing the German High Command that an enormous Allied force was waiting to cross the Narrows and land in the Pas de Calais. They misled the Wehrmacht to regard the Normandy landings on D-Day, 6 June 1944, as a diversion. They were not disillusioned until it was too late.

The Axis, of course, practised similar deceits, but the difference lay in the quality of the British rubber decoys. Most ersatz models were constructed of painted canvas over wooden frames. Dunlop's rubber fakes were markedly superior : lighter, simpler, easier to handle and more realistic.

A decoy which, when inflated, almost exactly duplicated a Sherman tank could be packed in a hold-all a little larger than a cricket bag. Its weight was 170 pounds, compared with the 35 tons of a Sherman. Only five minutes were required to set up and inflate one of these elaborate deceptions. The Americans simply copied them (with a slightly different inflation system). On this occasion they did not try to sell the designs back to Dunlop.

Barrage balloon material was used to make these decoys after it had become clear that the great German air offensive against Britain was finally and totally off the agenda.

The barrage balloon – *en masse* – was a Dunlop development as were a number of other devices connected with ARP : Air Raid Precautions.

Barrage balloons were huge silvery instruments, resembling fish, tethered by cables and flown over cities in order to trap unwary aircraft which tried to fly low in order to improve their aim.

In 1936, when the UK began, belatedly, to re-arm and to construct air defences, output was a mere two per week. The Ministry of Aircraft Production asked Dunlop to reorganize production. Under the management of Mr C. Heman output was transformed. New methods were introduced whereby panels, or layers, of Sea Island and Sudanese cloth were prepared with simple-to-operate jigs and tools. By May 1941 a Mark VII balloon was being completed every eighteen minutes of the day and night. In all, 28,000 balloons were completed, of which 4,000 were sent to the West Coast of the US and the Panama Canal to defend these areas against possible Japanese attack (in fact the only hostile Japanese missile to hit mainland USA was an armed balloon which killed a family in Oregon). All told, 65 million yards of dry cloth were proofed in Dunlop factories.

Manager Heman's key improvements were the utilization of floor space and the successful employment of untrained women operatives. They adapted quickly and showed the usual female supremacy in conscientiousness and dedication to the job in hand. They carried on with their work during air raids, prompting Lord Beaverbrook, the Minister of Aircraft Production, to send the management a message commending 'their magnificent example to all who are engaged on work of national importance . . . They have qualified as front line soldiers in the fight for freedom.' They also demonstrated a stamina which was often lacking among male war workers. From October 1940 to May 1941 the women workers at the Glasgow and Manchester factories producing balloons and dinghies for use in fighter aircraft had only one day's holiday. They were looking forward to three days' rest at Whitsun when a sudden order came in for material for 'K' type dinghies which were just beginning to be issued to air-fighter pilots. Ninety-eight per cent of the labour force opted to forego their holiday and work through the Whitsun break until the contract was completed.

This kind of patriotic resolve was wholly in the Dunlop tradition where the watchword could well have been 'Whatever is right for Britain is right for Dunlop'. It was a spirit which reinforced the flexible, family spirit of the company.

Patriotism and family feeling was much needed in the desperate days of the early 1940s. Dunlop plants were frequently bombed. During a raid on Manchester, one of the city's factories making barrage balloons lost 54,000 sq ft of roof – blown clean away. Other plants were hit: Fort Dunlop in Birmingham, the rim and wheel works in Coventry, the Edmonton clothing factory (hit by a V2 rocket only six weeks before the war's end), all causing death and injuries.

Yet the casualties were surprisingly light – half-a-dozen dead and a score wounded – and the production time lost blessedly limited, thanks in large part to Dunlop's well-trained ARP volunteers. Dunlop was a pioneer in planning air raid precautions. As early as 1935 D. R. Crabbe had been put in charge and the first purchases of equipment were made in 1937. By 1940 when the Blitz started the company's thirty-one factories were among the readiest in the land.

Fire was the greatest hazard and the Ministry of Home Security reminded the public (in June 1940) that 'one incendiary bomb, no bigger than the lead weight of a grandfather clock, is enough to burn

81

your home – and one Nazi plane can carry between 1,000 and 2,000 incendiary bombs . . . a single plane could start up to 180 fires.'

That was the measure of the threat. Dunlop met it by anticipating the precautions introduced by the Home Office and then improving on them. Dispersion was one method. Many products were turned out in garages, in brick-works, in a colliery. Dunlop pioneered the roof spotting scheme, whereby factories continued working after the air raid siren had sounded while local employees stationed on the roof observed German aircraft through field glasses. Only when the aircraft were seen approaching the factory did a local alarm sound. In this way production time was saved which would otherwise have been lost with workers taking shelter.

Dunlop's fire fighting and repair squads were also keen and efficient. Incendiaries dropped at the gas works adjoining the General Rubber Goods factory in Manchester were removed by a Dunlop employee, H.E.Furnival, at great risk to life. For this he was mentioned in the *London Gazette*. Miss Betty Quin, acting nurse in Dunlop's Coventry factory, was awarded the George Medal (the civilian equivalent of the DSO) for her brave work during the Coventry blitz of November 1940 which saw the destruction of Coventry Cathedral, as well as much of the city centre.

Occasionally there were mishaps. As when a London employee accused of being slow in getting black-out material in position emphasized her family's devotion to ARP by remarking to the Bench : 'My husband used to have a beard, but when we received notice that we shouldn't keep any inflammable material in the house he shaved it off.' She was dismissed with a caution.

The black-out alone involved a heavy strain on wartime workers – and was a heavy item in Dunlop's ARP bill, for the company had to buy enough material to cover 2 million sq ft of window (black-outs in factories remained in place throughout day and night so working conditions were sultry, to say the least).

Marching with ARP in resolve and endeavour was Dunlop's very own Home Guard. On 16 May 1940, two days after Anthony Eden's broadcast calling on all Britons, especially those with military experience, to form themselves into a local defence corps, 230 volunteers had presented themselves at the appropriately named Fort Dunlop. Many of these men had seen service in 1914–18 and, had the Germans landed, could have given a good account of themselves. Sir Ronald Storrs commented on this response : 'It was then that the Company's long-established policy of employing ex-Servicemen was seen to have been not only patriotic and just, but also farsighted.'

It was, again, the Dunlop spirit in action. At first – as elsewhere – there were few armaments and no uniforms (and within six weeks of the call 1,500,000 men were enrolled nationwide). The company purchased a dozen shotguns and some sporting types came forward with twelve-bores. Fortunately, Dunlop had a flourishing rifle range so practice with .22s could be advanced. In short order the Dunlop unit rose to 450 men under the command of Major N.H.Lawley MC (Garage and Test Fleet Superintendent).

Of course, the Germans never came. The Home Guard however remained in being long after the need for it had disappeared (it was said it was far too good a 'club' to be dissolved). Inevitably a spirit of levity crept in. The following is taken from the log book of Fort Dunlop for 7 December 1941, the day Pearl Harbor was attacked. It is signed by Lieutenant C.L.Bostock:

21.00 hours. BBC announced hostile acts by Japan. Guard turned out as a purely precautionary measure. All aid offered to the USA.[2] Troops warned of the dangers of fraternising with Geisha girls.

09.00 hours. Handed over the care of a troublesome world to Lieut. A.G.Perret, whom God Preserve.

As a piece of Punch plus P.G.Wodehouse that entry doesn't leave much to be desired. It was the kind of nonchalant self-mockery which took the sting out of working a fourteen-hour day and doing Home Guard duty in your spare time.

Altogether more than 1,100 Dunlop men joined the Home Guard, from start to finish.

Throughout the entire organization the war prompted a remarkable response: not least in the sheer thrill of technological innovation. A few examples must suffice for the numberless achievements of Dunlop's laboratories, technicians and engineers.

The first concerns the development of underwater suits for 'frogmen' whose task was to slip unobserved from small rubber dinghies (another Dunlop project) to blow up the underwater obstacles confronting the heavily loaded landing craft on D-day. These suits – which were also used with remarkable success in other cross-Channel operations, notably Walchern, and for attaching limpet mines to Japanese warships in the Far East – had to be light, flexible, totally waterproof and skin tight (to enable the wearer to move swiftly and to adopt different postures). W.G.Gorham, works manager of Special Products, was entrusted with supervising production of these extremely demanding suits. He had already overseen the development of the anti-'G' flying suit invented by Dr W.R.Franks which balanced the greatly increased internal pressure in the pilot's body caused by the downward rush of blood by applying an equal external pressure in the form of fresh water confined within the suit. This permitted British flyers to perform aerobatics – twisting and turning violently at high speeds – which their foes could not emulate. A virgin rubber weld of pure vulcanized latex provided the basic material, with interlining pipes moulded to body contours.

Now Gorham and his scientists came up with an outfit, so ideally suited to underwater operations that it was copied by ally and enemy alike. Fortunately the enemy did not succeed in identifying the process until very nearly the end of the war.

The contribution made by Dunlop to D-day was not confined to frogmen's suits. They also produced the Pneumatic Wave Controller, incidentally the largest device manufactured anywhere in the world by the rubber industry. They were made in units 200ft long and 25ft high, clamped with 500 bolts to a 700-ton keel of concrete, and anchored to the sea bed at the ends, and their purpose was to reduce 6ft waves to 1ft. These pneumatic pontoons of rubberized cotton, set in line broadside to the waves, absorbed the weight of water and created a quiet sea on the landward side.

And so it went on ... the Ectah airplane tyre and braking system which practically eliminated the danger of fire from static electricity. Dunlop made tyres, wheels, brake drums, brake units and controls. Much of the work in this field was carried out under Jo Wright at the Coventry and Dudley plants ... stirrup pump hose, Dunlop made 45 million feet of it to help householders douse the fires set alight by the Luftwaffe ... Semtex flooring material, used on warship decks to make them oil-resistant, non-inflammable, non-skid ...

Oh, and Dunlop also made Winston Churchill's mattress (Dunlopillo, naturally), and the former tennis racket factory at Waltham Abbey brought out straw dartboards for thousands of Service messes throughout the world. Such improvisation was prompted by the loss of rushes from Japan and China which provided the peacetime raw material for dartboards.

Improvisation was the name of the game in wartime Britain. Dunlop virtually took over tyre control during the conflict, providing the expertise for the government's Rubber Controller. When the plantations in Malaya were overrun by the Japanese, Dunlop scientists were already prepared with a conservation scheme of grinding suitable types of scrap – worn tyre treads – as replacement.

From 1943 onwards the US embarked on a colossal programme of synthetic rubber production. More and more of this substance found its way to Britain to make up for the absence of natural rubber. The Dunlop-inspired conservation system had achieved a 40 per cent saving in consumption even before the arrival of the ersatz variety.

Economies of this nature – they corresponded to a similar frenzy of cheese-paring in other sections of society whereby, for example, bacon rind was collected in bins at street corners and fed to pigs – were fine for war, but not so fine after it. American advances in synthetics (and their capture of British export markets in Latin America) were to prove a serious handicap to Dunlop in the years ahead.

As were the advances made by the rubber industry in German-occupied France.

The renaissance of French industry probably owes quite a bit to that period of regimentation between 1940–44. On the one hand French industry was forcibly reorganized so that it could play its part in the Nazi new order. On the other it was a patriotic duty to divert as much energy, material and research to non-war ends so as to deprive the German war machine of support. Both ways benefitted France. The labour force was disciplined without fear of strikes or political trouble, while innovation, for ultimate peacetime purposes, flourished. Storrs observed (in *Dunlop in War*) of the Dunlop factory in France during this period : 'Every conceivable method was adopted to conceal raw material and to make sure the largest quantity of finished goods reached the *French Home Market* . . . This was done so successfully that at least half of the factory's production never reached the Occupying Authority.' Dunlop's great rival, Michelin, doubtless practised the same patriotic manoeuvre, with still greater impact on future competition for, quoting Storrs again, 'Where the industry was French-owned the existing management was usually left more or less alone, but closely watched to see that output was maintained.' The ideal recipe for using war to prepare for peace.

Thus, while Dunlop UK scraped and saved and schemed to develop means of achieving wartime ends, France and the US were – for different reasons – able to prepare for post-war conditions.

In the Far East, Dunlop suffered severely through the Japanese occupation of Malaya. So did Dunlop employees, for the Japanese press had announced that Dunlop was a prime intelligence agency for the British Empire throughout South-East Asia.

Casting a more benign glow and prefiguring a happier future, a Japanese officer in Shanghai permitted a Dunlop 'godown', or warehouse, to remain trading. He had come across some Dunlop 65 golf balls in the place and, being an enthusiastic golfer himself, turned a blind eye to the plant's British ownership.

Elsewhere in the Far East, Dunlop flourished during the war, most of all in Australia where almost a whole new industry had to be created to meet the demands of the US forces who had gone there to prepare for the Pacific counter-offensive. In addition to building factories to supply the Americans with 18-ply tyres for earth-moving equipment and 47-inch tyres for large American planes, the Australians devised an inflatable pressure bag to raise sunken ships.

From Canada, South Africa, India, the empire of Dunlop made its contribution to the war effort of the British Empire.

The years 1939–45 were, in truth, Dunlop's 'finest hour' . . .

CHAPTER IX

AUSTERITY UNLIMITED

Dunlop emerged from World War II in a far, far healthier state and frame of mind than from World War I. The company had performed magnificently: breaking new technical ground, responding to every demand made upon it, flexible and far-sighted. In contrast to the shenanigans between Jimmy White and Arthur du Cros in 1919, kindly shrewd Sir George Beharrell remained in the chair.

Many young men who had experienced command and responsibility in the Services were applying to join the firm's management training schemes. The French, German and Japanese factories had returned to the group. The Malayan plantations were back in trim, anticipating growing demand for natural rubber.

Sir Ronald Storrs (in *Dunlop in War*) summed up Dunlop's position in 1945 thus:

> Dunlop is in some ways the best known name in the world. ... This vast concern is in effect a Department of Works that really produces work, a constructive Civil Service functioning without the standard percentage of undismissable ineffectives playing for riskless, effortless safety. ...

Some years later John Lord, a director of the group, was to characterize the public perception of the company: 'Good old reliable Dunlop, a familiar, solid name, like the General Post Office.'

'Department of Works', 'Civil Service', 'General Post Office' – those descriptions would come to haunt Dunlop decades ahead when in the 1980s it was dismissed for being just those very things: inert, unadaptable, Whitehall-minded (and actually headed by a former senior civil servant).

All that, however, lay in the distant future. In 1945 Dunlop seemed especially favoured among the great companies in the land. It was export-orientated. It had excellent labour relations and had evolved competent training schemes for workers and clerical, supervisory and executive staff. True, it was hierarchical (none of your 'all lads together' in a common canteen with everyone wearing the same uniform), but England in 1945 was still a deferential society, albeit with a socialist government.

Clement Attlee's Labour administration inherited wartime controls and perpetuated them as a system of government. Rationing of food, clothes and petroleum, allocation of raw materials, direction of labour (rarely enforced), priorities for earners of overseas currencies – all played into Dunlop's hands.

Here was the sheltered, protected market of the 1930s and the war years writ large. The group's intimate relations with officialdom and its cosy relationships with all other parts of the automotive industry enabled Dunlop to thrive. Unfortunately the very certainty of markets and the embrace of state direction of resources obscured the harsher realities of competition. The warmth of the Whitehall womb suffocated rather than germinated enterprise.

An early warning of things to come appeared as early as June 1946 – from France. Michelin, a tyre company of immense technical capacity, applied for a patent that would provide 'an outer cover which will give increased resistance to wear'. This was the steel radial-ply tyre, the legendary 'Michelin X' which doubled the life of tyres – and shortened the lives of tyre-makers. The technical background is well displayed by Eric Tompkins in *History of the Pneumatic Tyre* :

> Tyres wear out because they have to run misaligned (to produce the cornering force to push the vehicle round corners). So if we make a tyre which produces its cornering power at a smaller misalignment it should wear slower.
>
> The construction used was highly original, the operative part being a structure, immediately below the tread, consisting of layers of steel cord, built up as a rigid band. In order that this structure might have the maximum effect in guiding the tread of the tyre, so that it functioned as a rigid hoop, the casing below was made flexible, by building it of radial cords of rayon, which ran directly from bead to bead as horse-shoe-like loops, at right angles to the circumference of the tyre. Such tyres are commonly called after the radial casing, but it is the rigid breaker structure which gives them their long-wearing properties.

Actually two Englishmen, Gray and Sloper, had patented a similar idea thirty-five years before (shades of Thomson and J.B.Dunlop!) but, methods of successfully bonding rubber and steel together not being forthcoming, the invention lapsed.

Nor did the Michelin X meet with an initial roar of approval. Dunlop Tyres' technical staff, headed by Albert Healey, dismissed the radial tyre as 'a gimmick'. They were not alone. The mileage increase was there; it *did* last twice as long[1] as the cross-ply tyres. But the tyres had to be handled differently. They gave the impression of being 'on tramlines' which encouraged cornering at speed and this could prove dangerous.

Even so, Michelin X marked a turning point in tyre technology which set the world tyre industry on a whole new and ultimately loss-making course. For the Michelin X simply could not be denied. As *The Economist* journal was to observe, ten years after the tyre was introduced to the UK market in 1953:

> British car makers have shied away in the past from buying components at more than minimal costs (including tyres, of course). They are chang-ing their attitudes fast with the advent of the radial-ply tyre whose greater expense is more than compensated for by better wear and road-holding characteristics. These tyres are so different from previous types that the best results are obtained by re-designing cars around them.

Which is exactly what happened with Jaguar, Rover, Triumph and Austin belatedly – very belatedly – following years behind the Continentals. The only tyre of the period to contest Michelin's X was Pirelli's Cinturato which used a girdle of textile instead of steel. Dunlop executives were much impressed with Pirelli's riposte; an admiring respect which was to have fateful consequences some years later.

At about the same time that Michelin and Pirelli were taking the tyre market by the scruff of the neck, Dunlop suffered a small disaster with a tyre which had to be recalled because the Egyptian cotton involved in the manufacture was of deficient quality. This was the obverse side of the Empire connection and the Whitehall link. While not strictly speaking an Empire country, Egypt was still in the late 1940s regarded as a British responsibility. Large quantities of Egyptian cotton were stockpiled as demand slumped (tyre manufacturers were increasingly going over to rayon and nylon). The government asked Dunlop to be 'helpful'. Dunlop obliged. And the result was an embar-rassing failure which did Dunlop's reputation no good at all – and still brings blushes to ex-Dunlop executives who were not even con-cerned with the purchase of the 'duff' cotton.

As so often happens, the period of greatest apparent success was that of unseen peril.

Seemingly supreme in Europe – with Germany and Japan flattened and Italy a major war casualty – the British car industry muffed its opportunity. Poor quality cars, deficient in workmanship and design, flooded into such vital markets as Switzerland and Sweden (both neutral and wealthy) and wrecked the reputation of British products for decades to come. Dunlop, as the original equipment supplier to the British motor industry (and, as *The Economist* was to observe, a low-price supplier at that) suffered from the general disparagement of British cars. When overseas customers got the opportunity to purchase Volkswagens, Fiats, BMWs, Peugeots, Hondas and Toyotas, they deserted the British in droves.

The tremendous setback to the British motor industry – mitigated only temporarily by the outstanding, brilliantly designed Morris Mini – had, of course, a serious knock-on effect on Dunlop.

No one, admittedly, could have foreseen the fatal impact wholly secure markets, over-full employment and complacency would have on the automotive companies' performance when peace came in 1945.

Dunlop was certainly not immune from the feeling that all was for the best, so falsely widespread among the motor manufacturers.

The company took over the huge Speke factory in Liverpool from Rootes, the car maker who had used the plant for aircraft manufacture during the war. No one enquired why Rootes were anxious to vacate the premises. If they had, they would have discovered how much trouble that company had experienced with its labour force. True, many of them did not remain at Speke, being directed elsewhere, under the labour controls regulations then still in force. But Dunlop's presence at Speke was a deliberate social commitment. The company's *Dunlop Gazette* stated: 'Dunlop made history by being the first industrial organisation to take over a war factory *designed to give substantial employment in the Merseyside area where unemployment was an acute problem. ... The policy was to employ local people.* [author's italics].'

Initially everything went very well. The first general manager, David Collett, was tailor-made for the job. Tall, square-jawed, blue-eyed (Dunlop senior management seemed to come out of some 'jolly-good-chaps' mould – the Geddeses father and son, the Beharrells, and later joint MDs Campbell Fraser and John Simon – all tall and square-jawed), he seemed to epitomize the young men who had been tempered by war and learned the quality of leadership in combat. In fact, Collett had not been in the war – one hand had been badly shattered when, as a child, he picked up a detonator dropped by a Zeppelin in World War I. But Collett had acquired qualities of leadership in his nineteen years with Dunlop. At thirty-seven, he was comparatively young for the job of starting from scratch a rubber factory with a target employment of 8,000 workers. That, however, was in the Dunlop tradition of giving youth its head – the du Cros boys had been sent out to the colonies to found parts of the Dunlop empire in their twenties. Eric Geddes had interviewed Collett when, aged eighteen, he applied for a post in the company (as a statistical assistant) and monitored his progress over five years while he performed tasks, humble and demanding, in the organization.

Collett's whole approach to the Speke factory was motivated by the best possible ideals: to draw his employees into his confidence and to draw the company into the community. It was very much the spirit of 1945 – business in the service of the community and vice versa.

Communication between boardroom and factory floor was carried to the nth degree. Apart from the joint works council, there was an elected welfare council and a joint works committee, not to mention an engineering liaison group and a staff consultative committee. In addition, there was a fortnightly Speke *Newsbeam* sheet to provide a two-way flow of ideas and suggestions.

In conversations with me Collett claimed that this concentration on communication helped prevent serious disputes: during his four years there as general manager there was no lengthy stoppage. Continuous contact between trades unions, workers and management ensured that when disputes over piece-work arose they could be swiftly settled.

Initially the company subsidized trainee-workers' wages. As he, or she, improved the subsidy dwindled, until finally the employee was on his or her own and had to work harder to achieve the rate for the job. This caused much discontent which was allayed and eventually dissolved through discussion.

Another source of irritation was the length of the journeys many employees had to undergo to reach work. The old village of Speke was nine miles from the centre of Liverpool. In those austerity days there was virtually no private motoring (nor could the workers have afforded cars had they been availabe) so public transport shouldered the whole burden – which inevitably meant queueing, often for long periods, when there was an infrequent service.

Collett used the Speke *Newsbeam* to publish a map showing where most of his labour force lived. The local transport concerns responded – and the frequency pattern was altered to the considerable gain of the Speke employees.

Looking through the copies of *Newsbeam* of the late forties it is clear that David Collett had got it absolutely right for the era.

Issue No. 24 of September 1947 carried as its lead story the appeal by Sir Stafford Cripps, President of the Board of Trade, for a huge increase in exports. The target for the rubber industry was a fourfold increase in volume over the 1938, pre-war level. What that meant for the five divisions at Speke – footwear, tyres, belting, precision instruments and sports goods – was spelt out and the reasons clearly stated, thus: 'Belting is desperately needed for the Government's programme to mechanise the mines, without which the National Coal Board cannot obtain the increased output on which all industry depends. Golf and tennis balls and other sports goods are in demand overseas and represent a high export value in small bulk.' Then came the warning: 'Markets overseas want Dunlop goods because over many years we have built up a reputation for quality and reliability; any weakening of that reputation would be fatal.'

Yet the mixture of totalitarian controls, state direction of industry and confiscatory taxation (standard rate was 50 per cent and top rate 98 per cent) brought about the very end feared. Exhortation was no substitute for incentive, while central planning undermined self-reliance and the capacity to respond to the demands of the market. British industry *did* in these years gain a reputation for indifferent workmanship, late delivery, poor after-sales service and outdated design from which it took generations to recover. Dunlop was tainted with these failings.

However, within the context of the times, David Collett and his Speke workforce did their duty, 'and did it well according to their lights'.

Speaking at a London School of Economics seminar in the winter of 1947, Collett summed up his philosophy: 'It is not sufficient that management be progressive and broad-minded; it is necessary that employees generally are aware of the attitude and actions of management. The worker on the shop floor should be given . . . management plans for the future.'

He was helped enormously in building good labour relations by the family atmosphere created at Speke, by the union leaders with whom he had to deal and with the local (Labour) administration.

Dunlop was the real centre of social life in Speke: children's parties, dances, golf, tennis, football competitions, bowls, concerts, charity drives. The Speke *Newsbeam* was full of them down the years.

An old-time Transport Union leader in the form of Alderman Simon Marn kept a fatherly eye on the needs of his 'lads and lasses' but created no problems for management.

Liverpool's Mayor Hogan turned up at Dunlop dances – Speke's highlight, for the council estate had no other community centre to compare with it – dressed in white tie and tails. He was the mayor and, regardless of party prejudices, was resolved to uphold the dignity of his office.

The deferential society was alive and in good heart. When the Roman Catholic Archbishop Downey visited the plant, men and women knelt before him and kissed hands. To level up the tribute paid to 'the green', the 'orange' representative, Protestant Archbishop Garbett of York was invited to visit the works (Liverpool, like Glasgow, has strong Irish-Catholic and Northern-Protestant populations). This time there was no kneeling, but Collett noted that almost everyone who was introduced to the Archbishop, carefully wiped his hand before shaking that of the episcopal dignitary.

As with the church, so with the state. The Speke *Newsbeam* announced, in September 1946, that the Union Jack would fly from the factory's masthead on the following dates: Princess Elizabeth's Birthday, St George's Day, Empire Day, Queen Mary's Birthday, the King's Birthday, the Queen's Birthday, Armistice Day.

Dunlop's identification with the national interest was as complete during this period of austerity and socialism as ever it had been during the war or in the Tory-and-Empire trade era of the 1930s. It was never to be quite so close again.

When, in October 1949, David Collett was appointed general manager of the Dunlop Tyre Company of Canada (potential main board candidates were required to earn their spurs by managing companies in the Empire) the Speke *Newsbeam* spoke of him in glowingly fulsome terms:

> Unfailing inspiration ... won co-operation and loyalty by personally sharing – with characteristically sympathetic approach – the problems which are part and parcel of our great factory.
> Jolly good luck to a truly great leader and friend!

Ten, certainly twenty years later, such a gushing farewell would have been reckoned a parody. But in 1949 it was certainly genuine.

Collett and the Dunlop organization had brought nearly 7,000 jobs to Liverpool. Plus the opportunity to acquire skills (the company operated day-release classes for young trainees) and provided the social centre for the entire community. David Collett and his wife deserved the encomiums heaped upon them.

Moreover, qualities of leadership were among the most admired virtues of the day. They lingered on from the war and, in this period of socialist reconstruction, the ethos and language of the war – 'Export or Die', 'The Dunkirk Spirit', 'Battle for Coal' – lived on.

In the absence of powerful financial inducement, and with profit considered practically immoral, 'the bosses' were expected to act rather like officers; motivated by desire for honour, glory and promotion. There were 'perks' of course – company car, driver, luncheons, dinners, overseas trips and so on. But the salaried manager had no prospect of making real money and with rationing of almost every commodity, not much to buy even had he earned a fortune.

In these circumstances, job satisfaction loomed large as a recompense for working long hours and assuming heavy responsibilities. It was noble. But it was not business.

For the further British management moved away from concern for profitability, shareholder approval, customer satisfaction, the less able it became to compete in the harsh world of resurgent Germany, France, Japan and Italy who were just beginning to rise from the ashes of defeat. So long as the workforce remained quiescent – and workers in the rubber industry were far less troublesome than engineers (as at Rootes) or dockers – this absence of money motivation and the lack of bottom-line profitability discipline could just be borne.

But when David Collett returned to visit Speke as a main board director some six years later, in 1956, he saw signs of disturbing change in the attitude of labour and the unions. He recalled (in an interview with the author):

> There was distinct evidence of politicisation. We could no longer count on the old 'us' and 'them' – 'us' being Dunlop and 'them' being our rivals. Instead the 'us' was increasingly the workers and 'them' management. I always found Frank Cousins [left-wing leader of the giant Transport Workers] personally quite co-operative, but within the factory there was increasing polarisation. There were more disputes and work would stop even while the dispute-settling procedure was under way. Unions were competing for membership. There was altogether a more 'bolshie' atmosphere.

Decades later the growing labour troubles of Speke would play a significant part in the downfall of the first Dunlop empire.

By the early fifties the 'easy days' of assured markets, lack of European and Japanese competition and state paternalism, were over, well over.

And coinciding with changes in the commercial climate and labour relations came a most unwelcome development for the Dunlop Rubber Company – investigation by the Monopolies Commission.

CHAPTER X

'SUCH A HURTFUL REPORT...'

Businessmen meeting in secret have always roused the ire, suspicion and anger of everyone not in on the secret. It is natural to doubt the motives of profit-makers who seek agreement, one with the other, for the consequence is usually higher profits through higher prices.

Adam Smith, author of *The Wealth of Nations*, the prime champion of capitalism and free enterprise, warned against such collusion by businessmen way back in 1775. He taught that the very sight of businessmen in conclave should arouse suspicion. But his warning was intended to keep the conduits of competition free from the clogging effects of cartels, of producer associations.

The sovereignty of the consumer and the subservience of the producer to that sovereignty was Smith's constant theme. In contrast, socialist doctrine saw competition as the enemy of society, creating conflict where there should be co-operation, strife in place of harmony. Capitalists individually were bad enough; capitalists in unison spelt conspiracy and exploitation of their customers who were also, of course, producers.

It followed, therefore, that anything tending to create a monopoly was against the public interest (unless that monopoly was the state which, in socialist theory, could not operate against the public interest as it *was* the public interest).

In pursuit of this policy, Mr Attlee's Labour administration passed the Monopolies and Restrictive Practices Inquiry and Control Act in 1948. It was designed to prevent rascally capitalists from robbing the people. It was never intended to put a great British institution, such as Dunlop, into the dock.

Such however is what transpired. In October 1951 the Conservatives returned to office. They were resolved to liberalize the economy which had endured twelve years of 'War Socialism' and was so bound with controls – over 11,000 statutory instruments governing every aspect of economic life – that it had practically atrophied.

Thus, for different reasons, the Monopolies Commission appealed to both political parties. Why the Tories chose to make an example of Dunlop is not clear: probably it was a bureaucratic decision of the Board of Trade. When Reay Geddes, then a fairly new main board director, enquired of a senior Trade official why Dunlop had been selected, he was told 'Well, we had to start somewhere.'

Whatever the reason the Commission, composed of lawyers, economists, businessmen, trade unionists, reinforced by a formidable array of technical experts and civil servants, set to work in the autumn of 1952 to investigate 'The supply of pneumatic tyres . . . and to determine whether operations are against the public interest.'

For more than three years the Commission toiled at their task. Needless to say they were not welcomed by the Dunlop management. John Simon, then a young executive, was told by Ted Beharrell, the company's managing director, not to give any information voluntarily to Miss Gates, one of the Commission's investigators. 'Not even a pencil to write up her notes.'

What had Dunlop to hide? Plenty. As will be seen from the Commission's report which was published in December 1955. The point is, did that report, and subsequent action, damage Dunlop more than it helped to advance the national interest? What it certainly did do was shatter the conviction – or illusion – that what was right for Dunlop was right for Britain.

The Commission listed eleven tyre manufacturing concerns operating in the UK in 1955 of which five were foreign, Firestone, Goodyear and North British (US), Pirelli (Italian) and Michelin (French).

One of the British companies, India Tyre of Inchinnan in Scotland, was a Dunlop subsidiary having been bought over from US interests in 1932. Another, John Bull, was embraced later. A third, British Tyre and Rubber, ceased manufacturing tyres. A fourth went out of business. A fifth, Avon, flourished but on a comparatively minor scale.

All these companies had been members of the Tyre Manufacturers' Conference since the early thirties when excess supply and price cutting forced joint action to protect resale price maintenance.

Here it is necessary to outline, in some detail, the policy and practice of RPM, resale price maintenance, for it lay at the core of the whole tyre industry, and of most other products, for some fifty years from World War I to the late sixties.

Briefly it was a system which permitted the manufacturer to determine the price at which his product would be sold to the ultimate consumer. Rowntree, the chocolate-maker, for example, would state on the wrapper that its 2oz block of Aero cost 2 pence. That was the price charged in every part of the country, from John O'Groats to Land's End. Any retailer who breached that price, say by selling it for one penny to encourage customers to his shop, or charging three pence because there was no alternative outlet, could be penalized. Not only would he not receive Aero again (or any other Rowntree product) but other chocolate-makers would also cease supplying the retailer. This was known as the collective boycott. It was applied infrequently, but its very threat acted as a deterrent to any seller intent on using a particular product as a 'loss leader', i.e. a method of tempting customers by offering a brand bargain in the hope that they would buy other more highly priced goods.

What applied to the homely chocolate bar applied in treble measure to the infinitely more expensive products of the highly capitalized tyre industry.

R.C.Hiam, general manager of Dunlop's tyre division, outlined his company's case for the retention of RPM, or Fair Trade, in an address to the Birmingham Chamber of Commerce:

> Tyres are tricky things to handle and to service them properly the dealer needs skilled staff. He needs equipment like jacks, air compressors, balancing machines and so on, as well as a fair amount of space. He must be able to give advice and to make repairs. To do his job properly he must carry a fairly heavy stock, not all of which will turn over quickly. Unless he is given the protection of fixed margins such a dealer cannot possibly compete with the merchant who stocks only the quick-selling lines and who considers his job done when he has handed the goods over the counter and collected the cash. One of the objects of our policy is, therefore, to channel the distribution of our products through dealers who are equipped to handle them. In doing this we are not only protecting our own reputation, we are also safeguarding our customers.
>
> A firm such as my own has a strong interest in obtaining the widest possible distribution of its products. It is not enough that they should be available through a few big establishments in the towns. Again we can only have wide distribution by ensuring that the remote dealer gets his share of the business at a reasonable profit. Resale Price Maintenance makes for stability....
>
> If trade margins are cut to a point where they are no longer adequate there will be strong pressure on the manufacturer to lower the trade price and restore the dealer's profit. The only way the manufacturer can find this money is very often to reduce quality. If he has a number of competitors selling the same sort of article, the pressure to reduce

trade prices will be even greater as first one manufacturer and then another tries to win the favour of wholesalers or retailers. . . .

Interest in trade stability is very great in an industry like my own where capital equipment costs are heavy and where carrying surplus capacity to deal with artificial peaks of demand would involve a lot of sheer waste. . . .

What the critics of price maintenance all too often seem to want are uneconomically low prices. These are, of course, very agreeable to the customers but they don't last. The question of resale price maintenance has been examined by Government commissions on three separate occasions, the latest in 1949, and the manufacturers' right to settle the price of his products has been upheld. . . .

Competition in price is only one aspect of competition and I believe that is an aspect best left to the manufacturer whose reputation depends on marketing a product that people want at a price they are willing to pay. He alone, at least in an industry like ours, can know what a product ought to cost ; and only he can hold the proper balance among all the factors of quality, service, distribution and so on, as well as the price, that add up to a competitive product.

Mr Hiam admitted that there were arguments for the abolition of RPM. One was that dealers and retailers who could operate more efficiently ought to have the undisputed right to pass on the fruits of their efficiency to their customers in the form of lower prices. Another was that customers should be free to decide between minimum service at lower price and more service (or quality) at a higher. A third was that retailers were being feather-bedded and there was therefore no incentive to be efficient.

He claimed, however, that these criticisms were not justified in the tyre industry.

The very fervour of R.C.Hiam's defence of RPM suggested Dunlop's vulnerability to change. And change was the purpose of the Monopolies Commission investigators.

By 1952 there was a growing revulsion against controls and regulations. The system had created shortages and perpetuated rationing. In an age of over-full employment and inflation, it seemed quite wrong to harp on about the need for orderly marketing to sustain jobs and prices.

The Germans, the defeated foe, had cast controls and rationing to the winds and were bursting with prosperity, *falling* prices and record-breaking exports. Like the Russians, the British socialists had stinted the nation of goodies to ensure future abundance – and had failed to deliver on the future.

In the censure of resource allocation the practices of the twenties and thirties (when the case for orderly marketing was overwhelming) were subjected to condemnation.

The structure which Dunlop had created with such consummate skill was now about to be exposed to hostile examination.

With considerable relish the majority of the Commission exposed the trade secrets which Dunlop had long, and successfully, sought to hide.

The whole tyre business in Britain was threaded through with bodies which effectively restrained free competition : the Tyre Manufacturers Conference to which reference has been made ; the Accountants Panel ; the Society of Motor Manufacturers and Traders (with its Scottish equivalent) ; the National Association of Tyre Specialists ; the National Tyre Distributors Association ; the Tyre Trade Joint Committee ; the Cycle and Motor Cycle Manufacturers and Traders Union. The Dunlop Rubber Company was not the creator of all these bodies, but Dunlop's preponderance in the industry ensured that what Dunlop said went.

The Tyre Manufacturers Conference, the Commission decided, was the main vehicle for Dunlop's influence. But the company's preponderance in UK tyre manufacturing – 47 per cent of the whole British market by value – determined the group's focal position.

In its report the Commission recognized Dunlop's outstanding achievements, from producing the first aeroplane tyres in 1910 to the tubeless tyres of natural rubber and non-skid treads in 1953, plus vast research into synthetic rubber including a plant capable of producing 2,000 tons a year.

It also acknowledged Dunlop's role as the custodian of the 'corpus of knowledge' on rubber technique, passed on to Dunlop subsidiaries worldwide and even – through joint consultation in the tyre industry – to rivals.

That said, the disclosures of how Dunlop fixed the market came thick and fast.

There were the secret discussions with the Rubber Export Association of America whereby, since 1925, Dunlop and the US manufacturers fixed the export price of tyres on the wholesale price level of the US or the UK, whichever was lower. Dunlop agreed to keep the principal European producers – Michelin, Pirelli and Continental of Germany – in line. The company justified the price-fixing arrangements by saying that a price war with the Americans would have ruined the much smaller British tyre industry, as the US with its huge domestic market could have slashed export prices and so fatally undercut Dunlop and other British makers.

99

There was the secret purchase of a controlling interest in a number of major tyre retail outlets, so that Dunlop would have a network of its own subsidiaries while still being able to supply independent traders who would not suspect that Dunlop owned their competitors. This covert operation began in 1927 when Dunlop acquired 51 per cent of C.H. Brittain, tyre factors at Stoke-on-Trent. This was followed in 1931 by the purchase of W. Briggs and Co. at Salford and the nearby Rapid Tyre Services Ltd. In 1933 the controlling interest in Marsham Tyre Co. was taken. Smallbone Ltd with outlets in Reading, Oxford and Worthing followed. Finally in 1937 Dunlop bought out a group in Scotland while using their Briggs and Marsham subsidiaries to acquire a host of other traders so that, to quote the report, 'the whole of England, Wales, Scotland and N. Ireland is now covered with a network of outlets under Dunlop control'.

The extent of Dunlop's holdings was not known even to leading executives in the subsidiaries. Only the managing directors and accountants were privy to the deals.

So secretive was Dunlop that when it went into the retread business in 1938, it set up a subsidiary of the Marsham Co. so that its connection with Dunlop would not be known. The new company was named Regent Tyre and Rubber. Factories were established at Edmonton and Manchester to take casings from the Briggs group. Neither group knew that they were both Dunlop subsidiaries.

When, in 1953, Dunlop bought another remould concern, Tyresoles of Leeds and the East Midlands, it was obliged to make this purchase public as the Tyresole concessionaries were legally entitled to be informed of any change of ownership. But the directors of Tyresoles were not told that Dunlop owned Regent Tyres and Tyres (Scotland) so that the three groups operated under the impression that they were dealing with competitors rather than partners in the same enterprise. Had Dunlop acknowledged its ownership of Regent, it would also have been obliged to acknowledge that it owned Marsham, Regent's parent. And as Marsham was operating as a maverick, outside the rules of the Tyre Manufacturers' Conference (i.e. buying casings wherever they were cheapest) such disclosure would have been highly embarrassing to Dunlop, who laid down the rules for the TMC!

This complex network of dealerships proved extremely profitable to Dunlop. The gross yield on the investment in the distribution and remoulding trades ranged from a low of 7.7 per cent to a high of 43 per cent in 1951. It also enabled the company to enhance its already dominant position throughout the tyre industry. But then, as Dunlop executives explained, these arrangements acted as a cushion against the volatility of tyre production : a new development – the steel radial or the tubeless tyre – could require extensive re-tooling, and prices and stocks were subject to sudden and dramatic swings in raw rubber costs, fluctuating from 1s 1d (5p) per lb in 1948 to 4s 3d (21p) per lb at the height of the Korean War in 1951 and then down again to 1s 4d (6p) in 1954 after the Korean armistice. Material costs – including textiles of course – represented 56 per cent of the selling price of tyres in 1948 and rose to 71 per cent in 1951 – which had the effect of halving Dunlop's profit, falling as a percentage of capital employed from 21 per cent to 11 per cent. Dunlop, in common with other tyre producers, naturally sought stable, and substantial, profits wherever these were on offer.

The Commission accepted that there was some justification in the Dunlop case, which was fully laid out in paragraphs 450–76 of their report.

Dunlop's position – and that of the British tyre industry which it dominated in manufacture and distribution – may be summarized as follows.

Uniformity of prices is brought about by competition which forces others to follow the price leader. Dunlop initiates a price and others must match it because if they charge less, customers would assume their tyres were inferior and if they charge more they would lose customers. Such competition as exists must therefore be confined to discounts offered to traders who will then push the tyres of the company offering the heaviest discount. Orderly and informed marketing is achieved through the industry-wide Tyre Manufacturers' Conference and its Accountants Panel.

Dunlop claimed that this system enabled the industry to avoid a destructive price war (after which the exhausted survivors would need to *increase* prices to recoup their losses) while preventing monopoly through the existence of a number of producers, each promoting its own models based on competing designs embracing the fruits of independent research and development.

'It would,' said Dunlop in its submission, 'be an ill-founded suggestion wholly unsupported by the evidence, to infer that because after consultation prices are found to be identical they would be different were there no consultations. In fact, the TMC is merely a forum for discussion.' Well . . . .

On restriction on advertising, Dunlop explained that 'heavy expenditure on advertising is uneconomic to the industry and the public . . . some years ago the Government appealed to the industry to curtail such expenditure.' So they did, but it was a socialist government, which *did* regard advertising as 'a wasteful and unnecessary cost burden on commerce'.

In arguing, somewhat ingenuously, for an industry-wide agreement to curb advertising, Dunlop was not showing that natural intuition which it had shown in the past in its relations with Whitehall. The agreement of the Tyre Manufacturers' Conference of July 1954 was pretty extensive. The members – effectively all the tyre manufacturers in Britain – bound themselves not to: advertise in cinemas, on buses (other than London Transport), in trade magazines, municipal publications, timetables and so on. The purpose of this was to cut costs *and* deny 'perks' to retailers. Thus tyre workers pledged themselves not to give overalls to garage mechanics, nor even blotters to sales managers of outlets. 'Presents will not be given away (at Christmas or any other time) excepting inexpensive novelties....'

Such a self-denying ordinance might have earned plaudits all round had it not been that Dunlop was also paying considerable secret loyalty bonuses to British Motor Manufacturers for using Dunlop's original equipment.

Paragraph 465 of the Monopolies Commission Report outlines the company's justification.

> Dunlop say that the special allowances, paid at the end of each trading year to certain more important original equipment customers . . . sometimes means the sacrifice by Dunlop of more profitable business elsewhere (replacement) . . . . Dunlop find it necessary to make these payments confidentially because of the strong bargaining priorities of their customers and the threats of competitors to underquote Dunlop at any price. Dunlop have therefore devised the system under which the amount of the special allowance is not made known to the recipient until the orders for the next year have been placed . . . . This serves to keep these customers faithful.

The extent to which Dunlop had tied up the tyre trade in the UK – from uniform tendering for exports through controlled advertising, confidential rebates and secret ownership of major distributors – may be gauged by examples provided in appendices to the Monopolies Commission Report:

Letter from Dunlop to all British Manufacturers, 14 August 1950.

> Effective 21 August, we shall be increasing the price in our 'A' export list for car, giant, motor-cycle and tractor tyres by $12\frac{1}{2}$ per cent [there followed details] . . . . We trust you will be prepared to apply a similar increase and we shall look forward to hearing from you on this point in due course.

102

Letter from Dunlop to Manufacturer X, 31 October 1950.

I have been looking at your revised export list and I find that in the following sizes your new prices differ somewhat from our own.

Giant Tyres	Manufacturer X	Dunlop
40 × 9 14-ply cover	£44 2s 8d	£44 1s 4d
40 × 9 tube	£3 10s	£2 19s 8d
42 × 9 14-ply cover	£47 15s 8d	£47 19s 4d
42 × 9 tube	£3 10s 8d	£3 0s 4d

Perhaps you will kindly confirm that your list will be amended in due course.

Reply from Manufacturer X to Dunlop dated 2 November 1950.

I confirm that the discrepancies in the list are as stated and that these will be rectified at the earliest opportunity.

From Dunlop to Manufacturer Z, 20 February 1951.

There appear to be two errors in your export price list .... We shall be glad to hear from you that you will be amending these prices in due course.

Reply from Manufacturer Z, dated 23 February 1951.

Thank you for pointing out the error in the price quoted in our list for the 40XG cover. This has already been corrected.

(The second 'error' could not be similarly corrected as the specification was different from that of Dunlop's, so prices were not kept exactly uniform.)

For any trader stepping out of line on agreed prices, there was swift retribution :

Case No. 6/2838.

In April 1952, Dunlop reported to the BMTA (British Motor Trade Association) that a small trader in Lincolnshire was price cutting on giant tyres, to the annoyance of local traders. The BMTA thereupon instituted enquiries through distributors in the area and authorised a test purchase. This was made by a BMTA inspector who bought four covers, for which he was undercharged £1 16s. 8d. The trader was charged with under-cutting and making out a false invoice. He did not appear at the hearing by the Price Protection Committee, but wrote pleading guilty. He said he'd considered he had been trapped into helping someone who had pretended he thought the protected price too high. The inspector denied, however, that he had said the tyres were too dear. The trader also claimed that, as the big distributors cut prices, he had to do likewise to keep any business. He was fined £50 but said he was unable to pay this outright because of the bad state of business and offered £1 a month. When the BMTA said they would accept payment of £10 a month, the trader said he could 'just manage £4' and trusted the Association would meet him on this point. The BMTA insisted on £10 a month and pointed out that failure to pay any instalment by the due date would result in the trader's name being placed on the 'stop list' (that is, he would not receive tyres from any manufacturer).

To a later generation such punishment for doing the public a service by cutting prices would seem grotesque. But to people reared in the business world of the depression-scarred twenties and thirties and the war- and austerity-afflicted forties, such proceedings were considered perfectly normal and proper.

The Lincolnshire trader, far from being a benefactor to mankind, was undermining agreed prices and destabilizing business. He was 'letting the side down'. As well apply the moral standards of one era to another as ask why Boadicea did not use tanks to drive out the Romans.

In the early fifties the Dunlop Rubber Company and the organizations it had created – like the TMC – or with which it happily collaborated, such as the BMTA, were instruments of orderly marketing, fashioned after the bitter experience of unrestrained competition. Even the Commissioners did not endorse unrestricted competition, so influenced were they by conventional thought of the time. Indeed it is quite possible that had Sir Eric Geddes still commanded Dunlop, the Board of Trade would never have dared set the Monopolies Commission dogs on the tyre industry.

Civil servants held Sir Eric in deepest awe. They were scared of him. And with reason. In 1936, the Permanent Secretary of the Air Ministry, Sir Christopher Bullock, approached Geddes with a view to securing a goodly income in retirement by getting a seat on the board of Imperial Airways, of which Geddes was chairman. This was an unwise thing to do for Geddes was a stickler for proper behaviour and it was improper for a senior civil servant to try to get a job in an industry with which his own department was intimately related. Geddes reported Bullock's approach to the proper authorities, notably Sir Warren Fisher of the Treasury. An inquiry was mounted and the unhappy Sir Christopher was required to resign. The incident was a major talking point among the mandarins of Whitehall for many a year, so that it was extremely unlikely that any of them would have risked the wrath of the mighty beetle-browed Geddes.

On the other hand . . . revenge is sweet. By 1952 the famed Geddes–

Beharrell rule was over. A pleasant, but less dominating figure sat in the Dunlop chair. Clive Latham Baillieu (later Lord Baillieu) was an Australian businessman who had served with the Australian Royal Flying Corps and the RAAF in the Great War. His father had been on the board of Dunlop Australia. Political opponents said of him, 'When Baillieu is on thin ice he skates fast.' The son however needed no such skill. He was already an establishment figure, with many directorships, when he was asked to succeed Sir George Beharrell. A popular, likeable man (in the Dunlop tradition of big handsome bulldogs) he did not possess the awesome reputation of the Geddes–Beharrell axis. As a strong exponent of co-operation between state and private sector, he acquiesced in the Monopolies Commission investigation which gave civil servants the opportunity to probe the company of the man who had so harshly treated one of their own – with devastating results.

Even though the majority of the Commission were not zealously in favour of all-out competition, they still regarded some of Dunlop's methods as unacceptable.

The majority of Commissioners concluded as follows.

> Discussions on prices within the Tyre Manufacturers Conference reduce price competiton and are against the public interest.
>
> The system under which identical prices to the consumer are collectively maintained (resale price maintenance) is against the public interest.
>
> The system by which the TMC fix discounts is against the public interest.
>
> The maintenance of registers (of tyre users who had to abide by certain rules and standards) is against the public interest.
>
> Dunlop's secret ownership of the two retreading concerns, the Regent Tyres and Tyres (Scotland), hampers the efficient organisation of the retreading business as a whole. Such secrecy is, for that reason, against the public interest.

The Commission found that the confidential loyalty rebates paid by Dunlop were not against the public interest. Nor was Dunlop's price-setting regime for tyre exports. Nor yet Dunlop's disproportionate strength in the distributive trade.

In fact the Commission went so far as to declare: 'Apart from specific matters dealt with the Dunlop Rubber Co. have *not* used their dominant position in the industry to the detriment of the public interest.'

Welcome though that ultimate verdict may have been to the Dunlop directors, shareholders and workers, the damage had been done. Sir

Reay Geddes's words 'the hurtful report' would cast lengthening shadows over Dunlop's planning and policies in the years to come.

As a direct result of the Monopolies Commission Report, Dunlop's position in the home base was eroded. The company would no longer enjoy the unhesitating acquiescence of its fellow members in the automotive industry. It would be regarded, increasingly, in the press as being a monopolistic practitioner and, most important of all, it would lose that feeling of 'effortless superiority' and turn to image-making as a corrective to its previous reputation for autocracy.

With the benefit of hindsight it is possible to see 1956 as a watershed year in Britain's economic history (the Monopolies Commission Report was published in December 1955).

Until the mid-fifties the UK was in the enviable position of experiencing minimal competition from Germany and Japan. No real effort had been made to equip the economy mentally for the tests to come. Churchill's Conservative government of 1951–55 did privatize the steel industry, but until the Thatcher administration of 1979 that was the *only* industry de-nationalized throughout three Conservative governments, totalling thirteen years. In other words, the 'mixed economy' where the commanding heights remained in state control, was the norm for the generation of the fifties, sixties and seventies. And while efficiency was praised in the press, it was the efficiency stemming from bigness and appearance rather than that imposed by the disciplines of the market which evoked applause.

Dunlop in the mid-fifties was big, very big. It ranked sixth in the *Fortune* listing of UK companies, coming closely behind such massive concerns as Shell, Imperial Chemicals, British Petroleum and Unilever. By the mid-seventies it had slipped to thirty-fifth.

Let us now examine the factors which make companies wax and wane – and wax again.

CHAPTER XI

AN ESTABLISHMENT
COMPANY IN REPOSE

With the retreat from Empire signalled by the withdrawal from Suez
and the African colonies in 1956–7, media attention became increasingly concentrated on Britain's domestic economic performance.
Growth, growth at almost any cost, was the watchword.

The trouble with this philosophy was that the UK was singularly
ill-equipped to create inflationless expansion. Just as the absence of
competition in the immediate post-war period had induced a fatal complacency, so now the emergence of German, Italian and Japanese
rivalry found British industry, particularly the automotive industry,
wanting.

Technological competence, even inventive genius, was there in
abundance. What was lacking was the commercial follow-through to
exploit ideas, to turn brilliance into profit.

Let two examples suffice : Dunlop's wet-grip tyre and British Motor
Corporation's Mini motor car, both from the 1957–9 era.

Ever conscious of the need to advance road safety, Dunlop engineers
pioneered a tyre to grip the road under bad weather conditions.

Car engineers had begun to complain to tyre engineers that tyres
then available suffered from loss of grip at high speed in the wet.
The effect was described as 'going light in the wet'.

Dunlop had excellent testing facilities at Fort Dunlop, Birmingham,
and experiments were carried out where a one-week-old car was driven
to destruction within one week. Another new car was immediately
brought in as a replacement. The Dunlop engineers were determined
to solve the problem. And so they did.

High speed testing was abandoned. Instead a system of controlled
testing at moderate speeds – much more the norm for the average
motorist – was introduced. The investigation moved to Liverpool's
dockland which still possessed granite sett roads (the very same kind

of surface which had prompted John Boyd Dunlop to develop the pneumatic tyre). Working early on Sunday mornings – with the local fire brigade hosing down the roadways, in the unlikely event of there being dry weather – the Dunlop engineers followed the results intently and fairly quickly produced a ribbed pattern tyre tread with a higher concentration of knife slots. This design was improved with the introduction of Wet Hold Two (WH2) which was sent to the more clamorous car designers who had long complained. Their reception was favourable. But then came the anti-climax. 'There followed', says Eric Tompkins, the historian of the pneumatic tyre, 'one of those quiet periods, so far as Dunlop were concerned, during which it was imagined that the new tyre was being used as a goal to spur on other tyre manufacturers to efforts along similar lines.'

That, alas for Dunlop, is exactly what happened. The Germans brought out the *Sicherheit Schulter* (the 'safety shoulder') tyre, which had considerable success. The Americans came in with a butyl safety tyre, the tread of this synthetic material – a by-product of oil – providing a greatly improved grip on the road. The marketing of the butyl tyre as 'a mighty advance in safety' proved highly profitable and, while Dunlop followed up by producing a similar grip using a suitably modified GR-S tyre with a higher styrene content from the newly opened pilot polymer plant at the Fort, the commercial gain was minimal.

Even when Dunlop brought out a super-safe tyre named the Elite, the cash did not flow into the company's coffers. The Elite was so effective – it gave 45 per cent more resistance to wheel spin, 24 per cent better wet hold on cornering, 15 per cent more braking grip and eliminated squeal – that, inevitably, its on-cost was very high. Fuel consumption, for example, was increased by 2 per cent, and with fast motorway driving fuel consumption became especially noticeable. Tompkins comments sadly, 'The rapidly expanding motorway, which at that time was subject to no speed restriction, led to little interest in the Elite as a commercial proposition.'

Nevertheless, such superb technical designers as Tom French and Eric Gough continued their experiments, winning ecstatic praise from motoring organizations and prizes. Profits however remained static. The granite setts of Dunlop's test beds were not paved with gold.

As with tyres, so with the cars which wore them. The story of the British Motor Corporation's Mini illustrates the pitfalls of genius. The brainchild of designer Sir Alec Issigonis (born in Smyrna, Turkey, but British as his father was a naturalized Briton), the Mini matched the Ford Model T (1914) and Germany's Volkswagen (1936) in originality. According to Alex Moulton, inventor of the Mini's hydrolastic suspension and designer of the Moulton mini-bicycle, the car was christened by himself and racing enthusiast George Dowson[1] who first suggested 'Morris Minimus', in contrast to the pre-World War II Morris Major. Moulton suggested eliminating the 'mus'. And so 'Mini' entered the English language.

Initially both Austin and Morris, independent companies spatchcocked together to form the British Motor Corporation, manufactured their own versions of the Mini, the Austin one being known as the Austin Seven.

However, despite anguished misgivings by the advertising men, the term Mini took over totally.

The name suited the period. Britain, from being maximum was going minimum (the mini-skirt followed the Mini car) and this tiny vehicle seemed to sum up the best of the change.

It was the Suez crisis of October–November 1956 which dictated the change. When Colonel Nasser blocked the Suez Canal to sabotage the Anglo-French attempt to occupy the Canal Zone, the principal route for oil tankers to Western Europe was closed off. Petrol rationing returned to the UK. Although that was regarded as a temporary measure, the general instability of the Middle East suggested that oil supplies could be vulnerable to sudden interruption for the foreseeable future. Cars with maximum fuel economy suddenly became an urgent necessity. Alec Issigonis obliged.

He had been a keen exponent of the small car for years. He had helped to design the extremely successful Morris Minor. He was a staunch proponent of less-crowded highways (at heart, he thought the motor car an infernal evil) and manoeuvrability. The fuel-economy cars then in existence were generally noisy little glass bubbles, three-wheeled, single-cylinder models produced by the famous German aircraft manufacturers, Messerschmitt and Heinkel, who, by treaty, were banned from making war planes.

Issigonis had a short ride in one and resolved to have no more. According to Moulton, that determined him to make a car which would have four seats for adults, a four-cylinder engine and a four-speed gearbox, 'a proper car, not a motorized pram'.

Issigonis had his way. He built a functional box measuring 10ft by 4ft by 4ft, of which 6ft 6ins lengthwise was passenger space, 1ft 6ins for a boot, leaving no more than 2ft for the front-wheel-drive engine which Issigonis was obliged to take off the BMC assembly line. The only suitable one available measured 3ft 2ins from radiator to gearbox. Issigonis' solution was to mount the engine sideways between the two front wheels. He placed the four wheels – each measuring only 10ins in diameter – at the corners of his box to give as much space as possible to the passengers and improve still further the handling and stability of the car by engaging as much road space as possible.

The design was a triumph. The engineering work was fantastic. Within a year the Mini prototype went on the road and clocked up 30,000 miles through the winter of 1957–8. In July 1958 Sir Leonard Lord, chief of BMC, gave the order, 'Have it in production in a year's time.'

The order was carried out. The magnificent Mini appeared in large numbers from the summer of 1959. The British genius had borne wondrous fruit – with, however, two fatal flaws. Workmanship was faulty on many models, allowing rain to seep in when there was a welding defect in the two-section flooring. The second concerned pricing.

BMC's Mini should have earned the company a fortune. Two million were sold – half for export – in ten years, far exceeding any other British-made car. Yet BMC consistently lost money and was finally absorbed by Leyland, the truck and lorry maker. As Dunlop was the supplier of original equipment to BMC, losses in motor manufacturing rebounded on them.

The fact that the magnificent Mini was underpriced and its production lagged behind demand dented both BMC and Dunlop. Great inventive capacity – as exemplified by the Mini and the wet-grip tyre – clearly did not automatically mean big profits.

Engineers, it was felt, should be subject to marketing disciplines. Firms such as Dunlop and BMC should 'sell' themselves. The media taught that American ways and American practices should be adopted. Indeed in the late fifties and early sixties it was not impossible that American ownership, never mind American methods, might embrace the whole British tyre and motor industries.

In the automotive field, US firms held dominant positions. Ford and General Motors' Vauxhall held 40 per cent of the market. Rootes, one of the remaining two volume producers, was in dire trouble, with shrinking sales, extended credit and awful labour relations in its Clydeside factory at Linwood. Rootes was already in the sights of a third major American combine, Chrysler. In 1960 Rootes made one last dash for prosperity. The 'Imp' model, designed to compete with the magnificent Mini, failed to capture a significant segment of the market. Production was plagued by stoppages. By 1963 profits were being transformed into huge losses. Lord Rootes, the firm's father figure and principal salesman, fell fatally ill. The fight went out of the company. Chrysler, the only one of the top three US car manufacturers without a British subsidiary, owned Simca in France and was eager to develop its European potential. Rootes was ideal for this venture. It enjoyed preferential treatment by being near Glasgow, in an area of higher-than-average unemployment. The poor state of Rootes's finances, and the low morale of its management, promised an easy conquest.

Reginald Maudling, the Chancellor of the Exchequer, went out of his way to counter criticism of the fact that a Chrysler purchase of Rootes would put over 50 per cent of British car output in US hands. In February 1963 he declared categorically: 'If, as appears, there is growing opposition to American investment on the Continent of Europe [President de Gaulle was conducting a furious campaign against US economic domination at this point], let us make it quite clear that American investment and American know-how are welcome in the United Kingdom.' The Treasury's welcome was echoed by the Board of Trade which announced that 'existing [favourable tax] arrangements will be carried out exactly as with any other firm which is helped with inducements to go into developing districts'.

Chrysler purchased 30 per cent of the voting equity at twice the market value, and 50 per cent of the non-voting 'A' shares at three times their value. Shortly afterwards a full take-over was consummated.

Some years previously Harold Macmillan, first as Chancellor and then as Premier, had presided over the sale of Trinidad Oil to the Texas Oil Company and the minority UK shareholding in Ford to the parent company in Detroit.

Frustrated by de Gaulle's veto, in January 1963, from entering the European Common Market, the British government seemed intent on throwing the weak UK economy wide open to US penetration. In the preceeding fifteen years the pace of America's take-over had increased enormously, to *fifteen times* its pre-World War II size. In a chapter of a book headed 'Mrs John Bull's Diary'[2] a typical British housewife and her husband were shown touching nothing but American-owned products from the moment their Westclox alarm roused them at 7 am until they retired to the comfy warmth of their Monogram electric blanket at 11 pm.

And nowhere was that penetration greater than in cars and all to do with cars. American-owned oil (Esso, Mobil, Texaco, Murco) fuelled American-owned cars (Vauxhall, Ford, Chrysler) which were fired by American-owned sparking plugs, cleaned by American-owned Turtle Wax, started by American-owned ignition keys, and so on.

What more natural than that the tyres should be American-owned as well? Some, of course, were. Goodyear and Firestone were already, and had been for long, in the field. The very first American firm to establish itself in Britain was the North British Rubber Company way back in 1856. Yet there were still US tyre firms with no UK holdings. What if they were to bid for Dunlop? A change of ownership would not alter Dunlop's market share and bring about an automatic referral to the Monopolies Commission (which might have been the case with a Goodyear or Firestone approach).

In much of business strategic planning in the 1960s and 1970s the threat from across the Atlantic was a factor which had to be weighed in the balance. If American ownership were to be resisted, it had best be done by adopting American methods.

Clearly by the late fifties the old practices – first-class technical service combined with predominant control of the distributive trade – were not enough in themselves to ensure Dunlop's pre-eminence and independence.

Growth, diversification, marketing were to be the watchwords for tomorrow.

Organic growth and acquisition were one answer to post-war blues; Dunlop actually dropped the dividend in 1955, at the same time issuing £12 million in debenture stock to finance expansion (but also to increase the debt burden). The ten years from 1953 to 1963 saw startling developments.

1953 Tyre factory opened at Campinas in Brazil.
      Tyresoles Ltd (remoulders) acquired.

1954 Tyre factory opened at Whitby, Canada.

1955 Work started on opening up raw rubber plantations in Nigeria.

1956 Hose division factory opened in Gateshead.

1957 Synthetic rubber plant opened at Fort Dunlop.
      Chemical products factory opened at Birmingham.
      Dunlop Footwear Ltd formed.
      Golf-club maker, John Letters of Scotland, acquired.

1958 John Bull Rubber Co. (rubber-to-metal bonded components, couplings, etc., and tyres) acquired.

1959 Tyre factories opened at Bulawayo (Southern Rhodesia – now Zimbabwe), Ambattur (India), and Amiens (France).
      Slazengers, sports goods manufacturers, acquired.

1960 Brakes Division formed.

1961 Edgar Sealey Ltd acquired.

1962 Tyre factory opened at Nagoya, Japan.

1963 Tyre factories opened in Malayasia, Nigeria and Uganda.

By the early sixties Dunlop's organization looked like this:

Dunlop Rubber Co. Ltd – Divisions

Aviation – Coventry

Belting – Speke, Liverpool

Brakes – Coventry

Chemical Products – Castle
 Bromwich

Dunlopillo – Harrogate

Rim and Wheel – Coventry

Semtex – Brynmawr, Wales

General Rubber Goods –
 Manchester

Hose – Gateshead

Overseas – London

Tyres – Fort Dunlop, Speke and
 Leicester

Sports – Waltham Abbey

Below these came the manufacturing concerns – owing responsibility to their respective divisions ranging from cotton mills in Rochdale to India Tyres in Inchinnan, Scotland. Abroad, Dunlop had manufacturing subsidiaries in France, Germany, Canada, Brazil (hopelessly vulnerable to US competition), Malaya, New Zealand, Nigeria, Rhodesia, India, Japan, South Africa, the USA, plus selling companies in Belgium, Denmark, Italy, the Netherlands, Sweden, Switzerland, Peru, Ceylon (Sri Lanka), China, Indonesia and Pakistan. Dunlop Australia, a robust and thriving manufacturing concern on its own had associate status with a Dunlop shareholding of some 10 per cent. This later became Dunlop Pacific.

The Company had become globally the thirty-ninth largest enterprise outside the USA and, along with its associates, was operating 130 factories in 22 countries spread across the globe, providing work for 108,000 people, half of them employed in the UK. There were 120,000 shareholders spread throughout the world. The gross capital employed in 1960 amounted to £194 million. The Board of Directors was composed as follows:

Chairman
Sir Edward (Ted) Beharrell

Managing Director

Sir Reay Geddes

President (honorary title
for former chairman)
Lord Baillieu

113

Executive Directors: David Collett, T.E. Peppercorn, D.W. Hawkins, J. Wright, John Lord

Non-executive Directors: Sir David Bowes Lyon, Sir Alex Aikman, Sir Archie Forbes, Lord Weir, Lord Robertson.

These latter, embracing banking, engineering, transport, provided impartial advice and, where necessary, correction, that is in theory. For another view see p. 197. The executive directors were, of course, more experienced in the company.

The main board met once a month, to review major projects and determine policy. Guided by the excellent accountancy system pioneered by de Paula, the board executives plotted the course ahead, matching plans to expected revenues. Two key figures, who later became board members, in controlling this operation, were Maurice Coop, the company secretary, and Eric Holt, the financial adviser. They were men of caution. Members like Collett, Wright, Hawkins and Peppercorn were specialists: in personnel, tyre manufacture, engineering, labour relations. The dominant figure was the managing director, Reay Geddes, son of the redoubtable Eric, and the man with big, bold strokes, in contrast to the gentler, more retiring chairman, Sir Ted Beharrell.

It was Geddes who dealt with all sectors of Dunlop's senior management.

The organization fell into two broad categories. On one side were the general managers of the subsidiary companies and manufacturing divisions in the UK and managing directors of the overseas companies. They reported to one or other of the main board executive directors and were, of course, responsible for the profitability of their own concerns. In the second category were officials in charge of specialist divisions such as research, engineering, finance, personnel, publicity, purchasing. Their function was to advise general managers in their own concerns and liaise with their opposite numbers in other divisions or subsidiaries. This cross-fertilization was designed to improve comparability and enhance the two-way flow of ideas. Thus, accountants would exchange ideas through the finance division, with its HQ in London. Similarly research in say the chemical division would find application in the tyre division, as happened with the invention and development of 'Gentac', a vinyl pyridine latex which provided the only satisfactory method of bonding nylon to rubber, thereby accelerating the change-over to nylon casings in certain types of tyre. Products developed by the research division could indeed spawn new subsidiary companies, or even divisions: as with the brakes division (later absorbed in vehicles).

A Dunlop organizational handbook explained these lateral lines of communication with their apparent complexity, by drawing a parallel with an army system in which 'the commanding officer is responsible for the operations of his unit, and is completely answerable for the results, but can call on specialist services, such as the Royal Army Medical Corps, to keep his troops fighting fit'. The handbook went on to claim that the system was 'flexible and efficient'.

Its flexibility may be attested to by comparing the company's divisions in 1970 with those in 1950. After a decade of swift technological progress, new divisions – in hydraulic hose, oil and marine, plant and equipment – had emerged while others had disappeared (such as brakes) being absorbed in new species. Yet one is left with the feeling that organization for the sake of organization, that dreaded hardening of the arteries which is the death of commerce, was beginning to set in.

Max Aitken, the first Baron Beaverbrook, boasted when he took over the Ministry of Aircraft Production in 1940 that his mission was to 'smash organization'. That was an extreme expression impossible of fulfilment, but it did demonstrate the need to question empire building constantly. Thus in 1970 there were fourteen Dunlop divisions, against nine, ten years earlier, although profits as a percentage of capital employed had diminished.

Indeed even by 1960 there had been a severe deterioration of performance. Thus at the depths of the economic depression in 1933, Dunlop could point to 15 per cent profit on capital. By 1960 it had fallen to 7 per cent.

Although personal responsibility was not submerged – general managers were dismissed for failing to meet output and profit forecasts, and executives were fired (some thought unfairly) for endorsing excessive stocking of rubber – the general thrust of company policy was to deal kindly with shortcomings and to transfer executives to other tasks, thereby exacerbating the growth of over-organization.

In 1960 however this was not a matter requiring immediate attention, or even particular note. The company was truly 'sitting pretty': an establishment concern with a proven record of achievement and a constant technological itch to improve itself. . . .

Nowhere was this itch more apparent than in the development of sports goods.

By 1960 the Age of Leisure was dawning – or so it was said. Certainly participatory sport was booming and rubber was at its centre, for golf balls, tennis balls, footballs, and the footwear to go with them.

When Dunlop started making golf balls at the Fort much of the work was done by hand. Daisy Blake recalled how it was in the 1920s:

> In those days when they had the golf balls joined together and the core inserted ... they were put into very hot water for 30 minutes. They were then put into cold water to cool off for 10 minutes. They were taken out and the girls would use 'trimmers' – a little instrument with a wedge – to take off the thin rubber [where the two halves were joined]. After that the paint went on. Girls put the paint in the palms of their hands [they never touched the ball with their fingers] and rolled the ball around, finally dropping it on the tray. They trimmed and painted all day. After the balls had been hardened other girls stencilled. One of my sisters did stencilling and another did the paint. The only use of machines was in the core winding.[3]

For this Daisy was paid £2 5s. a week: a pretty good rate in those days when the average average male wage was £3 5s. Pay was based on piece-work and Daisy recalled: 'I never heard a miserable complaint ... so long as there was fair play and they had their weekly wage that was all that mattered.'

Forty years on production methods had altered dramatically. Practically everything was mechanized as this description of operations at Dunlop's Speke factory shows:

> Refrigeration plays an important part in the manufacture of a golf ball. The core of rubber-covered paste on which it starts is frozen solid for the first winding, in which 5ft of rubber tape are put round it. For the second winding 21 yards of rubber thread are wound on at full tension by an ingenious machine in which the ball is held between two oscillating rollers subjected to a jet of compressed air, the combination of forces turning the ball in all directions to ensure even winding. Then gutta-percha shells are fitted round the core, followed by a moulding process which leaves a seam and more freezing takes place rendering it brittle and easier to cut off, while a brushing machine brushes the ball clean of dust. [How different from Daisy's sister's hands!] Next there's a full-scale examination for all types of defects. Then comes painting [automatic of course] and a further series of five tests for resilience, weight etc.[4]

Not surprisingly it took three weeks to make a golf ball.

Twenty years further on and the production of golf balls had become a meta-science. The April 1985 *Golf World* recorded a 'revolutionary new concept in golf ball design' – the Dunlop DDH (standing for dodecahedron).

A requirement of any good golf ball surface pattern is to provide uniform aerodynamics – the ball must fly accurately and consistently no matter how it is aligned to the club face. . . . Not only has the surface pattern been designed for greater ball accuracy, but the unique use of four different computer established dimple sizes has produced a ball which has been shown in tests to go further than any other leading ball.

Neil Coles, the distinguished English golfer, provided the proof of the pudding by hitting the DDH an extra 20 yards. The American *Golf Digest* revealed that the DDH took five years to develop and cost more than $1 million to produce with its 360 dimples against the conventional 336. Or, as Bob Haines, the physicist and research and development manager of Dunlop, put it :

The 12 pentagon format enables us to get more seams on the ball. If you think of a cricket ball and how it can be made to move around in the air with only one seam on it, then it makes obvious sense if you can construct a ball with a lot of seams designed to conflict on it, you will decrease that movement. Some golf balls have only one seam, some have three, but the dimple formation of the DDH gives us ten. We claim, and intensive testing has proved, that this makes the ball the most accurate ever produced. It is a bonus that we have been able to construct a dimple pattern that also sends the ball further.[5]

Sixty years on from Daisy Blake, the physicist had taken over from the physical.

The point of this foray into golf is to demonstrate Dunlop's continuing effort on the frontiers of scientific and technological development. Be it in sports goods, tyres, consumer products, hose, footwear, aviation, chemicals, the board of 1960 could rely utterly on the technical supremacy of the men in grey jackets. They acknowledged no superior and few equals.

In tyres, for example, Dunlop in 1960 took first, second and third places in every Grand Prix race. One hundred Wimbledon Championship players used Dunlop 'Maxply' rackets. Ninety per cent of the world's airlines used Dunlop engine seals on their jet aircraft . . . and so on, and so on.

Yet problems there were. Despite diversification, tyres still represented 70 per cent of the company's turnover.

Ted Beharrell had played a major part in securing Dunlop as the prime – almost the sole – supplier of original equipment to the British motor car industry. He was justly proud of that and of the construction, in co-operation with other rubber manufacturers, of the synthetic rubber plant at Hythe which broke America's monopoly.

However, these developments were expensive and further increased Dunlop's vulnerability – to successful penetration of the British car market and to a decline in rubber prices.

Economic growth, research and investment were not enough. To keep up with the Joneses needed an image, a market strategy and a good press. Public relations was the answer.

CHAPTER XII

THE McKINSEY EXPERIENCE

James Campbell Fraser was brought into the Dunlop organization to give the company's image and marketing a much needed boost. He was to become probably the first 'PR man' to head a major multinational.

In business as in politics – or in the tennis club committee for that matter – the bright, ambitious newcomer is not a person universally loved : especially when he comes with an impeccable track record in communication, the buzz word of the late fifties.

Fortunately for Fraser his ability to get on with people, his complete likeability, broke down barriers and made him extremely popular.

Big, commanding, blue-eyed, square-jawed, in the classical Dunlop tradition, Fraser was born and brought up in Dundee in comfortable, but not affluent surroundings. He was, in the best Scottish mould, 'a lad o' pairts' – that is, he was excessively good at whatever he put his hand to. He was head boy of his Dundee school. He started to study engineering, but at eighteen joined the RAF. Returning to college, he switched to economics and, inevitably, got a First. In 1950 he joined the Raw Cotton Commission, an organization set up by the socialist administration to produce cotton on behalf of the British textile industry. The Conservatives claimed the Commission simply raised the price of cotton (the producers saw them coming and organized cartel selling) and abolished it as soon as they returned to office. In 1952 Fraser took himself off to the Economist Intelligence Unit where he quickly made a name as an incisive operator and first-class communicator. During his five-year term there he got experience with many different firms and industries, carrying out surveys for them and recommending management and marketing improvements. He also broadcast frequently, often two or three times a week, on Scottish BBC radio. 'That was great training,' he recalls. 'You had to be able to speak on almost any topic at a moment's notice.'

But Fraser was, in his own words, 'a driven man', driven by the spur of ambition. He got his chance in 1957 when he was approached by a management consultant, or head-hunter, Sidney Walton, who had been impressed by Fraser's work in the Society of Business Economists which he had helped to found. Walton arranged several meetings and then finally held out the appointment Fraser had dreamed about : control of Dunlop's corporate public relations.

PR had for years been regarded as a nasty American import whereby smarmy individuals bamboozled the press with a mixture of blarney and whisky and soda. 'PR types' were not held in high regard in Fleet Street.

Fraser's job was altogether different – and in doing it he was to help change PR's somewhat sleazy reputation.

His task was twofold : to raise Dunlop's standing in the City, principally among the increasingly powerful fund managers of pension funds, insurance companies, investment and unit trusts, and secondly to wipe away the stain on Dunlop's reputation caused by the Report of the Monopolies Commission.

That was a formidable challenge as the company had but recently passed its dividend and was in poor odour with the media. It was, however, a challenge Fraser met with gusto and a startling degree of success.

Of course, good PR can only be as good as the performance of the organization it represents. As Dunlop stepped out of the shadow of Michelin's X radial ply and financial results improved, Fraser's clear, articulate explanation of Dunlop's market strategy had the desired effect on financial editors and commentators as well as fund managers.

The Fraser technique, honed to perfection in the Society of Business Economists, was to bring a few people together for dinner at the discreet, well-appointed Stafford Hotel beside Dunlop's Ryder Street headquarters (known to initiates as Dunlop's Canteen). There he and Reay Geddes would discuss the company's future plans in the given political-economical context with journalists and City representatives.

Thus was formed public opinion concerning Dunlop and thus was cemented the Geddes–Fraser alliance.

In 1957 Sir Edward Beharrell was about to take over from Lord Baillieu as Dunlop's chairman. But the real figure of influence on the board, the master planner, was Reay Geddes. This Scot-by-succession (born in India and educated in England) immediately took to Fraser, the Scot-by-birth. Lord Beaverbrook and Harold Macmillan – also Scots-by-succession – had similar empathy with Scots who talked with a Scottish accent.

In 1957 Geddes had been ten years on Dunlop's main board. In appearance he was very much his father's son, but the rougher edges of the elder Geddes had been rubbed off the younger one. Public school and Trinity College, Cambridge (he came down without a degree), and innate courtesy had produced a smoother figure; albeit one with excellent mental equipment and iron resolve to map out clear lines for Dunlop's development.

It is always extremely difficult to follow in the footsteps of a distinguished father. Ted had followed George Beharrell, it is true. Both men, however, were of retiring personality: first-class administrators of a going concern rather than charismatic leaders in creativity.

Geddes senior had saved the Dunlop Rubber Company in the twenties. Geddes junior had a mission to lead Dunlop to more exciting, more progressive achievements in the sixties. In Campbell Fraser he saw an ideal lieutenant: quick-witted, intelligent, articulate, his intellectual equal – and a Scot to boot.

Reay Geddes saw himself as an industrial statesman as well as managing director of a multinational. That was later to be a source of bitter criticism of him by those (notably joint managing director John Simon and City contact man Tony Bullfield) who felt he had his eyes fixed on the far horizons when they should have bent over the balance sheet.

As the sixties advanced, Geddes with Fraser at his side, formulated a market philosophy for his company in the environment of a wholly changed economic scene.

Europe dominated his thinking.

This was hardly surprising, considering that the year he became managing director, at age forty-five, saw the signing of the Treaty of Rome which established the European Economic Community, or Common Market.

Suddenly, so it seemed at the time, a community of 200 million matching the USA had appeared on Britain's doorstep. What was to be done?

Initially the UK government acted coolly towards the newcomer. Interim arrangements were made with the non-Common Market countries of Europe, the Scandinavian states, Portugal, Austria and Switzerland, to reduce tariffs, and there was a move to develop Commonwealth trade which still, in 1958, accounted for four times as much as British trade with the six Common Market members: France, Germany, Italy and the Benelux combination of Belgium, Netherlands and Luxembourg.

By 1960, however, Cabinet views had altered drastically. The grouping with the smaller European states, known as the European Free Trade Association, EFTA, was clearly no substitute for the Common Market. For one thing EFTA was too small; for another the Common Market was not merely tearing down tariff barriers among its members but erecting a common tariff against the rest of the world. If Britain were left outside she would face a Continental combination horribly reminiscent of Napoleon's system which was designed to cripple English commerce: a conclusion that would not have been wholly displeasing to President Charles de Gaulle.

Against unconditional entry into Europe – a simple application to join the Community and accept its rules would have been sufficient – were two formidable arguments. The Common Agricultural Policy, the only actual working component of the EEC, was founded on a high-cost system of protecting the farmer by assuring him of secure, substantial prices for his produce. The customer had to pay, and this caused much anguish in Harold Macmillan's Cabinet:[1] Macmillan's deputy premier and rival, R.A.Butler, pointed out that the Common Agricultural Policy would wreck the cheap food system in the UK sustained by importing low-cost Commonwealth food while succouring the domestic farmer with subsidies. High cost food equalled many lost votes. Hence the chariness of the Tory government. There was also the question of Commonwealth relations. You could have the Commonwealth or you could have the Common Market. You couldn't have both, not when the purpose of the Common Market was to prevent Commonwealth temperate foodstuffs from entering a self-sufficient Europe.

The result of the Cabinet's deliberations on this dilemma was a sludgy compromise. In October 1960 Mr Edward Heath, the Lord Privy Seal, was charged with negotiating British entry into the Market on terms which would allow the UK to keep its Commonwealth relations and its cheap food policy. This was rather like applying to join a club on condition that you could re-write the rules. What Britain wanted was access to the *industrial* free trade of Europe, while avoiding the agricultural protectionism which was the very foundation of the Common Market.

Unkind critics pointed out how appropriate it was that someone bearing the unlikely title of Lord Privy Seal ('neither a Lord, a privy, nor a seal') should be burdened with such a forlorn hope. And so it proved. After fifteen months of futile negotiation, President de Gaulle applied the veto on Britain's application. For the remainder of the decade the Common Market issue was, in the words of Macmillan's successor Sir Alec Douglas-Home, 'a dead duck'.

For Reay Geddes and the Dunlop Rubber Company, however, European collaboration was far from being a dead duck.

Geddes, like his father before him, hankered after orderly marketing. He paid due obeisance to competition. But he was only too well aware of the surplus capacity in the European tyre industry and the constant threat of take-overs from across the Atlantic to believe that unrestricted competition alone would ensure Dunlop's prosperity.

The company straddled both Commonwealth and Common Market with factories in France and Germany and others in Canada, Australia, New Zealand, South Africa, India and Nigeria. But all the indications were that Europe would be the main centre of growth. Canada was wholly overshadowed by its giant neighbour. India and Africa were too poor to generate really big purchasing power. Geddes admitted (in conversation with the author) that a major failure in his term of office was paying far too little attention to Dunlop in Japan, where the most spectacular of all growth was experienced. Short of that, however, Europe was the target area.

To gear up the company for the challenge ahead Geddes, eagerly abetted by Fraser who had been promoted to market controller, called in McKinseys, the American management consultants.

McKinsey, with offices in New York, Washington, Chicago, San Francisco, Los Angeles and Geneva, was new to London. It was typical of Dunlop that it should be the first major British concern to commission an investigation of itself. The study was confined to the marketing of replacement tyres in the United Kingdom. And it was here that the company stood to gain most – or lose most. Tyres still accounted for some 60 per cent of Dunlop's turnover. Original equipment supply was *not* a money-maker, for brand loyalty to tyres hardly existed. The happy notion – which seems to have been held by Sir Edward Beharrell – that motorists would rush back to their dealer to demand Dunlop replacements for their tyres when they wore out, was not being fulfilled. Dunlop's share of the replacement market, at about one-third, was half its share of the original tyre supply. Motorists were more likely to blame the manufacturer when the original tyre wore out than ask for a same-brand replacement.

So dependence on original equipment, OE as it was known in the trade, made Dunlop vulnerable to brand rejection (memories of the tyre failure of the early fifties had not entirely vanished ten years on) while offering nothing in the way of brand loyalty.

Furthermore, the motor manufacturers were squeezing the company's margins on OE as price competition became fiercer, so it was vital to diminish dependence on original equipment and increase the market for the more profitable replacement tyres.

As the sixties dawned a mood of self-examination and fierce self-criticism settled on Britain. The media, notably BBC television, the *Sunday Times, Observer* and other serious journals, fed this feeling of inadequacy. The country's commercial performance was contrasted with the success stories from the USA, Japan and the newly emerged Common Market. A book at that time, *Anatomy of Britain* by Anthony Sampson, encapsulated the criticisms of class-ridden, indolent British management, the fit partner – or antagonist – for trade union bosses burdened with outworn ideas and outdated craft traditions.

Dunlop, as so often before, reflected the public mood. Reay Geddes, the real mover on the board, did not, however, subscribe to the prevailing pessimism among the opinion-formers in the 'quality' press. His view was that if there was something wrong you did something about it. The 'something' in Dunlop's case was McKinsey.

Their consultants were approached in August 1961. They worked for four months to produce an interim discussion document by December; the two reports embracing their findings and recommendations were delivered early in 1962.

McKinsey did a thorough, judicious, sensible job. In the perspective of history it is possible to glean the fundamental flaws in Dunlop's performance : almost all the results of fundamental decency allied to inertia.

McKinsey's consultants pointed out that in the vital sphere of distribution Dunlop, thanks to its acquisitions, was extremely well placed. The company had not, however, exploited its dominance. It had adopted a defensive attitude, permitting wholly owned subsidiaries to sell other, competing, brands.

In the easy days when demand exceeded supply and prices had been effectively controlled by Dunlop, such tolerant practices had not mattered. In this non-competitive atmosphere the number of distributors had grown to 1,300 with an annual average turnover of £40,000–£50,000, and 30,000 traders whose average turnover did not exceed £500 a year. These traders, of course, sold other motor accessories as well as tyres. Distribution costs were high because tyres were being sold in penny packets.

By 1961 the scene had wholly changed. Supply now exceeded demand. Prices were no longer maintained by agreement and prices were being cut vigorously to attract custom. McKinsey correctly foresaw the following developments :

Tyre manufacturers would increasingly tie up distributors in exclusive agreements. The number of distributors would diminish as would the total of traders. The consultants – who had toured the country with Dunlop salesmen visiting tyre depots – concluded that Dunlop should identify the best potential outlets, offer them programmes to win their loyalty and back them up with service to ensure their success.

But, inferred McKinsey, Dunlop was letting old loyalties weaken its drive. Three brands, Dunlop, India and John Bull were being marketed through the same channels. McKinsey declared that John Bull was being kept alive at the expense of the other two brands.

John Bull – a name redolent of Dunlop's own patriotic views – had been acquired four years previously. It was not company policy to buy in order to close. Yet from the best of motives, Dunlop was weakening its market penetration by holding on to a brand which had – according to McKinsey – little market appeal, and whose unit costs were double those of Dunlop and India.

Conventional wisdom argued against John Bull. But Dunlop's reluctance to part with a name and re-locate or dismiss staff was a potent reminder of the company's philosophy: 'What is right for Britain is right for Dunlop.' Unfortunately, patriotism was not enough in the case of John Bull. Nor, according to McKinsey, was Dunlop's conservatism concerning trade terms and resale price maintenance. The report declared :

Dunlop has been the leader in setting industry trade terms and has given strong support to the existing structure and industry register (of approved dealers). These terms and registers have, however, already lost much of their meaning under the pressure of competition.

There is increasing price-cutting to all categories of end users, and increased efforts by manufacturers to achieve greater market shares. Manufacturers offer distributor terms to large retailers who, by definition, should not qualify for them. They also offer additional quantity and loyalty discounts over and above listed distributor terms. . . . The retail price to the motorist is breaking down.

These developments are the natural consequence of a competitive market. Under strong competitive pressure prices and margins seek their true economic levels, and terms evolve which tend to remunerate various distributive outlets for the economic function that they actually perform – regardless of trade definitions. This change is as basic as the change in the distribution channels themselves. Thus, if a volume retailer can buy in quantity he can, and will, get favourable terms regardless of the formal industry structure. The present obsolete terms structure will probably be abandoned as the channels of distribution become more exclusive and more competitive. . . .

Faced with this situation, the Group should re-appraise its position as the primary supporter of the traditional terms structure. In a competitive market it must plan for, and be as prepared as any other manufacturer to offer economically-based rather than artificially-maintained trade terms.

In other words, Dunlop had to face up to the fact that its traditional way of doing business no longer sufficed in the age of supermarkets, mega-stores, and chain garages. Whoever could sell the most would get the best possible terms. Whoever couldn't sell all that much, for whatever reason – sparse population, unpopular site, lack of initiative – would get poor terms. 'That's the way the cookie crumbles,' as an American might have put it.

The breakdown of resale price maintenance, forecast in the Monopolies Commission Report six years previously, was now an accomplished fact. Within two years Parliament, under the prompting of Edward Heath, the Tory trade minister, would legislate to outlaw RPM in all essentials.

Dunlop's distributive system was based on recognizing and upholding resale price maintenance, on protecting the little man – as much to prevent large distributors dictating terms as out of sentiment – and on sustaining a structure which had allowed Dunlop to control the market, albeit in a thoroughly gentlemanly fashion.

Now exclusivity, 'sell only our products and no one else's', along with discounts based entirely on volume/value, were to replace the old informal methods of nod, wink, memo and arm squeeze.

No section of the group would be more affected by these reforms than the sales force.

According to McKinsey the morale of the 360-strong Dunlop sales organization was low. Significantly the trade riposted that, in contrast to the rest of the tyre industry, 'Michelin is singled out as an exceptional example of aggressive technical salesmanship'. No such vibrancy was visible in the Dunlop sales camp.

McKinsey distinguished four major areas of weakness.

Lack of definition of the job. Dunlop sales reps were more 'missionaries' than salesmen, calling on distributors from time to time to give them a pep talk. 'Customer relations', observed the consultants, 'has become a public relations task.' Dunlop salesmen did what was expected of them.

Inadequate planning and control. Field sales managers had so much discretion that practices varied widely, depending on the individuals in charge. One conducted regular sales meetings, another had held none for a year.

Insufficient direction and leadership. 'Communication between sales reps and management,' pronounced the McKinsey men, 'has been reduced to a minimum. Sales management generally considers its primary job to be the maintenance of good relations with distributors and large customers. Salesmen with whom we talked . . . related that it had been months since their management had been with them in their territories, and others could not remember when their performance had last been reviewed.'

Little opportunity for promotion. Only one representative in four was under the age of forty and many believed there was a policy of not promoting anyone over forty.

For more than thirty years the Dunlop organization had been run on the basis of orderly marketing: during the Depression, the run-up to war, the war itself and the controlled economy that followed. Technical expertise, utter dependability and a host of distributive agencies, large and small, many secretly owned by Dunlop, had secured the group a satisfying predominance. Senior sales management confined itself to keeping the big customers happy.

In doing this they were often extremely successful. Scotland was exceptionally favoured in the man who headed up the Dunlop operation: or, more accurately, the India Tyre sales pitch. Sir William Sinclair (the knighthood was for political services to the Conservative Party) was the very personification of the Dunlop image: cheerful, ebullient, silver-haired, ruddy-complexioned, ample-girthed – and extremely effective as the firm's spokesman in Scotland.

'Willie' Sinclair was so much of a personality and so highly regarded in Scotland that he was designated 'managing director', though elsewhere in the UK he would have been a mere sales general manager. Perhaps the fact that Scotland always liked to be treated in a special fashion also explained the grander title.

Nonetheless, Sir Willian Sinclair *did* represent, at its highest level, the Dunlop method of leaving sales to those well-versed in entertaining clients, solving their problems and generally oiling the wheels of industry.

The 'hard sell' was alien to the Dunlop creed. Now they were being told by the people they had called in to guide them that 'today's sales effort is costly and not very effective. . . . The first step must be improvement in sales management practice.'

So: 'The manufacturer's sales force will almost certainly be fewer in number *and more highly qualified.*' (Years later, when Dunlop bought the Angus hose and firefighting company, Angus sales executives deplored the quality of the Dunlop sales staff.) The report went on to recommend that, 'those who have the characteristics required for the future should be trained and encouraged. For those who clearly do not, plans should be made and opportunities found to place them elsewhere.'

There was no mention of dismissal. Possibly because McKinsey did not want to be associated with advocating such drastic measures – there was no guarantee the report would remain confidential – but also because any such measure would be anathema to Dunlop paternalism.

At this period too, trade union power precluded sacking for any but the most heinous offences. True, salesmen were not members of the powerful manual unions, but they could be sure of sympathetic support from that quarter. So, for all these reasons, drastic alterations in the role of the sales force, involving a reduction in numbers employed, was out of the question.

Indeed Dunlop was boasting of its record of increasing employment and of its success in sustaining the personal touch. A company bulletin about the same time that McKinsey was reporting, recorded these facts :

In the period 1949–59 the number of people employed by the Group in 20 countries rose by 20 per cent to over the 100,000 mark and the wages and salary bill rose by 110 per cent to £60 million a year. Every effort is made to ensure that each person on the payroll is treated as an individual and long service shows the success of this policy. In Britain, more than 28 per cent of the male staff and 15 per cent of the operatives have been with the company for more than 15 years (over 2,800 gold wrist watches have been presented).

It is interesting to note here the differentiation between 'staff' and 'operatives', between the white collar and, those who were later called by the American term, 'blue collar'. Dunlop were not alone in treating the two sections wholly differently. Progressive British industry as a whole provided office staff with generous pensions, job security, their own dining area. In turn, 'staff' were expected to work extra hours without extra pay. 'Overtime' was for the workers. This attitude was not imposed by employers ; it was accepted at all levels as the natural order of things. Craft and manual union leaders were not at pains to alter it – though they frequently decried the division in public – because workers would feel greater class solidarity and a full association with their union when they were separated from the white collar 'petit bourgeoisie'.

In turn 'staff' had prestige, plus pensions and security, and the women members were free from the foul language and lewd jokes

128

of the toilers. Not that Dunlop was a company which tolerated swearing. Certainly until World War II, as archive material makes plain, men using bad language before women were sacked. It was unheard of for women to use bad language at all.

Dunlop paternalism, or real caring, was shown in a multitude of ways. A bulletin proudly pointed out :

> everyone should know what is happening in the organisation and should feel that his opinion carries weight in matters that affect him directly. . . . Formal consultation is well advanced in the Group. In every unit of any size at home or overseas there are joint consultative committees, which deal with such topics as the application of national agreements, production problems, working conditions, accident prevention. Works committees have a very successful record. At Fort Dunlop the annual election of delegates normally attracts a poll of 90 per cent [Parliamentary elections rarely attracted a poll higher than 77 per cent].
>
> The Company's personnel officers help countless families in all manner of things from health and finance to legal matters.

Abroad, Dunlop outlined its social obligations, dutifully discharged.

> On the plantations in Malaya and Nigeria, the company provides housing for staff and workers and has built schools, hospitals, sports grounds. In many cases several generations of one family will have lived and worked on the estate. One of the factories in India, Sahaganj, also has its own village for workers with two schools, a hospital and a cinema.

The bulletin went on to outline the company's responsibility for further education in the UK :

> Younger men are always encouraged to acquire technical or professional qualifications at the company's expense. Separate apprenticeship schemes cover all the main factories and at the Coventry and Birmingham plants thare are modern apprentice training schools which include basic training in general machining and toolroom work over five years.
>
> Company policy is to fill vacancies by promotion from within. From the shop floor upwards courses are arranged for suitable men and women to take them a stage further up the ladder. General managers appointed in recent years have come up from such varied beginnings as junior production foreman, production planner, chemical laboratory assistant, sales trainee, cost accountant and engineer.

The bulletin went on to list other good works :

> Factories and offices are kept, as far as conditions permit, light, colourful and comfortable. The Company provides canteens, medical centres and premises and facilities for sports and social clubs.

Dunlop was among a handful of giant British concerns in sustaining an Old Dunlopian Association at Fort Dunlop. A letter, quoted in *Dunlopera*, sums up the affection for the firm by retired employees:

> It is very nice to know that the firm is not losing touch with the old employees. I get every issue of the Dunlop Gazette and, believe me, I appreciate it, take it from me. I thank the firm for thinking of me, in company with the older servants. Believe me, I am still a Dunlopian. Sgd, W.H. Shuttleworth.

Another letter declared:

> I am pleased to hear that a club has been formed, because when one has worked so many years at a firm the sudden loss of friendly contacts leaves a great gap in one's life. Frances M.E. Lane.

'Friendly contacts' and the whole family atmosphere of Dunlop sat uneasily with the McKinsey approach. Making the firm more efficient to face the challenge of growing competition could not truly be squared with sentiment.

McKinsey courteously avoided the issue on the sales force. But with depots and distributors, vital elements in cost accountancy and market predominance, its conclusions were clear: 'As the industry leader, you have much to lose from changes that you are not prepared for and much to gain from those for which you have a plan.'

The plan inevitably meant streamlining, which, in turn, meant eliminating economically unjustifiable outlets and ending old, friendly contacts.

McKinsey recommended as far as possible direct factory delivery to distributors exclusively trading in Dunlop tyres. The argument was irrefutable.

> Orders ... can be delivered more economically by direct shipment to many if not all areas. The capacity of the largest lorry delivering from factories is 10 tons and their average load is 8 tons. A lorry from Fort Dunlop to London making four 2-ton drops and returning to Fort Dunlop would result in far less delivery cost than the depot delivery alternative. In depot delivery, the lorry would have to travel the same distance with the same load. But he would drop it all at say Albany St (depot) and then return to Birmingham. The products would then be taken into stock, recorded, taken out of stock and delivered in smaller vehicles.

By following certain procedures, reported McKinsey's consultancy, big economies would result:

> They have been discussed with tyre division personnel and they appear reasonable.

Dunlop and India depots would be consolidated. John Bull depots would be eliminated. Seventeen Group depots would remain. Fast-moving stock, estimated at two-thirds of total volume, would be shifted direct from factories to distributors. Distributors would hold four weeks of stock in fast-moving items; delivery time from factory would be 2 weeks maximum. Depots would only hold stock of slow-moving items for delivery to distributors on demand. Depot service activities would be transferred to exclusive distributors thus eliminating depot service costs.

The estimated saving from this rationalization was £761,000 a year, including capital cost of inventory holding.

The McKinsey Report was a neat and necessary operation. It showed a proper awareness at board level, expressed through R.C. Hiam, the sales director of Dunlop's Replacement Company, to whom the report was addressed, of the need to meet swiftly changing conditions and mounting competition in the tyre market. Yet the report also symbolized the conflict between Dunlop's pride in combining employment growth and the iron logic of reducing employment to cut costs and meet competition.

This dichotomy was never satisfactorily resolved. Eventually Dunlop *did* reduce its labour force – quite drastically in the late seventies and early eighties – but never sufficiently or as part of a grand strategic design. It was piecemeal: too much of the 'willing to wound, afraid to strike' dilemma.

And the company's troubles to come were, of course, compounded by the huge over-capacity of the tyre industry in Europe and North America.

Still, before we deal with that, we should note one more superb example of Dunlop tyre technology: the development of the SP41.

The development of the SP41, and its successor the SP68, demonstrates the technical strength of Dunlop and its weakness for making the best the enemy of the good.

Using its marvellous worldwide experience the Dunlop tyre-makers came up with a Road Speed Model which combined hard-wearing properties, such as were required in India, with a racing aspect. The RS5, as it was called, won high praise and its pattern – a nylon casing for strength and the safety shoulder developed in Dunlop's German factory – enabled the model to perform exceptionally well at high speed in wet weather.

But then the boffins went one ahead of the market, a 'tyre too far', so to speak. In 1960 they introduced the Elite, 'a safe luxurious tyre embodying all that has been learned about high grip treads and very soft ride properties' as the advertisement had it.

The tyre was produced for a small range of luxury cars. It was a luxury Dunlop could ill afford. Its 'soft ride' increased fuel consumption by 2 per cent. It was doubtless a thing of beauty to the tyre technicians and a joy to the handful of people who rode on it. But in the age of mass motoring on mass motorways there was no place for the aptly named Elite. Commercially it flopped. It was all so reminiscent of the footstools and Venetian blinds in the heyday of horseless carriages for the gentry.

Now in 1962, however, came a real winner: code-named the C41 it combined in one standard tyre[2] 'three new and welcome features'. It had a 'Wet Hold 2' microslotted tread with many knifeblades in the mould. This pattern was combined with a high grip tread, advertised as 'road-hug rubber'. The third feature was the German-style safety shoulder. When these principles were extended to the radial-ply range the SP41 was born – and flourished.

It was at this period, 1962–64, that Dunlop again demonstrated its mastery of researching the causes of road accidents and discovering the solution. So it was with aquaplaning, loss of tyre grip on wet roads.

Evidence that this was a major preoccupation with road users came at the Motor Cycle Show of 1964. In a competition held there, entrants were asked to select the nine most important elements, out of a possible eleven, in the design of a motorbike. Eight thousand competitors, 27 per cent of the total, chose 'road hug' or 'tyre cling' as the most important component. Other countries were experiencing similar interest and concern about this aspect of road safety.

Dunlop's technical team of Tom French, Eric Gough and others got down to discovering the whys and wherefores of aquaplaning. The facts were not in dispute: tyres in the last stages of wear on the treads were extremely hazardous in wet conditions. But what actually happened?

Laboratory experiments established that worn tyres at a fairly low speed, say 30 mph, had time, on being braked, to sink through the film of water and expel the water from under the area of contact between road and rubber. As the speed of the car rose, a water wedge formed until the area of contact with the road vanished altogether and the tyre floated completely on the film of water where all braking grip was lost. We have aquaplaning.

Fascinating facts emerged.

At 60 mph in moderate rain each tyre has to displace eight pints of water *per second* from under the contact patch, which is no greater in area than the sole of a size nine shoe. Each gripping element is in contact with the road for 1/150th of a second as the tyre rolls by.

After the laboratory tests came the real thing: running a car on Dunlop's proving ground. To continue with Tompkins:

> The vehicle was fitted with a separate brake control on the front wheels, so that the rear wheels would keep turning and the car would run straight. The aquaplane slide was started by a short front brake application. . . . When the front wheels were locked momentarily they continued to slide in an aquaplane movement over the track. Close-up photographs and films were taken with cameras carried on outriggers on the car.

Subsequently the same demonstration was extended to heavy vehicles running on worn front tyres. The results were still more spectacular. And, of course, the danger of a massive vehicle aquaplaning on a motorway would have far direr consequences for other road users than the same event afflicting a private saloon.

Dunlop's team now went further. They set up an elaborate system for photographing the water distribution under the tyre contact by putting a glass plate into the track surface of the proving ground. The plate was covered with water containing fluorescein. Below the glass plate was a camera with electronic flash apparatus, triggered by the passage of the car. The results showed, in detail, the advance of the water wedge until aquaplaning supervened.

In a paper delivered in the USA, Tom French explained the consequences of the Dunlop experience.

> The few square inches of the tyre/ground contact are where everything starts and finishes. Tyre designers should be trained to get themselves mentally into this area, to know its complexities in detail and from the standpoint of this subject (the danger of aquaplaning), to forget tyres as we normally look at them . . . particular structures, design configurations, styling contribution to vehicles and so on. Everything depends on what is going on down on the ground.

Dunlop's research won plaudits round the world. Motoring correspondents and tyre designers beat a path to Fort Dunlop. Photographs and films of the company's achievements were despatched to every corner of the globe. And, by great good chance, Dunlop had the SP41 radial-ply tyre ready for launching. Within reasonable speed limits the SP41 gave complete freedom from aquaplaning. Furthermore,

Dunlop's possession of the testing technique at higher speeds enabled the company to advance on its competitors towards a still safer tyre.

This involved a series of small reservoirs on the tread surface at such distances, one from the other, that the water could travel to them in the time available. Which, for a tyre travelling at 60 mph, is one ten-thousandth of a second!

Tom French's patent covered a system of microslots, so arranged in number and distance apart, that the final water could reach them. His specification stated that 'the provision of slots ... operated as local reservoirs which have the function of soaking up water from the portion of the contact area of the tyre, acting like cavities in a sponge, mopping up the last drops of water, storing it, backed by the pressure of the air already in the slot, until the load comes off and the water is expelled.'

Tom French's patent was the basis of the hugely successful SP68, replacement for the SP41. The successor had the additional advantage of providing a 'magic carpet ride', to borrow from Dunlop's advertising agent. To quote Tompkins again:

> This illustrated once more that all the properties of a tyre are interlocked and that a modification of one property will immediately react on others. In this case high-density grip slots were added to the tread, primarily to increase wet grip. As a by-product we got a tread of exceptional flexibility, with a caterpillar-like capacity to adapt itself to the road surface.

Dunlop executives were euphoric. The SP range of tyres was a global triumph. Congratulations and awards descended on the company's master technicians.

Dunlop's own Baillieu Trophy (named after the former chairman) was awarded to the technical department under H.W. Badger 'for outstanding contributions to the competitiveness of Dunlop'.

The citation read: 'To have become world leaders in radial ply tyres [a hit at Michelin, perhaps?] as well as crossply is a substantial victory in the long, unceasing struggle.... The Baillieu Trophy is conferred in the full knowledge that the award can bring gratification, but never contentment.'

As the acknowledgements descended like confetti at a wedding it must have been difficult to avoid triumphalism, never mind contentment.

In 1965 the Automobile Association celebrated its Diamond Jubilee. No longer the hammer of the police the AA was in the business of prize-giving for road safety. The first of its Silver Medals to mark its anniversary went to Dunlop for 'the amount of detailed research and development ... in the field of road safety, investigations into braking problems and the development of tyres generally and the SP range in particular'.

Germany, West and East, hailed Dunlop's victory. At the Frankfurt Motor Show in 1967 the organizers had to ask the company to suspend its demonstration of how to counter aquaplaning because the crowds watching it were blocking the gangways.

Leipzig's International Spring Fair the following year awarded its Gold Medal to the SP.

It was as though, with Tom French's patent, the glory days of J.B. Dunlop and Charles Kingston Welch were being re-born.

Further good news came in the sixties with the great increase in road safety legislation. The consumer movement in America linked with environmental groups to form a powerful lobby. Ralph Nader, an abrasive propagandist, took on the automotive industry with his book *Unsafe at Any Speed*. Anti-big business feeling, which lies deep in America's puritanical conscience, flared up, and Congress and the Democratic administration hastened to enact regulations concerning the structure of vehicles, the performance of their key components and new safety devices.

In the UK the government followed suit, though at a much more demure pace. From April 1968 Motor Vehicles (Construction and Use) Regulations were brought up to date. For the tyre industry these were important, and profitable. Tyres were required to have a depth of pattern of at least one millimetre over the majority of the breadth and round the whole circumference of the tyre. In addition, tyres had to be free of cuts deep enough to reach the casing cords; there must be no exposure of the ply or cord structure, and no bumps or bulges were permissible on the tyre casing.

These regulations brought much business to tyre manufacturers and improved Dunlop's rating in the City.

Such relief, however, could be but temporary. Despite the increased business generated by safety requirements, and the steady but no longer spectacular growth in the British and European car market, tyre-making capacity was excess to requirement, and the greater the advances in tyre technology, the longer the life of tyres, and the more marked would that divergence become. Too many tyres were chasing too few motorists. Of the fourteen domestic tyre-makers listed in the Monopolies Commission Report of 1955, only two remained in 1968: the specialist small firm Avon and the giant Dunlop.

To remain a giant Dunlop would need to expand in those areas of rubber-related production favourable to growth or become a conglomerate, seeking to maximize returns by plunging into unrelated products and services.

This was the dilemma facing Reay Geddes when, in 1968, he inherited the chairmanship from Sir Edward Beharrell.

CHAPTER XIII

SON OF GEDDES

Although Geddes entered his inheritance in 1968 he had been effectively in control for the previous four years, when Sir Edward bowed out of executive duties. And for some years previously, as managing director, Geddes had been the most powerful personality on the board.

In his early fifties at the time when he emerged as *de facto* chairman, Reay Geddes was as much a man for his period as his father had been. When he gazed out of his large, tastefully furnished office on the fourth floor of Dunlop's headquarters in St James's Place, he dreamed dreams of a better organized business society in which well-being would be secured through the harmonization of conflicting interests.

He assuredly did *not* subscribe to the theory that struggle was the only real generator of activity and progress.

In an interview with me Sir Reay recalled that he had urged on Lord Watkinson, a senior Conservative minister, later a leading businessman, a plan for requiring every company to include social responsibilities in its articles of association.

In an unpublished paper, written after he had retired from active business, Geddes propounded the philosophy which, he thought, should guide multinationals. Economic advance, he argued, was the primary concern of society. 'Human rights begin with breakfast.' He dismissed the command economy as one 'with little or no response to complaint or suggestion, but with unfair discrimination and injustice'. And went on to define free enterprise as

an expression of certain human rights: the freedoms of association, of property and its profitable use, of expression and of contract. These give it legitimacy. Individual business people support human rights from conviction: their enterprises also do so from self-interest – accept-

137

ing that the rights and freedom which they enjoy are only likely to last if their reciprocal social responsibilities are discharged.

The primary purpose of production and trade is economic and also its *first social duty*: to go on serving the needs and wants of society in a self-sustaining and improving way, creating jobs and new wealth, raising standards of skill and human relationships, all with due regard for the effects on others of the actions or inactions of the enterprise itself. A business has no vote but has a duty to be a good citizen in the community, sometimes going beyond the minimum requirements of the law, but not to the point at which it begins to damage its primary purpose and duty. It also has a role as an 'expert witness', advising those who form opinion or policy nationally or internationally, on matters within its competence... But each business... exists and attracts the savings of others on trust for stated purposes only. It is a highly specialised tool. It has no power of general benevolence... a business-man must try to balance the various conflicting political, social and economic claims, for each has its ethical content.

Sir Reay Geddes concluded his musings – which were directed at churchmen critical of business behaviour in South Africa and elsewhere – with the observation that his notes were 'a short step towards convergence and understanding'.

One word missing from his notes was 'profit'. His philosophizings, often conducted at boardroom luncheons which preceded executive meetings, provoked one director, 'Bill' Bailey, to the caustic jibe that they'd had enough of 'Reay's ethereal bullshit'.

Yet Reay Geddes mirrored the Whitehall and Westminster consensus. His service as managing director and then Dunlop chairman coincided with the governments of the Two Harolds: Harold Macmillan and Harold Wilson.

Macmillan the aristocrat-by-marriage (his Scottish peasant roots about which he sometimes boasted having been severed nearly a century before he was born) was no lover of capitalism, 'red in tooth and claw'. His inter-war book, *The Middle Way*, separated him conclusively from the Tory Right Wing. His service in World War I – a brave man alongside many other brave men – had convinced him that the selfish pursuit of profit would doom capitalism to an early grave. He sought to save the system by neutering it. Compromise would mitigage competition, convergence of aims – brought about by joint trade union-employer associations – would create a consensus in favour of the 'mixed economy'. The corporate state would sustain the welfare state and all would prosper by going along the middle way.

There was – is – nothing ignoble about this ideal; though sceptical critics remarked that people who chose the middle of the road were apt to get knocked down.

Harold Macmillan's views would have saved much hardship and agony in the twenties. In the late fifties and sixties, however, they were not the remedy for a Britain on the slide rather than on the make.

The other Harold, Mr Harold Wilson, had no quarrel with Harold Macmillan's attitude. Wilson was a socialist out of calculation rather than conviction. He too was inclined to boast of his plebeian background, hinting that, as a child, he had gone without shoes (Macmillan neatly riposted that he had doubtless grown too big for his boots). But Wilson was an Oxford don who had spent World War II in the civil service and had taken on the world-weary coloration of the mandarin. He was much more likely to advance in the Labour Party (he had been a Liberal at University) than in the Tory Party and to progress in his political career he allied himself with the Labour Left. He was regarded as a real radical when he was, in fact, a pragmatist.

Both Macmillan and Wilson, who together dominated British politics from 1957–1976, were consensus-corporate men, deeply sceptical of enthusiasms. In effect, they wanted a quiet life for the country combined with full employment, as well as steady, if not spectacular, economic growth, rising, evenly enjoyed prosperity and effective social services.

Their chosen instruments for ensuring an economic system to pay for this were quasi non-governmental organizations, Quangos, which would indicate the course which should be taken. 'Indicative planning' was the term used. Along with 'mixed economy' (the coexistence of a huge state-owned sector with a free enterprise) it was a concept much admired during the Macmillan–Wilson era.

The 'chosen instrument' which involved Reay Geddes was the National Economic Development Council. Established by Harold Macmillan's Tory administration in 1962, the NEDC or Neddy as it came to be called (its opponents dubbed it 'Noddy', after Enid Blyton's somewhat pallid story-book character), Geddes was asked to serve, and took part in the deliberations which produced 'Growth of the United Kingdom Economy' – a sort of five-year plan for British industry.

By itself Neddy – and the myriad little Neddies it spawned, each representing a separate industry – did no harm. There was nothing wrong, possibly some good, in businessmen, ministers, trade union leaders and senior civil servants reasoning together. What was dangerous was the belief that their deliberations and conclusions were an achievement. They were not. They were a substitute for action. Worse, they camouflaged inaction.

Geddes, and later Campbell Fraser, were seduced by the sound of their own voices in bodies such as the Confederation of British Industry and the National Economic Development Council. Dunlop suffered. By going for the general, the particular lost out.

Yet that was the climate of the period. Macro-economics was the flavour of the decade(s).

Increasingly Reay Geddes became the industrial statesman. Starting with the Federation of British Industries – the predecessor of the CBI – Geddes graduated to Neddy and then was asked to chair an inquiry committee into British shipbuilding. He performed this function extremely effectively. It is easy, being wise after the event, to dismiss the inquiry's findings and recommendations as being naive and over-optimistic. At the time it was congratulated in the press and Parliament for doing a good job.

From the point of Dunlop's long-term future, however, Geddes's growing involvement in national, as opposed to company, affairs was a mixed blessing.

Top table economics were all very well: discussing global issues with political leaders, strolling through the corridors of power with distinguished civil servants, impressing the media in the thoughtful, articulate, penetrating fashion common to both Geddes and Fraser. But, in the homely American phrase, 'Who was minding the store?'

Dunlop profits throughout the sixties remained dull and lifeless; labour troubles were beginning to dog the company which had always prided itself on its industrial relations.

Signs of change, of growing militancy, had been noted by David Collett in 1956 (see p. 94). In 1958 a serious dispute broke out in Inchinnan, the India Tyres subsidiary in Scotland. The general manager – and prospective main board member – John Simon saw that work was being scamped to provide overtime, at overtime rates; for its correction John Simon ordered the practice to cease. It didn't. He suspended the ringleaders. The union shop stewards called the 2,000 production workers out on strike. He sacked the 2,000. Sensation!

According to Simon (in discussions with me), David Collett, the personnel director, opposed this intemperate action. The men were reinstated with assurances that they would behave in future, but Simon refused to re-employ a dedicated communist who was out to wreck the capitalist economy.

For a while Simon's name became a by-word in Scotland for forceful decisions. Glasgow Rangers, the famed Scottish football team, had as its manager one Scott Symon. Enraged by the team's performance at a match in Ibrox Stadium, a stentorian voice was heard: 'What this bloody lot needs is John Simon, no' Scott Symon.' The cry was taken up. And Glasgow humour overbore the sense of grievance created by Simon's action.

Yet his ruthlessness – or sturdy resolve – highlighted the clash between those who believed that management should manage, even if it meant facing down union militancy and those who clung to consensus and the emollient approach. Many years later, when unemployment had passed the 2,000,000 mark, the tough policy of sacking malcontents universally prevailed. In the full employment circumstances of the decades prior to 1980, however, no such clear-cut view existed.

Rootes cars at Linwood, near neighbours of Dunlop's India Tyre factory at Inchinnan, virtually bankrupted themselves resisting union demands and bearing a months-long strike which fatally disrupted production.

There was a double warning for Dunlop here. For Rootes had only gone to Linwood, close to Glasgow, at the invitation of the government, which sought to build up car-making capacity in Scotland following the siting of a steel mill beside Glasgow. This was all part of a well-intentioned plan to spread growth industries throughout the country. It was the indicative mixed economy in action. Unfortunately the militant workers of Clydeside proved too much for the weak management of Rootes to handle. In the end Rootes disappeared from the scene, being bought out by Chrysler of the US.

Abrasiveness à la John Simon might not be the solution; at least so argued those who did not want any suggestion of 'treat' 'em mean' to attach to Dunlop; but it was pretty effective.

Simon's career was not harmed by the Inchinnan imbroglio. He went on to the main board six years later, welcomed by Reay Geddes whose personal assistant he had been.

The events at Inchinnan did demonstrate, however, how hard things could become for a conern like Dunlop, heavily dependent on a domestic motor industry wracked with labour disputes and falling sales.

Reay Geddes (in talks with me) said how, in the late sixties, he became seriously worried about Leyland's prospects. As soon as he was chairman, in 1968, he moved to extricate Dunlop from agreements to provide British motor manufacturers with original equipment, which gave a poor return. The Mini, with its small wheels, meant that tyres wore out rather more quickly and this made drivers angry – with Dunlop.

Unhappily, even implementing the McKinsey Report recommendations did not improve Dunlop's position in the replacement market, once the effect of the government's tread regulations had run their course.

Tyres were simply lasting too long, and the cost of tooling up for another great technical leap forward was too high to contemplate. In these conditions, Dunlop had to go for diversification and expansion.

As soon as Geddes replaced Beharrell in 1968 the momentum of change increased palpably. Geddes had observed:

> Boards (group) work as their members, *especially the chairman*, make them work in frequently changing circumstances... It may sound odd that boards should be self-appointing and self-perpetuating. The present arrangement may not be perfect, but works well generally because the nomination is made by men who have a direct interest in the company's success because their own prospects and reputation are at stake and they will have to live and work with their choice.[1]

Reay Geddes now had the team of his choice, at least in the key posts. Campbell Fraser had done a two-year stint as managing director, New Zealand (the other executive board members had insisted that he could not join them until he had had 'field experience'). John Simon, who had advanced from Inchinnan via general management in Canada and negotiation concerning the Dunlop factory in Japan preceded Fraser on the main board by a couple of years. Both these men were in their forties. They would shortly be made joint managing directors and the 'constructive tension' between them would be an important factor in the Dunlop story.

In 1969 Dunlop decided to buy the George Angus group in north-east England, a highly successful concern specializing in fire-fighting equipment, hose and belting – the perfect complement to Dunlop's own hose division.

The trouble was, George Angus did not want to be taken over. And when Reay Geddes and his finance director appeared on the doorstep of Angus's Newcastle plant, the Angus board, prompted by its managing director, Colin Baker, straightway sought a White Knight. They found one in the asbestos firm of Turner and Newall who made a counter bid. Geddes, however, was not to be foiled. He raised Dunlop's offer to £34 million, and won.

John Simon has claimed – in talks with me – that 'the sum was twice the net worth of Angus at the time. Those who knew the business were not consulted. People like myself were told about it later. This was the first time that I started to doubt the efficacy of our decision-taking process.'

Well, that is one man's opinion, not necessarily shared by others who were on the board at the time.

The value of an acquisition depends on the potential development of the asset acquired. On paper it could appear expensive. In retrospect it could be a bargain buy – as BTR-Dunlop demonstrated in the late eighties.

George Angus's fate was to be subsumed in the general difficulties which attended Dunlop's future.

By its acquisition Dunlop had embarked on a policy of out-and-out expansion in an attempt to climb back to a position near the top of the industrial 'first league' which it had occupied in the fifties.

Geddes retained his belief in the social responsibility of business – and was, with Campbell Fraser, on the point of introducing a 'social audit' into Dunlop – but he had become increasingly sceptical of government initiatives and intervention.

In an address to the Institute of Management he expressed fears of state influence, '. . . uncertain in aim and in method. If the influence creeps through the private sector under some general powers, industry will be increasingly subject to special pleading in the constituencies, in Westminster and in Whitehall.'

Drawing on his experience of the shipbuilding industry into which he had carried out an enquiry, he illustrated the Fairfield experiment – a kind of back-door nationalization of the Fairfield Shipbuilding Company in Glasgow by the Wilson government – as an awful warning of what might happen to others.

> The case of Fairfield is instructive about 'creep'; the wish to make a temporary loan led to a shareholding by the State and then the trade unions, which led to nominee directors. The State director was then given a special power of veto in the Board, thereby cutting across the way in which a board of directors works with a chairman *primus inter pares* for the good of the enterprise as a whole.

The Wilson administration had, by the late sixties, lost faith in the 'white heat of the technological revolution' and lost face as scheme after scheme for the regeneration of British industry – from a grandiose National Plan through an Industrial Expansion Act to a Prices and Incomes Policy – failed to bring about the desired result. When union opposition forced Wilson to give up his plan to reform the trade unions, disillusionment was complete.

Looking about for a *deus ex machina*, the Labour government alighted on the European Common Market, an organization to which many of its leading members, notably premier Harold Wilson, had been vehemently opposed because it would erode British sovereignty, limit national planning and, due to the rules of competition in the Market's franchise charter, prove antagonistic to socialism.

However, 'something had to be done' and so the pro-Marketeers in the government – particularly Roy Jenkins and George Brown – persuaded their colleagues to re-apply for membership. Initial approaches were roughly spurned by France's President de Gaulle, but when he quit office in 1969 the prospects brightened. De Gaulle's successor, President Pompidou, had no built-in antipathy to the Anglo-Saxons, and the Commonwealth, now largely an echo of the imperial past, no longer presented a problem.

Europe would provide the universal solution to Britain's trade difficulties.

Reay Geddes was entranced at the concept. As his father had embraced one type of EFT – Empire Free Trade – so the son embraced another EFT – European Free Trade.

With the election of Edward Heath – a fervent advocate of British membership – and a Tory government in June 1970, the prospect of entering Europe became a certainty.

Geddes hymned praises of the prospective New Deal. He addressed the Institute of the Motor Industry on the subject of the 'European Dimension' in September 1970. 'All that the removal of tariffs (between EEC members) will do is make us feel more quickly and directly the consequences of our success or failure. That is what competition does: it shows the reality in clear relief.' And Europe promised all the competition Britain needed. 'Europe,' continued Geddes, 'has the population, the creative abilities, the education, skills and, generally speaking, the will to work. Only organisation, unity, is lacking.' He pointed to the United States of America as an example of what could be achieved,

> where the real loyalty is to the Union, the real oath of allegiance is to the flag of the Union . . .
>
> Our children see the rapidly developing network of motor roads binding Europe together. They take it for granted that passports are hardly needed on a motoring holiday round the Alps. Their miniskirts and pop idols are very much the same in Milan, Manchester, Mannheim and Marseilles. What is to be done in the next few years will be done for our children and their children more than for us . . . The European dimension can do as much for our spirit as for our industry. We have much to give. In a free and strong Europe we could give much more.

Here was the vision 'without which the people perish'. Here was Geddes Mark Two : the new blueprint for tomorrow.

Well before he gave that address to the motor trade, Geddes had launched the biggest project – his critics would say the grossest gamble – in Dunlop's history : Dunlop's own union with Europe – the unbreakable alliance with Pirelli.

CHAPTER XIV

THE FATAL UNION

Dunlop on the eve of its Italian marriage in 1971 was a huge concern; 'a billion dollar company', split into five groups: tyres, consumer products, engineering, industrial and plantations. These, in turn, were broken down into divisions, such as accessories, tyre distribution, chemicals, Dunlopillo, footwear, floor coverings, sports, textiles, aviation, plant and equipment, wheels, belting, domestic (including, for example, hot water bottles), marine, hose, plastics, precision, Angus fire armour, components. That is not an exhaustive list and it includes some 600 separate items.

The tyre division produced tyres for vehicles ranging from aeroplanes to Go-Karts, from earth-movers to prams. The accessories division offered anything from fan belts to mudguard flaps, from cycle saddles to insulating tape. Dunlopillo provided anything from mattresses and pillows to carpet cushioning and car seats. Footwear had everything from Wellingtons to bootees, from angling waders to hockey, golf and tennis shoes. Semtex could give you Piazza Tiles to Safeshine floor polish via weatherdecking. Sports covered all aspects of golf and tennis – the great names of Slazenger and John Letters vying with Dunlop's own brand name – plus bladders for footballs, punch balls for boxers and fishing rods for anglers. Aviation supplied air cooling systems for brakes right down to windscreen wipers. Belting of every conceivable type – conveyor, transmission, heat and oil resistant; washers and gaskets, silicone mouldings and silicone tubing. General goods proffered buckets and trays, wastepaper bins, coke hods and coal scuttles, wheelbarrows and road markers, bed sheeting and corset material, tarpaulins and garment proofing. From marine came inflatable life rafts and underwater swim suits, submarine escape equipment and buoyancy bags; from the hose division, all kinds and descriptions – brewers' hose and creamery hose, garden hose and aviation refuelling hose, vacuum cleaner hose and road tanker hose. There were all manner of bondings, bearings, couplings, shackle pins and shock absorbers. There were even toggle link rear suspensions, timing chain dampers and tensioners and transmission system torsional vibration dampers (!). There were O-rings and U-seals, washers and grommets, sleeves and bellows, shrouds and insulators. From newly acquired Angus came fire alarms, extinguishers, breathing apparatus, pumps, extension ladders, foam equipment and face masks, gauntlets, goggles and gaiters, hydrants and heat resisting clothing, harnesses and standpipes, sprinklers and fire engines. All that and the biggest single private landholding in the British Commonwealth – the rubber plantations of Malaya. John Boyd Dunlop would have been proud of his successors.

Dunlop seemed to cover every human need remotely concerned with the application of rubber – sitting, standing, walking, playing, travelling by air or land. It resembled a gigantic emporium: ironmonger, garage, shoe-shop, fire station rolled into one.

So what did it want with an Italian partner, or any other kind of partner? Why could it not make a go of what it had instead of embarking on a journey into the unknown?

The short answer is – tyres. Despite diversification, tyres still represented 52 per cent of Dunlop's turnover. Tyre production was still profitable, thanks largely to the requirements of road safety legislation in the UK and USA, but there was no guarantee that that would continue: rather the reverse, as technological advance lengthened the life of tyres and the newly developing countries (i.e. the old colonies) demanded first participation, then total ownership of the factories Dunlop had established in the British Empire.

A confidential study submitted to the board outlined further weaknesses. Profitability and cash flow had remained 'virtually static' (Dunlop profits ranged from £8.7 million in 1965 to £9.3 million in 1969, miniscule in relation to turnover and barely keeping pace with inflation) and were poor compared with American competitors. Gearing – loan capital as a proportion of the total employed – was high and this inhibited further borrowings. Dunlop's non-tyre businesses were, on the whole, small and fragmented, and the group was too dependent on the sluggish UK economy.

So – grand strategy had to aim at concentrating on increased profitability and particularly in making the tyre components of the business invulnerable to competition and possible American take-over by becoming one of the top three tyre companies in the world.

In the ten-year strategic plan it was taken for granted that Dunlop should expand as a multinational company 'offering promotion to the best qualified people, irrespective of nationality, viewing the world as one market, moving towards international ownership of the company's shares'. In this the study was echoing the definition by Dr Max Gloor of Nestlé: 'We belong to the world at large, if such a thing exists... a breed of our own. In one word we have the particular Nestlé citizenship.'[1]

In its worldwide mission Dunlop should 'extend into areas of high potential growth and acceptable economic and political risk; identifying the correct balance between established countries with a stable political and economic outlook and developing countries of Latin America, Asia and Africa offering high growth and profit potential, but subject to certain political and economic risk.'

Really big investment at Kobe in the late fifties and early sixties could have revolutionized Dunlop's earning capacity. John Simon recommended £12 million to push Dunlop's percentage of the Japanese market from 7 per cent back up to its pre-war level of 26 per cent. The move was never made and instead Dunlop started to hive off nearly half the Japanese enterprise to Sumitomo.

That opportunity having been passed up, Dunlop failed also to promote itself in the second area of explosive growth – the Pacific Basin economies of Hong Kong, Taiwan and South Korea. By what was to prove the most damaging decision, Dunlop went for Latin America, the mirage-land, littered with the bones of economists who forecast that 'El Dorado was just around the corner'.

Finally, the strategic objectives included 'obtaining access to freely transferable long-term funds and with the constituent parts of the group to develop access to wider financial markets... and to develop more effective control of existing financial resources'. (The failure to achieve this last objective was, alas, to wreck all the others.)

Given these aims, how were they to be realized? 'Pool resources with another group or groups.' Consequently detailed studies were made of a number of potential candidates during the latter part of 1968 and early 1969.

Campbell Fraser, who had joined the main board after successfully managing Dunlop's plant in New Zealand, was charged with the task of finding a suitable mate. He recruited an active and able team. Among possible partners were the smaller American rubber companies, Uniroyal, Goodrich and General. They were ruled out because US anti-Trust legislation would not permit an existing tyre company operating in America – as Dunlop was doing at Buffalo – to buy up competitors.

Anyway, Europe beckoned. Michelin was No 1 in Europe. Their

profits were above Dunlop's and the combination of the two companies' technical and commercial expertise would have been breathtaking.

There was, however, one insuperable obstacle. Michelin had no intention of linking up with anyone, least of all an Anglo-Saxon enterprise. Michelin was to French industry what Charles de Gaulle was to French politics. The patriarch of the family, François, knew English but would not speak it in conversation with Englishmen.

On the home front there were complementary firms such as Tube Investments, the engineering concern. They however were UK-orientated, with small growth potential, and had no great record of profit-making. The same argument applied to Lucas.

A somewhat bizarre partner was suggested by joint managing director John Simon. He put forward the notion of a linkage with Rio Tinto Zinc, the British-owned international mining enterprise. Simon records that he had been in Rhodesia on routine business and learnt that RTZ were looking for extra resources to fund the development of their Empress Mine which produced nickel and emeralds. This was the period of Ian Smith's rule and companies could not repatriate their funds from Rhodesia. Dunlop had such blocked sums and they could have been applied to RTZ's operation in return for a stake in the mine. According to Simon, Sir Val Duncan – a friend of Simon's – proposed going much further. He suggested that, instead of a simple local arrangement, Dunlop and RTZ should merge worldwide.

It is difficult to see what logic lay behind this proposal. There was no common bond as both firms were vulnerable to political risks in underdeveloped areas of the world. Simon recalls, 'When I reported my conversation (with Val Duncan) to Reay Geddes he poured cold water on it, saying that he had never heard such a ridiculous suggestion in his life.' Reay had a point!

Fraser and his team came up with BICC: British Insulated Calendar Cables. BICC seemed ideal. It was slightly smaller than Dunlop and could therefore be absorbed fairly easily, without creating the prickly jealousies which could bedevil the disputed take-over of an equal. BICC's market capitalization was £136 million against Dunlop's £171 million. But the cable company was more profitable, yielding a return of 13 per cent on net funds employed against Dunlop's 11.1 per cent. This meant BICC could provide improved liquidity for the combined concern. It was also complementary to Dunlop in that it was a cable manufacturer of considerable note and would have brought balance to Dunlop's manufacturing portfolio. In addition, BICC was strong in Australia where Dunlop's holding in the well-managed and successful Dunlop Pacific was a mere 10 per cent. The way would thus have ）een opened to entry into the Pacific region, so sadly neglected in the past.

It is difficult to resist the conclusion that BICC would have been best for Dunlop. But BICC had a fatal drawback in Reay Geddes's eyes. It was a British, not a European company – and in 1969–70 Europe was all the rage in British commercial and political circles.

The retirement (and shortly afterwards, death) of President de Gaulle had opened Europe to British entry. The fractured Commonwealth no longer represented a workable alternative. Britain's trade was increasingly directed towards the Continent (the proportions had altered from 3 : 1 in the Commonwealth's favour in 1959 to 2 : 1 in the Continent's favour by 1969). Whether in the institutionalized Common Market Six, or the much more informal European Free Trade Area of the Eight, it was plain that the UK was, commercially speaking, already part of Europe.

Geddes was a dedicated European, as his speeches and writings showed. Fraser too saw the overwhelming argument for the European dimension.

'The bigger the better and, biggest in Europe, best of all' could have been the slogan of the month. With the highly developed antennae for what the media said, Geddes and Fraser were entranced with Europe. They echoed the sentiments expressed by Lord Stokes, chairman of British Leyland, the car-maker : 'A company cannot survive in international markets without size, without marketing and service outlets, and without the advantages of scale for research and development.'[2]

It was Geddes who came up with Pirelli – at a lunch preceding a board meeting. According to Simon, Geddes announced, 'they [Pirelli] are our class of people, our style of management'.

Geddes went on to explain that the Dunlop–Pirelli partnership would be a 'union', not a merger or a take-over. This provoked a fierce rebuttal from Simon, who averred that as in marriage, there must be a dominant partner. Geddes just as fiercely rejected Simon's argument.

Geddes had a good deal of justification for his stance. Although mergers and take-overs were much in fashion by the late sixties, they did not have an impressive record. John Kitching in the *Harvard Business Review* of 1969 estimated that only one in four mergers in the USA succeeded. Christopher Tugendhat in his book *The Multinationals*[3] reckoned British experience was even more doleful with one in nine a success. The catastrophic failure of the amalgamation of two US railway giants, Pennsylvania and New York Central – within two years of joining up the combined Penn-Central filed for bankruptcy – added grim point to the warning about mergers.

Only two trans-frontier business mergers had taken place since the Six formed the Common Market in 1958, one between the German photographic concern Agfa and its Belgian counterpart Gevaert, and the other between two minor aircraft companies, the German VFW and the Dutch Fokker. Considering that one of the principal reasons for establishing the European Community was to facilitate trans-frontier mergers to resist American take-overs and competition, two fairly insignificant partnerships in ten years was hardly a dazzling performance. Dr Albert Beken, a Belgian director of Agfa–Gevaert, admitted that the company had two marketing directors. 'This makes it difficult to reap the rewards of efficiency.'

But very, very different were two unions which owed nothing to the bureaucracy of Brussels: the Anglo-Dutch Shell Company and Unilever, another Anglo-Dutch venture, had been flourishing for decades before the European Economic Community was a gleam in the eye.

If Britain's Shell Transport Trading and the Netherlands' Royal Dutch could make a go of the oil industry and Britain's Lever Group and the Dutch Van Den Bergh could flourish in commodities from groundnuts to soap, margarine and packed foods, then surely Dunlop and Pirelli could prosper in rubber, a business in which they had both been involved for eighty to ninety years? (The fact that Shell and Unilever were Anglo-*Dutch* combines while the union with Pirelli brought a Latin into partnership would prove crucial later. At the time, however, the new Anglo-French partnership to produce Concorde seemed to augur well for Anglo-Latin partnerships.)

Anyway, the case for linking with Pirelli was enormously strong and, in view of later bitter criticism of the Dunlop executives who carried it through, the case deserves to be given in full.

The two companies were similar in size and profitability – bumping along the £9–10 million market on average for the years 1965–69. A *union*, as against a take-over, would not bruise national sentiments. Together Dunlop and Pirelli would move to No 2 spot in the tyre world, immediately behind Goodyear. Centralized research would yield savings and technical advance. Each company, despite a common tyre base, could provide diversification for the other, Dunlop into cables, Pirelli into sports goods and plantations. Both companies complemented each other geographically, Dunlop being strong in northern Europe and the old Empire lands of Asia, Africa and North America,

Pirelli flourishing in Latin America and southern Europe. In short, $2 + 2 = 5$.

Fatuous remarks about Italians keeping three sets of books and being liable to Mafia pressures were roundly countered – by Reay Geddes and others – who pointed to Italy's superb economic perform-ance in the sixties which far surpassed that of Britain.

Moreover, Dunlop and Pirelli had collaborated before: unhappily in the thirties, as Sir Maurice Coop was to recall to Reay Geddes as a warning, but much more cordially in the early sixties when, along with Germany's Continental Tyre, the three companies had discussed co-operation in research and development to counter Michelin's predo-minance and American competition. Additionally, Dunlop had made offtake arrangements with Pirelli in Italy and Greece to take Pirelli products while Pirelli had reciprocal arrangements with Dunlop of France.

Consequently, on 13 March 1969 (the Ides of March, though no one at Dunlop's HQ in St James's Ryder Street thought about that at the time) Reay Geddes proposed to Leopoldo Pirelli that their two companies should examine a merging of their interests. Leopoldo replied in a favourable fashion stressing, however, the need to preserve the separate existence of the Swiss company 'for political, family and control' aspects. On 8 May Leopoldo sent a definitive answer stating that they favoured a 'union of equals' and that subject to the approval of the two boards, negotiations could begin.

Giovanni Batista Pirelli, a twenty-five-year-old engineer, opened the first Italian rubber factory in Milan in 1872, about the time Italy first became a unified independent state. The firm prospered, subse-quently branching out into cables, bicycle tyres and car tyres, at the turn of the century. Pirelli went overseas two years later, establishing a cable plant in Barcelona, the first of thirty-four factories in thirteen countries operating under the Pirelli brand name. The companies in the European Community were controlled by Pirelli SpA (Societa per Azioni) and those outside the EEC Six by the Swiss-based company in Basle, the Societé Internationale Pirelli (SIP). Pirelli in the late sixties had 50,000 shareholders in Italy with 51 factories employing 35,300 people. Pirelli, in the UK alone, employed 4,300 workers in tyre and footwear plants at Carlisle and Burton-on-Trent plus a further 5,200 engaged in cable manufacture in Hampshire.

The Pirelli family controlled 11 per cent of the equity and chairman Leopoldo dominated the board. A confidential report to Dunlop execu-tives involved in the negotiations concluded: 'The Pirelli Board, con-

George Beharrell.

hes Joseph Magennis, VC,
arly frogman's suit by
G. Goreham, 1945.

Inflatable dummy tank, 1943.

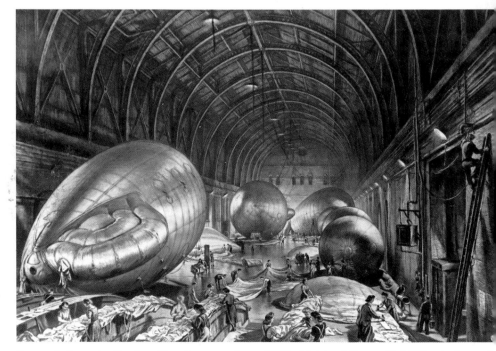

Barrage balloons by Dunlop, Manchester, as drawn by Sir Muirhead Bone, official War Artist, and presented by Dunlop to Manchester City Art Gallery, 1946.

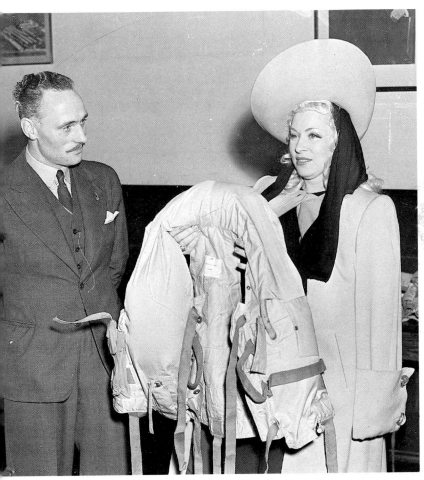

Miss Mae West with a 'Mae West', Fort Dunlop, 1947.

Sir G. Edward Beharrell.

Her Majesty Queen Elizabeth, the Queen Mother, at Speke, 1957.

'Le Mans 24 Hour, 1953' – Jaguar XK120 wins.

Above: Kay Stammers with Dunlop Maxply Racket, 1937.

Right: Ten different Dunlop golf balls, showing the development of surface patterns from the Feather to the Dunlop DDH.

Below: Sir Reay Geddes.

Sir Campbell Fraser.

Injection moulded
Dunlop Rackets.

Above: Tennis ball at the moment it is hit. High-speed photography is used to assess the torsional stiffness of the racket's construction.

Right: Denovo I Runflat tyres on test. The A1 number plate is genuine and does in fact still belong to Dunlop.

Below: Alan Lord.

Concorde landing on Dunlop's wheels and brakes.

Sir Owen Green.

sisting of four executives and 9 non-executive directors, is inclined to be gossipy and the impression was drawn that the Board was not a very great help to him [Leopoldo] in policy.' That could not however be said of those involved in the negotiations with Dunlop. They were hailed as men of exceptional talent and diplomatic skill, notably Emmanuele Dubini, Pirelli's managing director and a relation of Leopoldo Pirelli. Campbell Fraser's opposite number, Dubini was one of the 'wise men' fairly advanced in years, on whom the Pirelli company relied for advice based on the wisdom of experience.

At the heart of the prospective union were the two chairmen, Sir Reay Geddes and Leopoldo Pirelli. If they had not 'gelled', Pirelli and Dunlop would never have come together. Their close relationship, based on mutual respect and affection, meant that they were committed to the union in a far more personal way than their fellow board members. Critics of the union maintained that Reay Geddes was so entranced with the prospects – and the pleasant working relations he had with Leopoldo and the Pirelli people generally – that he would brook no opposition to the scheme.

Leopoldo had insisted on equality. Reay Geddes would go along with that in every sense and would not hear of any suggestion that one party must dominate the other, as put forward by John Simon.

Both men were used to working closely – perhaps too closely – with governments and civil servants: Geddes through his activities in the Economic Development Council, CBI and shipbuilding inquiry; Pirelli because he could do no other.

Ever since Mussolini's day Italian industry had been subject to a considerable degree of state supervision. The Istituto per la Ricostruzione Industreale, IRI, was the 'guarantor of the public interest' and would look askance at any diminution of sovereignty of Italian companies (much the same applied to the Industrial Reorganisation Corporation which the Labour Government had set up in the UK – a further factor in the need to stress equality). Leopoldo also had to contend with the fact that the really big private enterprise concerns in Italy – Montedison, Olivetti, Fiat, Pirelli – were constantly harassed by the Communist Party, the second biggest in the state and the largest in Europe outside the Soviet Union. A link with Dunlop would give Pirelli some relief from state and communist badgering.

Where Leopoldo Pirelli was on much stronger ground than Reay Geddes was through the family connections. As Leopoldo said in a letter to me (12 July 1988): 'The real advantage [of being a family concern] stems from the continuity in leadership and in the principles inspiring the action of the company's shareholders, its Board and its management'. It also meant that Leopoldo could be flexible and would put the family's interest at the head of requirements in any deal. Switzerland loomed large in Pirelli calculations. A glance at the political situation in Italy explains why.

The Foreign Office gave Dunlop a private summation of the Italian political scene in 1969. On a comforting note it reminded the British executives that Italians tend to overdramatize their politics and that the number of governments the country had had since the war did not necessarily reflect the political, far less the economic, realities. Indeed Italy was able to afford her unsatisfactory political system (a multiplicity of parties resulting from proportional representation) because of rapidly rising economic growth. Anyway, Italian private enterprise looked to the Common Market rather than the nominally conservative Christian Democrats – who had constantly to seek coalition partners – to sustain capitalism.

On the reverse, or downside, Dunlop's board was reminded that the increasingly militant trade unions were likely to hoist wages, that there was continuing expansion of the public sector at the expense of the private one, and that a centre-left coalition might succeed the existing centre-right combine.

So delicate was the political situation in Italy that Leopoldo Pirelli requested that the then British Chancellor of the Exchequer Roy Jenkins, a fervid supporter of European union, should not mention the negotiations between Dunlop and Pirelli when he met the Italian Finance Minister, Signor Colombo.

Amazingly, the secret negotiations which began in May 1969 remained confidential until released to the media nine months later. Most meetings between the working parties were held in London hotels and outside of Pirelli's HQ in Milan so as not to arouse the interest of the press or suspicions of competitors.

Security, however, did not prevent Roy Marsh and a few of the younger Dunlop executives from preparing a light-hearted comedy, on Shakespearian lines, which included in the Dramatis Personae the Gnome of Milan (Leopoldo Pirelli) and the Laird of Dunblane (Campbell Fraser). Most of the talking came from the 'divers men of Waterprice' – a completely non-disguised description of the accountants, Price Waterhouse, who were made to say that they had completed their labours

> on the strictest principles,
> passed down to us from our fathers,
> to reach a degree of understanding
> passing comprehension.

This was no more than the truth, for the tortuous negotiations that continued for many months beyond the public announcement of the union, concerned taxation and accounting principles.

For example, Dunlop followed UK practice, even overseas, and their accounts, including subsidiaries, were prepared according to British Companies Acts and Stock Exchange requirements with an audit carried out by British chartered accountants. The published accounts represented a fair reflection of reality.

Pirelli, on the other hand, operated in southern Europe and the South American countries where legal requirements were far less stringent and accounts were arranged to minimize tax liabilities. Thus in Latin America, Pirelli valued stocks on a 'Last In, First Out' basis so that, in a period of rising prices – and Brazil especially was subject to rampant inflation – profits were much diminished. The tax office there encouraged this procedure which was the opposite of UK methods based on 'First In, First Out' valuation of stock. Moreover, because Italian shareholders expected any surplus to be distributed in dividends, Pirelli had to build in depreciation and stock provision in times of plenty in order to sustain dividends when business slumped.

To solve this problem the parties agreed, at a meeting in Milan on 27 January 1970, to set up an independent valuer – Price Waterhouse – to work with the companies' auditors (Whinney Murray for Dunlop, Fides for Pirelli) to establish a common code to achieve a 'marriage of equals'.

The British government and Treasury – Sir Douglas Allen to the fore – were extremely helpful in amending the Finance Act to facilitate the union. They were certainly lobbied often enough by Sir Reay Geddes who became quite a familiar figure round Whitehall as he pushed and pushed for alterations in capital gains legislation.

Most ingenious accounting methods were used to eliminate obstacles, as happened in India.

The Indian government let it be known that Dunlop India would lose its status of a British subsidiary in India if it allowed ownership to be shared with another concern. So a 'mirror company' was established. The shares in Dunlop India were retained by Dunlop Holdings Ltd – now the master company – but a new company, Dunlop Investments Ltd, was created, entitled to receive from Dunlop Holdings 'amounts equivalent to any amounts received or receivable by Dunlop Holdings from, or in respect of, existing manufacturing and associated companies of Dunlop in India'.

Perhaps it is not surprising that there are more chartered accountants (110,000) in the UK than there are sailors in the Royal Navy!

Gradually the outlines of agreement became clear; the ultimate form of union would be on the lines of Anglo-Dutch Shell. Essentially Dunlop was to acquire 49 per cent of Pirelli's interests in Italy and other European Community countries and 40 per cent elsewhere in exchange for the transfer to Pirelli of equivalent interest in Dunlop's operations in the UK, Europe and worldwide. There were some exclusions, notably Dunlop Sport (to equalize profits) and Dunlop Rhodesia because of the political difficulties there.

The final negotiations, in November 1970, involved intense efforts by the two top teams: Dunlop's comprised Sir Reay Geddes. Messrs Campbell Fraser, Eric Holt, Peter Grant (representing Lazards, the merchant banker), Horace Ward, Stanley Wright, Tom Wyne; Pirelli was represented by Leopoldo Pirelli and Signors Dubini, Bellorini, Martinenghi, Cattanea and Caccio, of their merchant bankers, Mediobanca.

The Pirelli side were anxious to have matters brought to a close for they feared that pending capital gains legislation in Italy would make the union impossible. When it was accomplished by 31 December 1970, John Simon was later to claim that Reay Geddes had been so startled by this ultimatum that he demanded the Dunlop team work 'all night, if necessary' to reach heads of agreement. These were initialled at 4 am on 10 November 1970. The scrawled piece of paper bearing the signatures of Leopoldo Pirelli and Reay Geddes was given to Campbell Fraser as a keepsake. On 21 December 1970, the Italian shareholders of Pirelli approved the union.

In his letter to shareholders, part of the notice of an Extraordinary General Meeting of Dunlop share and stock holders at the Hotel Meurice, London, on 30 December 1970, Reay Geddes spelt out the advantages of the union.

We live in an age of change. Not only in the market place where change is real enough but also in the wider area of international relationships. Dunlop's attitude is to welcome change and to learn and profit from it.

One certain area of change is Europe. Most of Western Europe is in process of closer economic integration. In which event, economic frontiers will diminish in importance and may disappear.

We do not believe that time will be on the side of those who wait to see how the process unfolds. Success will go to those who retain the initiative and command the greater resources.

The one requires the support of the other. Dunlop itself cannot command the resources necessary to obtain a reward commensurate with the initiative it undoubtedly possesses. Nor, by itself, can Pirelli who share our philosophy and who are similar to us in organisation and management methods. To each of us the choice of partner is as natural as it is mutual.

After outlining the difficulties of the tax structure 'which will add some 3 per cent to the tax charge', the message ended with a ringing declaration :

We are not looking to the present nor even to the immediate future. Our sights cover not just the next few years but the decades beyond. The decision is now because the opportunity has come now. It is a historic decision which requires both judgement and faith. Judgement that the union of Dunlop and Pirelli in the form proposed will enable those responsible for their management to bring together the businesses of the two groups. Faith in their ability to achieve the enormous advantages that a successful union will bring.

Here was a re-echo of father Eric's call for vision and partnership. Forty years ago it was the wide horizons of empire which prompted the missionary urge. Now, for the son, Europe was a-calling.

Yet scarcely was the ink dry on the heads of agreement – duly ratified 7 – 3 in a matter of minutes by the ten shareholders who bothered to turn up at the EGM – than menacing problems arose.

The circular convening the Extraordinary General Meeting had been specific about profit forecasts.

Due to the prolonged strike sustained in the first half of 1970 and to the industrial disputes which have bedevilled the UK motor industry over a large part of the year, the profit contribution by Dunlop in 1970 is expected to be substantially below that of 1969 (when it was £9.3 million). *Pirelli expect their profit contribution to be slightly higher than the comparable figure for 1969 (£6.2 million).* [Author's italics]

Alas, when the central committee of the union, comprising the four executives of Dunlop and the four top executives of Pirelli met, John Simon (who along with Campbell Fraser, Reay Geddes and Eric Holt represented Dunlop) recalled :

It was a short meeting. As we were putting our papers away Leopoldo Pirelli pulled out a small sheet of paper, put it under Reay Geddes's nose and said, 'By the way, Reay, these are our latest forecasts for this year.'[4]

Instead of the profit from Italian operations which Dunlop had been led to expect, the figure of a £7 million loss was disclosed. Thus within two months of the union being operative, on 1 January 1971, the foundation of rising profitability on which it was based was fatally cracked. The loss rose to £18.4 million. It was never to be bright morning again for the Union of Hope.

Did Pirelli know, or suspect, that they were about to make a huge loss when they reached agreement with Dunlop in November 1970? Did Pirelli deceive their partners?

Sir Reay thinks not. He said to me: 'Pirelli didn't know, although they *should* have known. The accounting system was at fault.' Leopoldo Pirelli told me,

> I do not believe the accounting system was at fault in not anticipating the 1971 losses.
>
> The previous year [1970] had been a bad year both for the Italian economy as a whole and for Pirelli's activities in Italy. The outlook for 1971, however, had been for a rise in GNP of some 7 per cent, in spite of a persistent uncertain labour situation. This forecast was also made on the occasion of the February Dunlop board when the first management plans were presented which, in a much less optimistic assessment, forecast a small loss for Pirelli activities in Italy in 1971. At the October Dunlop board, instead, we had to acknowledge that, contrary to expectations, the Italian GNP was flat and the political and labour situation was such as to affect badly the results of Pirelli's activities for 1971 which turned out to be much worse compared with the February forecast.
>
> We can therefore be blamed for a wrong appraisal of the Italian economic scenario, not for the inaccuracy in our accounting system.

Recriminations are not wholly valueless if they establish why errors were made, and how to avoid them in future.

The impartial observer is driven to the conclusion that both Reay Geddes and Leopoldo Pirelli – who continue to enjoy most amicable relations – were so intent on pushing through their *historic* agreement that they were not prepared to let temporary difficulties stand in the way.

'Our sights cover not just the next few years but the decades beyond', to re-quote Reay Geddes's message to shareholders. Unfortunately the 'next few years', so airily dismissed, sealed the fate of the union. It may be that 'where there is no vision the people perish'. It is also true that where there are no profits, the visions perish.

As the political-economic skies darkened over Italy, Pirelli's financial outlook darkened with them.

Those on the Dunlop board who had voiced apprehension about the union, now voiced outright disapproval.

The confidential report on the union negotiations had this to say about the final stages: 'The details (of the agreement) were presented to the Dunlop Board at a special meeting on Friday November 19, 1970 and after keen questioning from Executive and non-Executive Directors was finally approved *without any great show of enthusiasm* [author's italics].'

John Simon who, along with Campbell Fraser, was about to be nominated Dunlop's joint managing director, has remained adamant that he was opposed to the union from the start.

Why then did he not vote against it? He says[5] that when he joined the Dunlop board in the mid-sixties the then chairman, Sir Edward Beharrell, told him it was a tradition that board decisions 'never went to the vote'. It was the chairman's role to sense the mood of the board and then to confirm accordingly. A vote in such circumstances was unnecessary. As is normal in most public companies, the chairman makes sure that he has enough shareholders' proxies in his pocket to ensure that his policies prevail at AGMs or EGMs. While a miniscule ten people had turned up at the EGM to ratify the Dunlop-Pirelli union, the vast majority of the proxies – representing 22 per cent of Dunlop's total shareholders – approved the partnership.

So Simon's excuse for not carrying his opposition to the point of a vote (which could well have been leaked to the press) is that it was alien to company traditions and would have been a meagre and futile demonstration in face of the proxy strength of the board.

What is on the public record is that the board unanimously recommended the union while it privately conceded that members of the board were far from enthusiastic.

Simon claims that the project was steamrollered through by Geddes and Fraser and that members such as Eric Holt and Sir Maurice Coop were thoroughly dubious, and other directors were swayed towards the deal by the power of persuasive arguments and excessively optimistic forecasts of Italy's economic prospects.

Victory has a hundred fathers; defeat is an orphan.

The ultimate failure of the Dunlop-Pirelli union has led many commentators to blame it for Dunlop's demise as an independent company in 1985. Is such a conclusion justified, and why did the union fail?

Leopoldo Pirelli wrote, eighteen years after the event (in a letter to the author):

I believe, with the benefit of hindsight, that we did not choose the best structure. In fact it was a mistake to think that a Mr 51 per cent would feel equally involved in his 49 per cent interest managed by

159

another Mr 51 per cent. We should perhaps, right from the beginning, have concentrated the whole tyre activities, both in Europe and overseas, into one separate company which should have been jointly owned but managed by the best man the Union had at its disposal in the tyre field.

Furthermore, other jointly-owned product companies should have been established, grouping the common activities in the diversified products sector : but this was not a problem of paramount importance as the one of creating a single tyre company.

Yet when I put it to Dr Pirelli that a simple take-over by Pirelli of Dunlop, or of Pirelli by Dunlop would have been the best solution, he was still adamantly opposed.

I do not believe that a straight take-over either way would have been possible because of the financial position of the two groups at the time ; in addition, neither shareholders nor management of either group would have agreed upon being absorbed by the other.

It is unlikely that Dunlop shareholders would have objected to a Pirelli take-over. They had been poorly rewarded for decades in the way of dividends and only ten bothered to turn up at the Extraordinary General Meeting to endorse the union. Dunlop's management might have been a different story. Apart from the natural fear of being elbowed out of their jobs, they had a fierce pride in the Dunlop name and its reputation. This was especially true of the line managers and the technicians upon whom the reputation had been built. Still, they would all have had to make the best of things.

The real objection to a straight take-over or complete merger seems to have lain with Pirelli and the tortuous Italian political situation. It was the Pirelli team who had insisted on a 'union of equals'.

Returning to Leopoldo Pirelli's observations about the need to make a single tyre company headed by the best men in the union, that is surely undeniable. Contesting Michelin's predominance in the European tyre market (in the seventies it held about one third) was imperative. That could really only be done through a single organization ruled by a single-minded individual to match the relentless drive and self-interest of François Michelin.

In that sense, John Simon's warning that the union would fail unless one or other partner were dominant, provided wholly correct.

As it happened, everything went wrong with the tyre market, especially for the Dunlop-Pirelli partnership. Pirelli produced a tyre which failed to please. The Arab-Israeli war of 1973 and the subsequent use by the Arabs of the oil weapon to put pressure on the West sent oil prices soaring. Commerce went into a tail-spin (the British Stock Market fell to one-third of its value in a few months in 1974). The whole tyre market went into the doldrums as over-capacity pulled everyone down.

Italy's political situation steadily deteriorated. The Red Brigades started assassinating 'capitalists' and many Italian industrialists looked longingly for an approach from a US firm which would enable them to take off for the relative safety of America. Pirelli's foresight in setting up a Swiss corporation seemed providential.

Yet well before these external hammerings the union, conceived in hope and trust and optimism, was doomed.

It was predicated on profitability. Pirelli Italy kept on making losses, from a promised profit of £3 million to a certain loss of £18.4 million by the close of 1971.

From the day in March 1971 that a Dunlop executive on a boating trip with Pirelli opposite numbers got wind that Pirelli's losses were mounting – not diminishing as had been hoped – the union began to rock.

Reay Geddes remained resolute. He took legal soundings about the possibility of keeping the share exchange – which was not finalized until June 1971 – down to a nominal, 5 per cent level, until events improved in Italy (it was *Italy*, not Pirelli's involvement worldwide, which caused the union's collapse). However, the momentum of the process could not be reversed. The full exchange went through.

The shock to Dunlop shareholders of having to absorb Pirelli losses, instead of sharing in rising combined profits, was considerable. On the Dunlop board there was open dissent.

According to an *aide-mémoire* prepared by John Simon:

> The cross linking is such that Dunlop Holdings [the top company] depends on Dunlop Ltd for its principal source of earnings to service the parent company's dividend. But Pirelli own 49 per cent of Dunlop Ltd and therefore – out of every pound generated to service Dunlop Holdings, 49p automatically goes to Pirelli. The net result is that Pirelli has an assured source of income irrespective of whether or not it makes any profit on its own and Dunlop Holdings only gets half of anything Dunlop Ltd generates.

Simon went on to list other weaknesses of the agreement: Pirelli's investments in Latin America were politically risky and – much more importantly – '... inflation in Latin America is such that money brought home is a very different thing from profits declared in the territory and used for consolidation purposes.'

Legally the union could not be broken unilaterally. Reay Geddes and Leopoldo Pirelli both insisted that 'you don't go into a marriage talking about divorce'. However Pirelli *did* agree to major amendments to limit the damage being inflicted on Dunlop's profit and loss balance. The method chosen was to convert Dunlop Holdings' 49 per cent share in Pirelli into preferred shares. The cumulative losses of Pirelli would fall on the *ordinary* shareholders. In all other respects the preferred shares were to rank equally with the ordinary. This freed Dunlop of Pirelli's 1971 losses, but meant that profits in future years would have to be sufficient to offset this loss before the joint concern would be in profit. In short, it was deferring the loss in the hope that the good times in Italy would soon return. Recriprocal arrangements were made concerning Dunlop preferred shares to Pirelli.

This did not satisfy John Simon. He wanted a complete break with Pirelli. He insisted that his fellow managing director Campbell Fraser accompany him to see Reay Geddes. One July morning they bearded him in his office.

What follows is the Simon version, with his flair for the dramatic.

> Campbell turned to me and said : 'There's nothing I can say to the Chairman, John. After all, I was the architect of the bloody thing.'
>
> I said he need not say a word, just come. This he agreed to do.
>
> With that, Campbell and I went along to see the Chairman. We settled round his table and then I said : 'Reay, I've come to ask you formally to break the Pirelli Agreement before it breaks us.'
>
> I was standing by ready to receive a broadside, but instead he turned to me very quietly and said, 'Tell me how, John ?'
>
> I replied, 'Well, Reay, as we both know, there is no legal way out of the Agreement,[6] but in my book an agreement is an agreement to agree between two willing partners. If those same partners agree to disagree then surely that provides the way out. So it's a matter for you and Leopoldo to resolve on a man-to-man basis.'
>
> With that, Geddes rounded on me saying : 'If you were Leopoldo Pirelli what would you do ?'
>
> I replied in an equally harsh voice : 'Reay, if I were Leopoldo I would dig my claws deep into you and I'd hang on to the death.'
>
> Reay said : 'Then what are we talking about ?'
>
> The subject was closed.

The following March at a central committee meeting of the union Simon formalized his demand for a drastic change.

The thrust of Simon's plea (he claims it had the active support of two other members of the Dunlop contingent, Michael Bexon and Horrie Ward) was that the figures were so weak that they were tantamount to an admission of failure for the union, at least in its early

162

stages, and that urgent action must be taken concerning 'P2' – the codename for Pirelli of Italy. 'As things stand at the moment in P2,' ran his statement, 'we are committing resources which have no reasonable hope, in the all-important short term, of even recovering their service charges – in other words, we are on the slippery slope of overtrading [spending beyond one's capacity].' Simon continues, in recall: 'There was absolute silence. No one said a word. The meeting broke up.'

Something else broke up: the relationship between Reay Geddes and his joint managing director, John Simon. The next day, in Simon's recollection, the two men had an 'eye-ball to eye-ball confrontation' in Simon's room. Geddes – again this is Simon's recollection – accused Simon of 'setting the union back 12 months on its tracks'. Simon retorted: 'You can negate anything that I say. But, I beg you, man to man, to break the Pirelli Agreement before it breaks us.'

Clearly one or other would have to go. It was Simon who went. Sixteen years later he admitted he should never have resigned. In fact, he quit to join the board of the British Leyland Motor Corporation. He was not an outstanding success there, though he can argue, quite plausibly, that so many other factors were operating against the British car industry that Henry Ford himself could not have turned things round.

Equally, Reay Geddes was at the mercy of external events. At the precise period that Pirelli's Italian losses were bringing grief and anguish to the Dunlop doubters, Edward Heath was negotiating Britain's entry into the Common Market. Even staunchly anti-Market commentators – such as the Express Group of Newspapers, then controlled by Sir Max Aitken, Lord Beaverbrook's son – were commending the Dunlop-Pirelli union as a fine example of trans-border European co-operation. Opponents of the Common Market pointed out that the most successful examples of industrial collaboration – Anglo-Dutch Shell and Unilever, Anglo-French Concorde, the Anglo-German-Italian fighter/bomber – owed nothing to the institutionalized European Community, but were rather the spontaneous consequence of commercial or defence requirements. The pro-Marketeers retorted that such joint efforts were but the symbols of things to come. *Both* groups applauded the Dunlop-Pirelli union.

To admit its failure would have been to undermine faith in trans-European partnership and repay, in scurvy form, the help advanced by government – Conservative and Labour – to facilitate the union in the first place.

Simon's departure probably had as much to do with the difficulty of keeping two such talented competitors as Fraser and himself in tandem (a director of Lazards, Dunlop's merchant bankers, said the dual role could not be sustained for much more than a year).

The Pirelli issue was simply the catalyst which prompted the resignation. Did Simon go, or was he pushed? As he had the distinct impression that Reay Geddes was both grieved and angered by his, Simon's, departure for Leyland, the conclusion must be that there was no question of him being squeezed out. He may well have blundered in resigning. He was no victim of conspiracy.

With Simon gone and Eric Holt retired there was no real, articulate opposition to the union left on the Dunlop board. There was little enthusiasm for it either.

And with good reason. For, over the years, the dream turned into a nightmare. Everything that could go wrong did go wrong. Pirelli of Italy proved a constant drain on Dunlop's resources and the hoped-for benefits of joint working never bore fruit.

The last spasm of optimism in 1978 – arising from a proposal to the profitable overseas arm of Pirelli located in Switzerland to make an outright bid for Dunlop – died when the Swiss-based concern made it plain it wanted nothing to do with the European tyre business.

By this time gross over-capacity and consistent losses had forced three European and two US subsidiaries to abandon tyre manufacture. By this time too Sir Reay Geddes' retirement from the chairmanship of Dunlop had removed the most resolute champion of the union. He made way for Campbell Fraser in 1978, ending more than forty years' association with the company, some thirty of them at the top level. Unlike his father who died at the peak of achievement, Reay Geddes retired when his brightest prospect – the Pirelli union – had been blighted.

The final obsequies on the union were delivered by Campbell – now Sir Campbell – Fraser in his 1981 letter to shareholders. Despite the gloss inseparable from most chairmen's reports, it made sombre reading.

Fraser's letter listed the bad news:

Dunlop Ltd. The principal European operating subsidiary is operating at a loss . . . part of Dunlop Ltd's losses have until now been attributed to Pirelli.

Dunlop Ltd needs additional capital to finance its operations. Pirelli is unwilling to provide any of the required funds. The situation has now been reached where Pirelli's investment in Dunlop Ltd has been eliminated.

The published accounts for 1980 show consolidated losses attributable to Dunlop shareholders of £15 million.

While Pirelli has derived an increasing benefit from Dunlop Companies other than Dunlop Ltd, in recent years, the good results have been offset by losses in Pirelli (in Italy) and in Spain and Argentina.

In cash flow terms Dunlop has paid considerably more to Pirelli in respect of investments and dividends than it has received and in the past five years Dunlop has experienced significant cash outflows as a result of the Union. These will cease with dissolution.

Apart from this catalogue of woes there was but a modicum of good news – technical exchanges, joint purchasing. That was about all.

Sadly Fraser, the architect-turned-demolisher, concluded :

With Pirelli Italy's decision not to invest further in Dunlop Ltd the remaining interest of the parties in each other would have become so fragmented as to have little practical significance. In these circumstances, continued pursuit of the original aims of the Union has become increasingly unrealistic.

In this, Fraser seems to confirm Leopoldo Pirelli's description, in his letter to me, of the fundamental weaknesses of the 51–49 per cent distribution. Where Fraser parts company with Pirelli is over the single tyre company, bossed by the best single individual from either company. Fraser reckons that would simply have exacerbated the problems and drained still more of Dunlop's resources into the bog of Italian losses.

As it was, Dunlop was now in dire trouble. Pirelli concurred with the dissolution, albeit reluctantly, but the damage had been done to Dunlop's balance sheet which was as red as (mistaken) predictions for Italy's political future.

In the division of cash at the break-up of the union, Dunlop received some £19 million from Pirelli. It was small consolation for the destruction of a scheme on which so many hopes had been pinned and so much of Dunlop's finance squandered.

Why did it fail? Why, when so much time and thought had been expended on looking at the Anglo-Dutch Unilever and Shell Oil type of partnerships – both of which have flourished mightily for generations – did the Anglo-Italian model fall flat on its face ?

Perhaps because it *was* an Anglo-Italian model. The British and Dutch had a great deal in common. Both derived their capitalist and commercial thrust in the seventeenth century from the Protestant ethic. For a period both shared the same king, William III, the champion of the Protestant cause in Europe. Both countries showed acquisitive instincts and merchant venturesomeness – expressed in their vast maritime empires and global trade. Both were 'northerners'. Not too much should be made of this latter characteristic – Anglo-German rivalry and two World Wars is an antidote to racial sentimentality – but in business a common view, based on shared experience, is a useful asset. Above all, Britain and the Netherlands were outward-looking. There were no political restraints placed on the mutually fruitful collaboration of the Samuel Oil interests and Royal Dutch nor on the Van der Berghs with the Lever organization.

In the days before there was a Common Market Commission, a Brussels bureaucracy and an institutionalized scheme of things to bring about trans-European mergers, British and Dutch companies showed what could be done by the application of common sense and self-interest. It is an ironic commentary that the Dunlop-Pirelli union should have collapsed in the first decade of British membership of the European Economic Community and that this glaring failure may well have contributed to the utter dearth of trans-European mergers since.

The goodwill and sincerity of the major figures on both sides of the union is not in doubt. But the differences between north and south, Anglo-Saxon and Latin temperaments, should not be underestimated. They almost certainly made the union far, far more difficult to achieve than the Anglo-Dutch partnerships.

Accounting methods, Pirelli's Swiss dimension and the sheer bad luck of Italian recession and extremist politics coming at the time they did, undoubtedly hastened the end of a noble experiment. But maybe, in 1970, Western Europe was not ready for a match between the North Sea and the Mediterranean. Whether that is so or not, the dissolution of the Dunlop-Pirelli union inflicted a fatal blow to Dunlop's plan to survive through growth.

By the time Sir James Campbell Fraser became chairman (the knighthood followed the job, in keeping with the Dunlop tradition of always having a 'Sir' in the chair) survival had become the name of the game.

CHAPTER XV

THE MAN FROM PR

When Campbell Fraser 'assumed the ermine' he was fifty-three years old and had nineteen years' service with the company. His strength lay in his outstanding talent for bringing people together, for resolving differences and collating and articulating the views of his board. He was, and is, kind, benign, affable, extremely popular and a notable speaker. His weakness lay in the fact that he was 'the man from PR' (public relations) – as he was once described by a director of Rothschild's.

Fraser had done more than anyone to give Dunlop a 'corporate image'. Back in 1962 he had sketched out the famous D arrow symbol on the back of an envelope while waiting for a meeting at Dunlop's German subsidiary. He had worked tirelessly to cobble together the Dunlop–Pirelli union at the insistent prompting of Reay Geddes. Once John Simon had gone, he was the obvious and undoubted successor to Geddes. But he still operated under the shadow of his predecessor and of the mighty Geddes-Beharrell dynasty which had ruled Dunlop's destiny for the better part of half a century.

Fraser could never truly be his own man. He was, by nature and experience, a communicator, when Dunlop needed an inspired accountant.

Not that he did not swiftly become acquainted with figures and the dire warnings they foretold.

In his first message to employees on taking over the top executive post in 1976 (in a booklet entitled 'Report to Dunlop Employees'), he observed on the company's £19.3 million profit :

> In relation to our world-wide sales of £1,289 million it is modest enough.
>
> In the UK the margin of profit on every £1 of sales ... was only just over 6½ per cent. That is before paying tax and interest on borrowed

money. And when we allow for inflation our profit was reduced to less than one half-pence in the pound. There is little cause for satisfaction here.

The making of adequate profits in real terms is vital for future investment which, in turn, is necessary to sustain the level of employment, let alone create new job opportunities. Faced with tough price controls ... The key to increasing profits is higher productivity....

There followed an account of a company's operations which could have been adopted in schools throughout the country to demonstrate how capitalism works in practice, rather than in the theoretical models presented to students in economic text-books.

The booklet explained inflation-adjusted accounts (the method adopted by Dunlop in parallel with historic profit and loss accounts) in this way :

Assume you make your living selling tyres and that you have a stock of only one tyre which cost you £5. You sell that tyre for £7 and you have made an operating profit of £2 in historic accounting terms. But if you are going to continue in business you will have to replace your stock and buy another tyre. Because of inflation the replacement tyre costs you more, say £5.50.

Although you make a 'historic profit' of £2 when you have replaced your stock you will only have £1.50 in your pocket. That £1.50 is the inflation adjusted profit and is a much more realistic figure than the historic profit.

This same principle of charging replacement cost is applied to the depreciation of fixed assets ... in historic terms, assets, say a motor lorry, are valued on the basis of what they cost when they were new. In inflation adjusted terms they are valued on the basis of what they would cost if bought at today's prices, a much more realistic figure.

As a result of inflation adjustment Dunlop's attributable profit falls from £19.3 million to £7 million.

In short, Dunlop was making a profit of about *two-thirds of one per cent* on turnover.

Fraser's guide to economic reality also touched on the Bullock Report which recommended greater trade union representation on company boards to ensure industrial democracy. Fraser demurred at the proposal. But that it should be made at all was symbolic of the period ... Inflation accounting ... falling profits ... price controls ... power to the unions.

In 1976 Britain was reverting to the siege economy. A Labour government with a tiny majority – it disappeared altogether at the close of that year forcing Labour into a pact with the Liberals – was entirely at the mercy of the mighty trade union leaders. Ministers were trying to hold down the pressure cooker of inflation which was rising to the level of 30 per cent per annum by price controls, while condoning wage increases which soared ahead of inflation and fuelled further inflation.

The British economy was being fearfully distorted, largely because the trade union chiefs enjoyed overweening power without accountability. In 1969 a previous Labour government, also under Harold Wilson, had produced a policy document on trade union reform entitled *In Place of Strife*. Wilson was defending a large majority, but was acutely aware that it was vulnerable to the charge that Labour was 'soft' on the unions. He told his Party :

> This plan is essential to our economic recovery, essential to the balance of payments, essential to full employment. That is why I have to tell you that its passage into law is essential to Labour's continuance in office. There can be no going back on that.

'Going back' is precisely what Mr Wilson was obliged to do. The union chiefs would have nothing to do with his code, designed to make unions accountable at law for contracts freely negotiated and providing workers with protection against compulsory unionism. Wilson, stung by this opposition, exclaimed to the union leaders : 'Take your tanks off my lawn.' To no avail. The 'tanks' remained. Wilson hoisted the white flag and *In Place of Strife* was withdrawn.

As he had feared, electoral defeat followed his surrender to union intransigence. When the victorious Conservatives introduced legislation similar to *In Place of Strife*, both wings of the Labour movement re-united – to condemn the Tories' industrial relations measure. 'Kill the Bill' was the slogan, and killed it was when Labour narrowly won the second election of 1974. In its place was passed an Act *increasing* the legal immunity of unions by covering strike action in the UK prompted by the overseas operations of multinational companies (such as Dunlop). Greater legal protection was also afforded unions which induced a breach of contract. The Labour Party, clinging to office with a finger-tip majority of four seats, was in no position to do anything other than obey its paymasters.

Yet by one of those paradoxes which make politics so fascinating – and frustrating – this very subservience laid the foundations for the counter-revolution against union abuse of power. Inflation and uncompetitiveness brought their members unemployment. The toll of workless doubled to 1,000,000 between 1973 and 1976, and doubled again between 1976 and 1980. Full employment, which had helped wreck the Wilson-Heath schemes to impose discipline on the unions, vanished, to be replaced by the spur of unemployment to bring recalcitrant workers into line: a bleak reminder that human nature needs the stick as well as the carrot.

But until the combination of changed circumstances and Margaret Thatcher wrought a transformation in UK attitudes in the eighties, Dunlop and other British companies, large and small, had to face shrinking real profits, mounting inflation, reduced competitiveness and union obduracy.

In Dunlop's case this was compounded by a huge increase in tyre imports, mainly from low-cost Eastern Europe. During the first six years of the 1970s the number of tyres entering the UK from Eastern Europe rose from 70,000 a year to 685,000. At £4.82 each tyre, they were brutally undercutting the steel radial tyre of the domestic manufacturers. The outlets owned by the big UK tyre-makers – Dunlop and Goodyear – were actually selling these imports at the expense of their parent organizations' products because the profit mark-up was so enticing.

While cheap (probably dumped) imports cut into the home producers' share of the UK market, Michelin passed Dunlop in supplying British-owned cars with tyres, both in replacement and original equipment.

Sir Reay Geddes had freed Dunlop from its prestigious but costly role of being the automatic choice for very low-priced original equipment tyres. Car-makers were free to choose – and increasingly they chose Michelin, without depressing the price either.

At this moment when French sharpness-plus-quality and East European quantity were threatening Dunlop with disaster, that superb engineering skill and inventiveness came, once again, to the company's aid.

Forever seeking better, more economical and, above all safer tyres, the master craftsmen of Dunlop came up with the Denovo, a 'run-flat tyre'.

Safety was the prime factor. An inquiry in the early seventies had revealed that 25 per cent of the spare wheels carried on cars running on the road were themselves deflated, or that the necessary jacks and wheel-nut spanners were missing. It was found that 75 per cent of women drivers regarding changing a wheel as a task beyond their capabilities.[1] The likelihood of the car going out of control following a puncture needed no emphasis. So clearly a run-flat tyre would fulfil two purposes: make for safer motoring and, ultimately, do away with the need for a spare wheel, thereby cutting the cost of a car (and incidentally its length and fuel consumption).

Motorways added to the hazards of driving with the danger of multiple crashes resulting from blow-outs and the risk of changing a wheel on the hard shoulder, given the appalling lane discipline of some motorists who indulged in crazy speeds.

Tom French, the company's tyre development manager, had such thoughts going round his head when he started doodling on a paper napkin during a long plane trip.[2] He wrote down his idea in a mix of English and Russian – which was certain to baffle anyone who happened to glance over his shoulder (what with the Denovo conceived on a napkin and Dunlop's corporate logo on the back of an envelope, the company was certainly economical with paper).

In a lecture which he gave in 1974 French outlined the aims of the 'total mobility tyre'.

> Having ensured that the motorist survives the loss of air from his tyres the objective is to give him guaranteed mobility to continue his journey safely at specified speed and distance without the irksome or sometimes impossible task of changing a wheel. The vehicle designer can then eliminate totally the inconvenient and space-consuming spare wheel and send it to join the starting-handle and other now forgotten encumbrances into the strange limbo of automobile history.
>
> It is a prime initial objective in parallel with 100 per cent assurance of safe mobility to render the deflated tyre a 'fail safe' component, so that if it were deliberately or inadvertently abused in terms of speed and distance, or by ultra-severe driving, its ultimate failure would not be dangerous.

Dunlop's superb technical experience was available to Tom French and his team. As Eric Tompkins, the indispensable guide to tyre technology, reminds us, the background included the design and production of run-flat army tyres in World War II and the study of the effects of friction from Dunlop's experimental work on aquaplaning.

In addition, the world champion racing driver Jackie Stewart had tested out certain devices at speeds up to 140 mph.

A word here about motor racing. As mentioned in previous pages, Dunlop's experimental work owed much to the skill and courage of racing drivers. The company had, over the years, built up its image through massive participation in the sport – from sponsoring individuals and races to huge and insistent identification through the famous 'Dunlop bridge' at the tracks. At one time Dunlop was the *only* manufacturer of Grand Prix tyres. But by the late seventies the cost of involvement in motor racing was outpacing the company's resources. One and a half million pounds a year was being applied, according to Roy Marsh, who had board responsibility for this activity. Top-class drivers were being paid £50,000 per annum to drive Dunlop tyres and they were liable to leave at a moment's notice for a rival firm. The price, alas, was excessive. So Dunlop quit the field of motor racing which it had adorned and promoted for so long.

To return to Denovo, the main features, summarized from Eric Tompkins *History of the Pneumatic Tyre*, were: thick tyre walls, the rubber compounds used having low hysteresis so that heat generation was held to a minimum; tyre beads so designed that they locked onto the profile of the rim and could not be dislodged sideways even when the tyre was deflated; a lubricant to cut down internal friction when the tyre ran flat, in two forms – the first a gel, coated on to the inside of the crown of the cover, and the second a liquid, contained in small canisters, carried on a light harness on the rim surface. The liquid was released by a pressure valve which offered greater radial accuracy than was obtainable in the normal wellbase wheel made from a rolled strip with a welded joint in it.

The Denovo was expected to run for 100 miles at 50 mph in the event of a routine nail puncture and for 50 miles at 40 mph in the case of a really wicked puncture.

Following the production of a prototype, unveiled to the press, there followed exhaustive tests. The law had to be altered to allow tyres to run in a deflated state. The police co-operated manfully, running hundreds of deflated tyres for 10 million miles, with over 100 punctures occurring at predictable intervals. Tyres were run flat for 70 to 80 miles without the driver once losing control.

The prizes for technical achievement started coming in. In 1973 the Automobile Association presented Dunlop with its Gold Medal. The Engineering Council conferred the MacRobert Award on Dunlop 'in recognition of an outstanding contribution by way of innovation in engineering, physical technologies and physical sciences which has enhanced, or will enhance, the prestige and prosperity of the United Kingdom.'

Once again it was 'Dunlop in the service of the nation.'

Unhappily 1973 was also the Year of the Yom Kippur war between Israel and the Arabs. In retaliation for Western help and sympathy for Israel, the oil-producing Arab states first initiated an embargo on oil exports and then increased the price of oil fivefold. Just as the Denovo won recognition from the car-makers (Leyland offered it as an option on certain Rover and Princess models) so motorists radically

reduced their motoring and manufacturers looked for ways to econo-
mize on production costs.

On both counts the Denovo suffered. Even the proud record presented by Gordon Shearer, director of Dunlop's tyre technical division
– a mere half of one per cent dissatisfied customers out of 110,000
Denovo tyres on the road – could not improve the tyre's saleability.
Improvement followed improvement : 'Polygel' replaced liquid canisters in the inner surface of the tread area. Polygel lubricated the deflated
tyre and sealed small holes. The wheel was re-designed, producing
a locking system which made it virtually impossible to dislodge the
beads during any road manoeuvre. This became known as the Dunloc
system. Dunlop's pioneering work on the run-flat could be applied
to any type of tyre and so contributed greatly to general road safety.
Second generation Denovo tyres had, to quote Tompkins, 'all the
classical attributes' : simplicity (three components instead of thirty),
lower cost, lower weight and, most important, compatibility with existing tyre designs.

To drive home Denovo's outstanding characteristics, in November
1979 a team took a Fiat Mirafiori car (Italian, French and Japanese
car-makers were fitting Denovos) with a deflated rear tyre and drove
it from Fort Dunlop to the Fiat works near Turin, a distance of over
1,000 miles. A few months later a Chevrolet Chevette was driven
from Boston to Los Angeles (nearly 4,000 miles) with a rear tyre
deflated.

Denovo roused worldwide interest and turned attention everywhere
to the benefit of getting rid of the spare wheel. Ideas abounded, from
the applied US scheme of carrying a deflated spare which could be
inflated by use of a gas cartridge to the visionary project of making
a car tyre from a one-shot injection of some fantastically water-resistant
plastic.

Commercially, however, Denovo just couldn't take off. While the
Fiat in Europe and the Chevette in the States were demonstrating
the tyre's remarkable run-flat virtues, the Shah of Iran was being
ousted from power by fanatical Islamic priests who brandished Iran's
huge oil resources as a weapon to be used against the industrialized
and decadent West. Down, down went oil sales from the Persian Gulf;
up, up went oil prices, soaring ten times above their level in 1972.
In 1980 came the war between Iran and Iraq (another major oil supplier) and motoring became yet more expensive.

Twenty years earlier, the Mini car had come as a godsend to the
British motor industry. It coincided exactly with Premier Harold Macmillan's election boast (in 1959) that the country was enjoying unprece-

dented prosperity – 'You've never had it so good'. Motor demand was rising at a wondrous pace, not only in the UK but on the continent among people, especially young ones, who had only dreamed they would own a car. The marvellous Mini made the dream come true.

No such happy fortune attended the Denovo. It came on stream as a saturated market retreated in face of doubled, trebled, quintupled and finally tenfold oil price increases. The Mini was made for expansion. The Denovo – with its potential for eliminating the spare wheel altogether – drove the tyre industry into still deeper contraction. For the paradox was that every improvement in tyre technology reduced the demand for tyres. The car industry might keep growing on the basis of 'keeping up with the Joneses', (the rear window sticker on the Mini – 'My other car is a Porsche' – echoed the snob value of having the latest model) but whoever heard of anyone boasting about their new *tyre* model?

Sir Campbell Fraser and his board saluted the skill, design and craftsmanship which had created the Denovo: they could derive no joy from it. The company's balance sheet held a bleak, depressing message. And so did Britain's economy.

To take the latter first, it was being confidently asserted in overseas financial circles that only North Sea oil was preventing an economic collapse in the UK. This – as is usual with the Hollywood-style exaggeration of financial pundits – was a long way from the truth. But the slow, steady British decline showed no sign of being halted. Just the reverse: trade union militancy was making headway everywhere. In large sections of manufacturing or extracting industry, nothing could be done without the assent of the unions.

The most flagrant restrictive practices – and occasionally downright cheating – were tolerated lest any attempt to increase productivity or require a fair day's work for a fair day's pay should rouse the ire of union bosses. The British car industry was particularly afflicted and strikes, especially at BL plants, were practically a daily occurrence: which made life very unpleasant for Dunlop, one of BL's main suppliers.

Labour Prime Minister Jim Callaghan regretted this indiscipline. A former Royal Navy chief petty officer, Mr Callaghan was much in favour of discipline. He was, however, still more in favour of the trade unions.

Most of Labour's finance came from union affiliation fees and direct support for Parliamentary candidates. The Party had been founded at the start of the century to be the political arm of the labour, or trade union, movement. The whole *raison d'être* of the Labour Party was to serve the unions. At Labour conferences, the union chiefs disposed of block votes which totally controlled Party decisions and largely controlled election to the Party's National Executive. Jim Callaghan himself was a trade union nominee. As a member of Harold Wilson's Cabinet, he had seen the futility of defying the unions when Wilson was obliged to withdraw proposed legislation, *In Place of Strife*, in face of union opposition. Callaghan had no intention of being the first Labour premier to preside over the dissolution of the Labour–union partnership.

So almost invariably employers buckled under to union demands. Although Dunlop had had generally good industrial relations in the past, the situation in the late seventies required radical action. In January 1979 the company closed the great tyre-making factory at Speke, Liverpool.

Massive protests broke out, headed by the local Protestant and Roman Catholic bishops. It was 'immoral' of Dunlop to close a factory. It was not, apparently, immoral for night shift workers to sleep on the night shift – for a major cause of Speke's closure was the awful productivity of the work-force. It was common – indeed it was almost obligatory in those days – to lay most of the blame for poor output on management. 'There are no bad soldiers, there are only bad officers' was a phrase frequently employed by media commentators.

So far as British labour relations were concerned, this was simply not true. There were heaps of bad workers – and many of them were to be found in the north-west of England and in the Clyde Valley in Scotland, the sites of two major Dunlop plants : Speke and Inchinnan. Speke was closed in 1979 followed by Ichinnan in December 1981.

Speke's closure coincided with what was to become known as the Winter of Discontent. Employees in the public sector launched widespread strikes in the hospital services, street-cleaning, undertaking. The dead remained unburied. The sick were not admitted to hospitals. Garbage choked the streets and rats scuttled among the debris. A huge public revulsion against the unions' abuse of power surfaced – made all the more ferocious by Jim Callaghan's innocent query, on returning from an international gathering in the sunny West Indies : 'Crisis ? What crisis ?'

The rickety Lib-Lab pact – Labour was by 1979 a minority government – cracked over prospective legislation to give Scotland and Wales their own parliaments (this exercise in irrelevancy, creating yet more politicians and civil servants, was described as 'trying to save a drug addict with an injection of bubonic plague'). The government fell and at the subsequent General Election, the Conservatives under Margaret Thatcher came to power.

This was of more than academic interest to the Dunlop board. Shortly before the election, Campbell Fraser and his fellow directors sought the help of the government in rescuing Dunlop's finances from the hammering they had taken from the union with Pirelli and from the depressed state of the tyre industry. After painstaking examination by the Department of Industry, the Labour administration recommended that of the £50 million needed to see the company through the 'long hard slog' (Fraser's words), part should be raised by a rights issue and part through investment by the National Enterprise Board.

To quote Fraser again : 'This nationalization through the back-door was not acceptable to the Dunlop Board.'

No doubt the Labour government would have interfered with Dunlop's management, but what they were proposing was not so different from the methods used by the non-socialist Italian government to bolster Pirelli and by the socialist French administration in the early 1980s to keep Michelin afloat – despite the fact that François Michelin was a fierce foe of socialism and state control.

The advent of the Tories meant an end to nationalization, by the backdoor, front door or down the chimney. It also meant the end of the National Enterprise Board. From now on British companies would learn that the days of comfy state subsidies were over. Neither feather beds ('easy to get into, damned hard to get out of') nor Dunlopillos were going to be supplied. 'Stand on your own feet', 'Compete', 'God helps those who help themselves', were to be the orders of the day. The Thatcher Revolution was under way.

The most the new government would do was to offer aid amounting to £6 million contingent upon the company attracting new investment. No such investment was forthcoming. Nor was any likely, as Britain, in common with the West, swung into a recession largely generated by another oil price rise, brought on by Iranian fanaticism.

Fraser, a strong believer in economic growth, now had no alternative but to cut, cut, cut. The number of employees in the UK fell from 43,000, when he had taken over in 1978 – and incidentally presided over Dunlop's best-ever year – to 22,000. Worldwide, they declined from 108,000 to half that number in the same period. The Cork factory was closed. Activities in Nigeria were curtailed. The French operations went into a disastrous retreat.

Dunlop reported a loss, on current accounting, of £26 million for 1979, and £42 million for 1980. They were not alone in this spiral

176

of misery. Globally fifteen rubber factories closed between 1978 and 1981.

In all this Campbell Fraser saw the hand of Michelin – the company which had dogged Dunlop since 1895 when it had overtaken the British inventor of the pneumatic tyre by being first in the field with a pneumatic tyre for automobiles.

In an article in the *Economist* (3 November 1984), Fraser listed the options for François Michelin at the opening of the eighties decade. As leader of the most successful tyre company in Europe Michelin had 35 per cent of the European car tyre market and 45 per cent of truck tyres. He could build up a new European force to meet trans-Atlantic and Japanese competition ; approach the European Economic Community for aid to reduce the industry's over-capacity – presumably to pay redundancy ; and, finally, do nothing and allow 'the hurricane of market forces' to clear the ground.

Michelin chose the third option. The other two were pretty weak anyway. The failure of the Dunlop–Pirelli union was hardly a recommendation for another grand European partnership and the EEC, saddled with subsidies for grain mountains and wine lakes, was in no position to finance tyre towers.

Aside from America's Goodyear, Michelin appeared to be in the best position to survive the hurricane. Goodrich, Uniroyal and Firestone, all from the US, were in headlong retreat from Europe. Germany's Continental had not shown a profit on its tyre activities for fifteen years. Pirelli had lost heavily in the seventies. Dunlop's losses on tyres for the two years 1979–80 amounted to £48 million. Sooner or later most of Michelin's rivals would go to the wall. The strategy seemed gilt-edged, and clearly working to Michelin's benefit and to Dunlop's terminal disadvantage.

It was at this unpromising juncture that a fresh factor appeared on the scene : the Malaysians.

Dunlop's connection with the Malayan Peninsula (Malaysia was a later twentieth century amalgam embracing Borneo) went back seventy years and more. The plantations were a well-managed and profitable part of the Dunlop empire. The company did, of course, take a considerable proportion of its rubber supplies from its own estates, but also bought on the open market and, likewise, sold on the open market.

Life on the rubber estates in the twenties and thirties was lonely for the European managers (many were bachelors) and their wives and there were strict taboos so far as mixing with the 'natives' was concerned. Somerset Maugham probably caught the flavour of the plantations best in his short stories on the Far East. With the forties the scene changed completely. As Japanese forces advanced swiftly down the peninsula in December 1941, much criticism was voiced in England of the 'whisky-swilling planters' who had so neglected their civic duties that there was no real civilian resistance to the invaders. This was part of the 'class war' theory sedulously spread by certain newspapers in Britain during hostilities. It built up an unfair picture of soft-living colonial masters and down-trodden Coloureds. Fed back to Malaya – not least by British troops who reoccupied the country in 1945 – such propaganda fed dissident Malay (or, more usually, Chinese) groups. Bruised nationalism and communist elements fused to create a terrorist offensive against the British presence in Malaya and the Malay establishment. London declared a State of Emergency. Isolated plantation managers were murdered, road and rail communications were sabotaged, large-scale guerrilla raids were launched on villages. By 1950 a full-scale war was raging in the Malayan jungles, involving 100,000 British and Empire troops and Malayan militia. By 1955 the war was won.

During the whole seven years of the Emergency not one Dunlop manager left his post. The World War II slur was totally expunged.

Malaya was now set on the path to democratic free-enterprise independence. Gradually British managers were replaced by Malayans, and as they inherited the nine-hole golf course they took up the game with a passion only excelled in the Pacific by the Japanese.

One such golfing enthusiast was Ghafar Baba, secretary-general of the United Malay Nationalist Organisation, the political party which came to power when the British handed over control.

It was this same Ghafar Baba who, in 1978, headed an elusive group of Malaysian businessmen and politicians who began buying large chunks of Dunlop stock.

It was understandable that Malaysians would want to own their raw material – Dunlop's plantations were in Malacca, Ghafar Baba's home state. As Dunlop's indebtedness to UK and foreign banks grew, there were, at any rate, strong arguments for selling the plantations to strengthen funds and reduce borrowing. There was also a suggestion – never confirmed – that some Malays had been insulted by Dunlop estate chiefs in the past and nursed a grievance which could have explosive political results.

Throughout 1979 and 1980, Far East purchases of Dunlop shares proceeded apace. Sellers were mainly British institutions whose fund managers read the Dunlop profit and loss accounts and didn't like what they read : notably the fact that dividends were being paid out of reserves.

Dunlop's shares, apart from those owned by institutions, were in the hands of some 50,000 shareholders of whom three-quarters owned fewer than 1,000 shares. A bid of, say, 120p per share would prove very acceptable to shareholders when, in 1980, Dunlop's shares stood at 90p – and were going down. Ghafar Baba, his associate C.A.Eng and their colleagues in Goodyield Holdings of Malaysia, were emerging as the principal single holder of Dunlop shares. Their bankers were urging them to go the whole hog and buy out not merely the Dunlop plantations but the entire Dunlop group. What a reversal of fortunes that would be : the servant turned master, the pupil become the teacher.

Not that the Malaysians would try to run the whole show. They could recoup the purchase price by selling off tyre operations, say to Goodyear in America, Continental in Germany and end the transaction with a comforting profit.

Rumours of this possible strategy reached the Dunlop board in April 1980 when Julian Bexon, son of Dunlop's director of Eastern affairs, reported that Ghafar Baba, Mr Eng and associates had 20 per cent of Dunlop's shares – more than twice the next biggest holding, that of Prudential Insurance. Sir Campbell set off for the Department of Trade to ask for an inquiry into the Malaysian holdings, which could fundamentally alter the whole character and future of the group.

UK law required any individual or association to declare itself if it owned more than 5 per cent of a company's shares. But there were many ways to circumvent such regulations by nominee holdings with a number of banks, by loose, unofficial groupings where, for example, each group could hold say 4 per cent but together could form a dominant 20–29 per cent. Beyond that latter figure, British law required a full bid. So far as is known, Pegi Malaysia, as the formalized concern came to be known, never exceeded 26 per cent.

Clearly, however, the Malaysian factor had to be met head on, especially as the Trade Department's inquiry seemed unlikely to yield much more information than Dunlop was already getting from its contacts in Malaysia.

In July 1980 Ray Nairn of Sime Darby, the commodity firm, informed Tony Bullfield, a senior Dunlop employee with City connections, that the Malaysians were 'really determined'.

Roy Marsh, a board member and close colleague of Campbell Fraser, arranged to meet Mr Eng in New York. The rendezvous was later changed to Amsterdam.

Marsh found Eng to be a 'strange inscrutable fellow'. They agreed that Sir Campbell Fraser should have talks with the three major figures controlling Dunlop stock in the Far East: Messrs Baba, Eng and Khoon.

They duly came together at the Fairmount Hotel in San Francisco. Fraser does not recall that he was brusque with the Malaysians. Marsh, however, believes he was.

Certainly there was no reason for cordiality. The Malaysians were acting in a shadowy, if not underhand fashion. The big formidable Scot may well have reminded them of the dominating Caledonian figures of the past. The meeting was *not* a success. The Malaysians wanted places on the board. Fraser was unwilling to grant them, or recommend them, unless they came clean as to who owned what in Dunlop and for what purpose.

Later Fraser was to 'go public' with his views in an address to shareholders:

You will have read of share buying from the Far East, especially from Malaysia and Singapore. We believe that is now between 28–30 per cent of the Company's shares held in the Far East [it was probably not quite as much as that]. Dunlop has been international in its operations almost since its inception and the Company has, in the nature of things, always had some overseas holders. But the present proportion is certainly far greater than ever before. One of the reasons I cannot be more specific as to the actual percentage of shares held in the Far East, is that many of these shares are not only held in nominee accounts but are often traded in the form of bearer certificates. In a number of cases it has proved impossible for us, or for the inspectors appointed by the Board of Trade, to discover the true beneficial owners. *In my opinion it is not desirable for a company or for its shareholders in any part of the world, to be unable to discover the true beneficial identity of substantial shareholdings* [author's italics].

Of the shares in the Far East the Company has been notified that one group, Goodyield Plaza and its subsidiaries in Malaysia, has an interest in 17.5% of the Company's equity. But it is worth noting that this group also holds its shares through nominees – the name of Goodyield Plaza does not appear on the Company's share register. The group, which at present is in the process of transferring its Dunlop shares to a publicly quoted Malaysian company within the same control, has publicly stated that its interest in Dunlop is that of a long-term investor.

Well, it would, wouldn't it? Messrs Baba, Eng, Khoon and colleagues were undecided what they wanted, but the idea that they were long-term investors in one of Britain's most unexciting stocks would tax the belief of the most credulous.

What they *didn't* want was Sir James Campbell Fraser as chairman of the board. When finally they did get representation – Messrs Eng and Baba – their earliest efforts were applied to getting rid of him.

Campbell Fraser had the support, the strong support, of his fellow board members in resisting the tactics of a group of speculators. He would have held the same astringent views if they had been British, American, Italian or French. The Malaysians may, however, have sensed a racialism that did not exist.

They were, however, further angered when, in August 1981, Dunlop sold its Malaysian plantations to a Chinese-Malaysian concern (United Malay Industries) for £60 million. Chinese-Malays are not best beloved among Malay-Malays.

A scenario had now been prepared for a drift to disaster. A divided board, with Malaysians confronting the rest, faced a deteriorating commercial and financial situation.

Most of the board were Fraser appointees or, anyway, had been promoted to glory during his chairmanship : Anthony Harvey, executive in charge of diversified products ; Colin Hope, executive in control of the tyre operations in Europe ; Roy Marsh, executive with responsibility for strategic planning and corporate affairs ; Ken Johnson, OBE, executive whose duties embraced the group's operations outside Europe. Most of the non-executive directors were of the same vintage.

According to Sir Maurice Hodgson, a newcomer from the chair of ICI and therefore not prejudiced one way or the other, 'They were a sound workmanlike competent board who struggled against the odds without losing their cool.'[3] If a board reflects the chairman's will, and it probably does, then Fraser's board was not without endorsement from an experienced and neutral observer (fierce criticism would come later). Against that were two factors : one, the Malaysian directors wished on Fraser by the power of the Malaysian shareholding ; the other, one he had wished on himself : his own managing director, Alan Lord, CB.

Alan Lord, in the Dunlop tradition of big commanding individuals, was also in the Dunlop mould of distinguished public servants. A Second Secretary at the Treasury, he had clearly made his mark in Whitehall. However, he chafed at the lack of real decision-making in the Civil Service and eyed the free enterprise sector with increasing favour.

Fraser had met Lord at Sunningdale where industrial chiefs and senior civil servants were wont to foregather during the seventies' high noon of corporate planning. He had been mightily taken with Lord's grasp of industrial realities and his ability to tackle fundamentals. Fraser regarded it as something of a coup when, in 1979, he persuaded Lord to join the Dunlop board as managing director.

Initially the relationship was sunny – Lord attended the wedding of Fraser's elder daughter – but as problems multiplied for Dunlop the partnership soured.

There were differences over strategic objectives and though neither man will really criticize the other, or at least go on record as doing so,[4] there were growing personal divergences, aggravated by external factors.

A leading one was Fraser's presidency of the Confederation of British Industry. A born communicator, Fraser revelled in the opportunity presented him by presiding over the CBI. It gave him a national platform to air views which were shared by most British industrialists. He captured top television coverage and national headlines by categorizing current wage claims as 'bonkers' (though he was to rue the phrase when his own pay came under scrutiny).

Fraser's critics allege that he expected Alan Lord to bear the heat and burden of the daily toil at Dunlop. In fact Lord was Chief Executive and responsible for profitability though Fraser does admit that his CBI job meant he did 'take his eye off the ball'.

At this very moment, 1979–81, the CBI's role was undergoing a significant change. Under a succession of administrations from Harold Macmillan onwards and particularly during the reigns of Messrs Heath, Wilson and Callaghan, the CBI had enjoyed a prestige comparable with that of the TUC.

In truth, neither body could deliver (giving point to the gibe of Frank Cousins, head of the Transport Workers Union, to Reay Geddes that he, Cousins, mattered a lot more than Geddes). But both were perceived to be the spokesmen of the employing classes and the toiling masses and were frequently accorded an importance in Downing Street which neither deserved.

Under Margaret Thatcher a great change was about to take place. The market was to replace 'corporation politics' as the determinant of trade union power and individual company influence. If firms could not stay afloat by their own efforts, they would be allowed to sink, regardless of the effect on employment.

So if Fraser thought that by recruiting Alan Lord he was getting someone with an inside track in the corridors of Whitehall, it was only to discover that the inside track was no longer worth having.

So the elements of doom accumulated: the disruptive Malaysians, willing to wound but afraid to strike (they had cooled on the idea of taking over the whole Dunlop concern fearing, perhaps, their inadequacy and the hostility of the City establishment) ; the soaring indebtedness of Dunlop to the banks – passing the £300 million mark in the early eighties ; the rupture between Fraser and Lord ; and, overshadowing everything else, the stubborn and worsening over-capacity in the European tyre market.

Pirelli, with its family flexibility and numberless leads to the Italian government, and Michelin, with its resolute one-man leadership and the implacable will to do down its competitors, would stand the pace. Dunlop could not.

The deficits – miniscule compared with Michelin's £1 million *a day* annual loss – were not to be borne by widely spread shareowners who had begun to look at Dunlop dividends much as Oliver Twist did at the prospect of a second helping. First the interim was passed ; then the final. Even the most patient, inert stockholders could not be expected to forego income indefinitely.

What was to be done ? Only one answer offered a real solution – sell the European tyre industry.

But to whom ? The great established US firms Goodyear and Firestone had cash-flow troubles of their own. Goodyear was facing an unwanted take-over bid and Firestone was so vulnerable that it succumbed to a take-over some years later. The Continental companies, Pirelli and Michelin, had no desire to add to tyre capacity. That left just one potential purchaser. The Japanese group, Sumitomo Rubber.

Sumitomo Rubber was part of the gigantic Sumitomo combine comprising forty-three major concerns ranging from mining to shipbuilding and from electronics to banking and including, of course, rubber, with a turnover of £60 billion per annum and a workforce of more than 300,000. It had had contact with Dunlop since 1960. In that year Dunlop made two basic mistakes in its relations with Japan. It failed to spend the £12 million recommended by an inquiry in depth into the company's Kobe subsidiary and it failed to realize – in common with most of Western commerce – the extraordinary capacity of Japanese industry.

For fifty years Dunlop had manufactured in Japan : starting with tyres for rickshaws and advancing to sophisticated rubber products of all types. But by 1960 Dunlop's share of the rubber market in Japan had shrunk from 26 per cent to 7 per cent.

John Simon, who headed the 1960 inquiry into Kobe, and Reay Geddes (who was later to admit that the lack of new investment in Japan was one of his biggest sins of omission) agreed that the only alternative to investment was to take a Japanese concern into partnership. Sumitomo was the choice. Talks were begun at Dunlop's overseas HQ building in St James's.

Simon recalls :

> They were very formal, very detailed and of necessity drawn out because, notwithstanding the fact that all the Japanese spoke perfectly adequate English, each step in the proceedings had to be automatically translated back and forth, point by point.
>
> We soon learnt that it is impolite – in fact positively bad-mannered – to say 'No' in Japanese. So when they wanted to indicate a negative they would say 'Yes, however'. [This doubtless helps to explain the inordinate length of negotiations.]

The upshot of the 1960 transaction was a deal which gave Sumitomo 45 per cent and Dunlop 40 per cent (the remaining 15 per cent being split between bank and public) of a new company named Sumitomo Rubber Industries. Dunlop protected its brand in Japan, won a rich fresh source of investment and earned useful fees for technical aid. Sumitomo were launched into tyre manufacture with a ready-made product welcomed worldwide.

At that juncture it was regarded all round as a jolly good settlement. No one then could have foreseen that twenty-five years later the Japanese pupil would take over the British master and that Sumitomo would inherit the Dunlop tyre empire in Europe, North America and even in the homeland itself.

But then no one could have foreseen the incredible impact of Japanese discipline and dedication on the global technology market. Without fully knowing it, the Dunlop management had hitched itself to a shooting star.

So it was to Sumitomo – now comfortably in control of the joint company – that a distraught Dunlop board turned in the crisis days of 1982–83.

Alan Lord took charge of the negotiations. He reckons he did a very fair job. His later chairman, Sir Maurice Hodgson, considered he had done extremely well. But the man who was his boss in the early phase, Sir Campbell Fraser, was concerned that the Japanese take-over was going to take far too long.

Finally, in September 1983, Sumitomo Rubber Industries acquired Dunlop's tyre operations in much of the world for £112 million. The story that had begun in a Belfast yard ninety-five years earlier was closed – although a new chapter was about to begin.

Nine months before the Sumitomo deal was closed, Sir James Campbell Fraser had quit the chair of Dunlop Holdings.

He was forced out by the Malaysians and he went to a chorus, a hurricane, of criticism from press and angry dividend-less shareholders.

Most of it concentrated on Fraser's 21 per cent increase in salary, paid in June 1983[5] at a time when workers were being sacked, plants closing down, profits vanishing and shareholders going without dividends. One of them, Vernon Morrell, demanded Fraser's resignation complaining, so the *Daily Mail* of 27 September 1983 reported : 'Why have I so many Dunlop shares (600,000) ? It must be because I have a hole in the head.'

The press gleefully recalled how Fraser, as CBI President, had described excessive pay rises as 'bonkers'. Andrew Alexander, the *Mail*'s city columnist quoted, with approval, a shareholder who provided Dunlop's AGM in May 1984 with these significant statistics. In 1977 the company's directors earned £237,028. In 1983 their income totalled £733,466. During this same period the value of shares fell by half; the number of employees by one-third and profits and dividends vanished completely. At this meeting another shareholder declared: 'How can companies expect loyalty from employees when the directors set the example they do ?'

Particular fury was directed at Fraser's 'golden handshake' of £137,000 and his Rolls Royce (though he had to pay for that). The London *Evening Standard* joyfully collected quotations from Sir Campbell's past speeches promising better times for the company 'just around the corner'. The trade unions – Municipal and Transport – weighed in with caustic comments that Sir Campbell had been telling them that all was well with Dunlop tyres when he and his managing director Alan Lord were actually negotiating with the Japanese to sell them off.

Sir James Campbell Fraser suffered the slings and arrows with commendable stoicism. His critics said he could afford to – with his £53,000 p.a. pension, his pay-off and his other directorship. But there was a deeper reason for Fraser's refusal to strike back at his tormentors. He had committed enormous gaffes – not least accepting a pay rise (even though it was partly compensation for lost future income from Pirelli) – but he also accepted that he was the scapegoat for a host of blunders, missed opportunities, and the sheer weight of external factors. Victory has a hundred fathers. Defeat is an orphan. Campbell Fraser happened to be the man in charge when the cumulative pressures on Dunlop took effect and so he had to bear the cumulative blame.

Newspaper financial writers concentrated on the 'disastrous'

Dunlop–Pirelli union as the basic cause of Dunlop's troubles and scolded the Geddes–Fraser axis as the author of its woes. Yet financial writers had been among the promoters of trans-European mergers in the days when the Dunlop–Pirelli union was being prepared. Diligent search of newspaper files may unearth cogent condemnation of the union when it was first announced. This researcher has not discovered any.

The irony is that Fraser, the man who made his career through public relations, should have been brought low by the very people he had set out to cultivate. In the eyes of the press and some shareholders, Fraser went from Dunlop 'unwept, unhonoured and unsung'. Some of his fiercest detractors almost added 'unhung'. It is worth noting, however, that companies not noted for retaining failures, such as British Petroleum and BAT, kept Fraser as a director and he was invited to join other boards in the years after 1983. Hardly the mark of Cain.

Fraser was succeeded as Dunlop chairman on 1 January 1984 by Sir Maurice Hodgson.

CHAPTER XVI

THE CRISIS OF 1984

The new chairman surveyed a bleak and cheerless scene. As he was to recall,[1] 'If I had my time over again I wouldn't do it. One needed one's head examined to take over Dunlop in the state it was in.'

Dunlop's capital was down from £379 million in 1982 to £252 million in 1983 after savage cuts. The company was in hock to a consortium of forty-two banks to the tune of more than £350 million – with every prospect of that sum doubling in a twelve-month period.

Right from the start Hodgson was in trouble: barracked by enraged shareholders at the AGM (he taped the meeting to make sure there would be no doubt about who said what to whom) and pursued by suppliers who wanted their money and by the banks who wanted assurance for their loans.

While Sumitomo's purchase of the loss-making European tyre industry promised some relief (the French branch had gone into liquidation and cost the Japanese one franc) there was no answer to the steady collapse in morale.

Interest on bank debts was draining the company dry. It could not afford to invest in new equipment. It was even accused of trying to renege on the payment of redundancy money to workers at one of its Welsh plants. There was some doubt about meeting electricity bills and Roy Marsh remembers 'putting creditors' names in a hat' to decide priority of payment. It was a repeat performance of the crisis of 1921; except that this time there was no Mr Szarvasy nor Sir Eric Geddes on hand to mount a rescue.

How had Dunlop, one of the greatest names in world motoring, got into such a mess?

Sir Maurice Hodgson lists arrogance as one of its deadly sins. 'They set up factories everywhere; they were indiscriminate. They thought that Dunlop couldn't fail.' Another mortal failing was the dominance of tyres. 'They couldn't face up to the awful concept of getting out of tyres. It dogged them all their working lives.'

Pomposity probably also played its part. Dane Sinclair, son of Dunlop's redoubtable Scottish boss Sir William Sinclair, recalled how Peter Rossiter once asked him: 'How far up does a helicopter need to be for the passenger to see how many fingers are being waved at him?' This particular director had made a habit of descending on operational plants like a visitation by Jove. It was claimed that marketing and production rarely spoke to one another. One sales manager, it was said, distinguished himself by wearing smart suits and declining to visit factories. Sumitomo's personnel and production director Ian Sloss, who worked in Dunlop's industrial relations in the 1970s, mentioned another fatal flaw: bureaucracy.[2]

> It was rife. We were told one Thursday that we should apply quality circles (a form of quality control) the next Monday. Everything was managed by remote control, with often ludicrous results. All our wage bargaining was centralised. By the time divisional industrial relations officers arrived at the meetings it was usually all decided. On one occasion they were going to award a 10 per cent pay rise. I said we couldn't pay that and insisted on a vote, which I won. We were compromising on everything in industrial relations. We bought peace at any price, yet we were losing money.

So, did arrogance, pomposity, bureaucracy and centralization help to bring Dunlop low? Yes, they probably did, and one could add inflexibility, inertia and complacency to bring the deadly sins up to seven. Or one could say it was a simple case of hardening of the business arteries. Or 'clogs to clogs in three generations'. Or, as was said of Austen Chamberlain, 'He always played the game and he always lost.'

Dunlop played the national game with commendable consistency: solid for Empire trade, protectionism and market-sharing in the depressed twenties and thirties; superbly responsive to the demands of rearmament and the challenges of World War II; loyally 'going for export' in the days of austerity and control; and then finding changed circumstances and a colder climate, with the investigation of its affairs by the Monopolies Commission.

Even then, Dunlop played the game, implementing the break-up of its cosy distribution system, employing McKinsey to improve its tyre sales system and its accounting methods, and finally going all the way with government in the new thrust towards Europe. The fatal Pirelli union was, after all, a direct result of the official policy of linking-up Common Market companies, fervently supported by much of the media.

Where Dunlop parted with official policy was in 1979 when Margaret Thatcher became Prime Minister. Bluntly she let it be known that the days of lame dogs whimpering and nuzzling up to spend-easy governments were over. Her simple message was that generosity with other people's money (the taxpayers') was no virtue and she didn't intend to operate a benefit scheme for firms in trouble.

This sudden descent into the free market-place after generations of controls and economic engineering provoked intense opposition, particularly from the trade unions who were stripped of privileges dating back seventy years, but also among employers who had grown fond of the Whitehall muzzle. Dunlop, as an establishment firm *par excellence*, was deeply hurt.

Would it have survived as an independent entity if Mrs Thatcher had followed the bail-out methods of her predecessors, or offered the same degree of support the Italian and French governments offered Pirelli and Michelin? No. Margaret Thatcher would not have been Margaret Thatcher if she had simply followed her predecessors. She was in the business of changing courses, not administering a system of which she heartily disapproved. An idealogue, she had no intention of pursuing the very policies of fudge, nudge and consensus which had got Great Britain Ltd into dire straits to begin with. In these circumstances Dunlop had not the slightest chance of receiving a sympathetic hearing at 10 Downing Street.

François Michelin, detester of state interference, *did* get help and understanding from his French socialist government in 1981. But then it was a believer in backing concerns in trouble if for no other reason than to curtail unemployment. Much the same applied to Leopoldo Pirelli in Italy.

Thatcher was quite ready to accept unemployment on a very large scale indeed (3.5 million) in order to squeeze out inflation and teach the British that if they would not work harder, they would have to bear the consequences.

Dunlop was one of the consequences, or, rather, Dunlop *in the state to which it had become accustomed*.

After he had left the group, Campbell Fraser took on the chairmanship of a small concern which built nursing homes. He told me: 'It is only when you're faced with buying a cheaper car for yourself in order to get the necessary finance for the business that you really appreciate the need for economy.'

Dunlop never appreciated the need for economy. It had gone first-class for so long that it could not adapt to changed conditions. The company had had it far too good for far too long. Profit, the bottom line, the principal reason why business exists, had been pushed aside. As marketing manager Peter Soddy put it: 'We were making tyres then finding out where to sell them, rather than making them with customers in mind.'

Even with a complaisant prime minister and a generous injection of cash Dunlop would have had to change drastically.

Sir Maurice Hodgson grasped this in short order. He made it clear to the banks that he was not going to be a broker's man, getting the best price he could for the different parts of Dunlop. He backed his managing director, Alan Lord, all the way. 'If Alan goes, I go.'

In the end, the banks said, 'You go.'

Sir Maurice was a non-executive chairman. He did not even have a written contract. He was a tried and acclaimed ICI chief but his age – well over 60, the normal Dunlop retiring age – clearly precluded him from the long drawn-out task of trying to put the company back on its feet. The search for a successor had yielded an able American, Eugene Anderson, who was with Celanese, US. The banks, however, were intent on a 'big name', someone who had established himself as a company doctor who could achieve not so much a cure as a resurrection. Their choice fell on Sir Michael Edwardes.

Edwardes' critics say he put himself forward. Sir Michael himself is adamant on the point: 'I was approached by Sir John Trelawny of Executive Search.' A Citibank executive – Citibank were one of the eight-strong advisory bodies by which the banks controlled Dunlop operations, including paying VAT on time, and delaying the Electricity Board! – claims that he too suggested Edwardes for 'high profile leadership'.

There was no doubt about that. Far from high himself – Edwardes stood no more than 5ft 3in in his socks – he became an internationally known figure when he took over the strike-racked, loss-making British Leyland car firm in 1977. He said then, 'I don't have any ambition in life except that BL should be saved.' It was. Though he later deprecated excessive admiration for his achievement by remarking that it was media exaggeration that he had taken on the unions, 'magnified out of all proportion'.[3]

The *Wall Street Journal*, America's powerful media voice, was in no doubt about Edwardes' qualities: 'Patching up Dunlop will be Sir Michael's biggest challenge since his 1977–82 chairmanship of BL, but colleagues and bankers are betting he will succeed again.'

That certainly is what the banks were betting on. They had been immensely impressed with Edwardes at BL. But that was not all. After his stint with BL and a year with Mercury, the communications firm, Edwardes had gone to ICL, the British computer firm. There he had organized its take-over by Standard Telephones and Cables (STC), forcing the bid up from the equivalent of 77 pence for each ICL share to 90 pence.

The banks wanted Edwardes. Edwardes was willing. And his terms were law. So – out went the old Dunlop board.

On 7 November 1984 a letter was delivered to Sir Maurice Hodgson. It was from Messrs A.R.F. Buxton of Barclays and P.A. Gille of National Westminster, Dunlop's banking minders. It referred to the Price Waterhouse report of the previous February, which had recommended immediate strengthening of the Dunlop top management team, and then said :

> The Advisory Group of Banks would wish to see Sir Michael Edwardes appointed as a director and executive chairman and Mr Robin Biggam and Mr Roger Holmes [who had been with Sir Michael in previous challenges] appointed to top management positions. It would also wish to see the resignation of Mr Alan Lord.

Assurances were given concerning the prospects for capital reconstruction and the letter concluded by expressing understanding for Sir Maurice Hodgson's resolve to resign the chairmanship, but hoping he would stay on for the time being 'in order to ensure a smooth hand-over to Sir Michael Edwardes in due course, which is what we all want'.

Next day, 8 November, the minutes for the meeting of the Dunlop board of directors held at noon, included the following items :

> The chairman's [Sir Maurice Hodgson's] letter of October 25 to Barclays and National Westminster seeking assurances concerning the company's ability to continue trading and the assurances being given. [Here it is germane to point out that a few months previously Dunlop had almost been forced to halt trading in face of a threat by its virtually bankrupt French subsidiary to sue the parent company for failing to keep it going.]
>
> The letter requesting board changes expressed as a condition of proceeding with the capital reconstruction – that is, those board changes outlined in the banks' letter of the preceding date.
>
> The appointment of Mr Lord as Deputy Chairman in consequence of the previous item.' [This was an attempt to keep the services of Alan Lord in a different capacity. The effort did not succeed.]
>
> Termination of the service contracts of Messrs Gardiner, Harvey, Lord and Marsh with immediate effect.

191

Compensation to be arranged for the above.

Clarification of the wishes of each of the non-executive directors in relation to the new board which will probably result in each of them resigning. [They did.]

Sir Maurice Hodgson to resign as Chairman and as a director with effect from the end of 8 November 1984.

A statement to the press and Stock Exchange announced the appointments and the departure of the non-executive directors, Sir John Baring, Sir Arthur Knight, Mr William Menzies-Wilson and Sir John Read. The ages of the two new men Robin Biggam (finance) and Roger Holmes (strategic planning) were given as forty-three and thirty-six respectively.

Sir Michael Edwardes was now the undisputed king of Dunlop Holdings plc. The little birdlike South African-born boss was not everybody's pride and joy. His habit of subjecting executives to psychological tests was not universally applauded; nor was his tough attitude towards options, saying, in effect, 'if my team and I get this right then we deserve to be rewarded through the shares whose value we have enhanced' – this was to lead to violent criticism the following year. Detractors also alleged that Edwardes was a prima donna, adept at getting media coverage, and one who enjoyed the limelight excessively.

Nonetheless the *Wall Street Journal* saw him as 'Britain's medicine man of strong management' and quoted a subordinate : 'By the look of it he's going into Dunlop the same way he did at BL. He's attacking the problems from Minute 1.'

As with the crisis of 1921, the first task was capital reconstruction. The banks had £400 million at loan risk. They were willing to take some equity, although the institutions who had had quite enough of Dunlop's bad dividend record insisted on preference stock. Michael Edwardes, Robin Biggam and Roger Holmes negotiated option rights at 14p per share, or 5 per cent of the company's capital. This provoked fierce denunciation, notably from Anthony Beaumont-Dark, a Conservative MP, and from the *Daily Express*. The three later gave up their option rights (Michael Edwardes sued the *Daily Express* and won an out-of-court settlement).

Edwardes moved swiftly to convince banks and shareholders that matters were being taken in hand. He rejected approaches from Ronald Jarvis, a Midlands businessman who proposed a new equity deal. A similar take-over attempt had been made previously by the redoubtable John Simon, who in collaboration with Sarasin International Securities made overtures which were rejected.

Instead Edwardes concentrated on cash-flow, closing down Dunlop's expensive London headquarters and selling off those tyre divisions not yet committed to Sumitomo – the US (a management buyout, later purchased by Sumitomo), New Zealand, India – to a total of £200 million.

Within a few months he had brought borrowing down from £400 million to £80 million.

Acting with furious speed Edwardes met 150 banking representatives to assure them that things were under control. He and his colleagues had discussions with 110 institutions, to persuade them to invest in the 'new' Dunlop. The 50,000 employees and the 40,000 small shareholders who had stayed loyal to the company (a curious combination of inertia and genuine affection) were assured the company had a future.

Then, early in March 1985, the really crucial event took place. Sir Owen Green, chairman of BTR, made his move. He offered to take over non-tyre Dunlop lock, stock and barrel.

CHAPTER XVII

PICKING UP THE PIECES

Unlike the tiny Sir Michael, Sir Owen Green is a big, firm-jawed man in the Dunlop tradition. He also keeps up the near century-old Dunlop custom of having a knight in the chair.

Sir Owen headed BTR Industries, a conglomerate of domestic and overseas concerns largely, but not wholly, concentrated in the rubber-plastics-engineering industries, with a spectacular history of growth : organic as well as by acquisition. In the ten years from 1974 to 1984, BTR's earnings per share rose from 0.8p to 12.2p. (They doubled in 1984–1988).

BTR (British Thermoplastics and Rubber) was earlier known as British *Tyre* and Rubber and was founded in 1924 as a subsidiary of the American corporation, BF Goodrich of Akron, Ohio. For the next two decades it followed a path remarkably similar to that of the much bigger Dunlop.

It acquired works for the manufacture of tyres and golf balls (later becoming owner of the famous Spalding brand). It branched out into hose and footwear manufacture. In 1934, in common with many other US firms hit by the Depression, Goodrich abandoned manufacture in the UK. (This was the period of the great American withdrawal – from a position where they controlled a host of British concerns, including much of the British electricity industry). The Goodrich name and trade marks were dropped, being replaced by British Tyre and Rubber, BTR. The following year BTR took over James Lyne Hancock Ltd, the oldest rubber manufacturing business in the UK founded by Thomas Hancock, inventor of vulcanization.

On and on went acquisitions, licensing agreements, joint production : Bestobell machine belting, couplings for aircraft engines, 'stonite' rolls for paper-making. Then, in 1956, BTR made the vital decision to end tyre-making. The board concluded that 'falling demand

and low profitability indicated that the investment needed would not show an adequate return'. That decision unquestionably saved BTR from extinction. Ironically, Dunlop at this juncture, was considering buying BTR which was regarded from the lofty eyrie in Ryder Street as a rather scruffy carbon copy of the World's No. 1 rubber firm.

Two years later BTR – the 'T' now standing for Thermoplastics – acquired the Oil Feed Engineering Company and, more importantly, one Owen Green, its financial director and general factotum.

Green had been with the company a mere two years, having qualified as a chartered accountant after wartime service in the Royal Navy. Born in Stockton-on-Tees, this hard-headed Northerner was thirty-three when he embarked on his career with BTR. The two grew together. In 1968 he was appointed managing director, by which time BTR had expanded into Canada, Germany, Sweden and France. Australia was added to the list in 1969, and Switzerland, Holland and the US followed. Acquisitions succeeded one another at an increasing pace. But the biggest prize of all waited until 1984 when Green was knighted and appointed chairman and chief executive (two years previously he had been named Businessman of the Year). At the end of 1984 Green saw his opportunity. Dunlop was ripe for the plucking.

He had already acquired a 25 per cent holding in the preference stock and was therefore in a position to be heeded. Towards the end of January 1985 he made his move. He lodged a bid for Dunlop's ordinary shares at 22p per share. It was no more than a sighting shot. Sir Michael Edwardes dismissed it as 'grossly inadequate and opportunistic'. The banks, the real determinants of Dunlop's future, were not pleased either. But the next month Green assured the bankers that he too favoured reorganization of the company's finances to meet their demands. 'The banks', declared Justin Dowley of Morgan Grenfell, adviser to BTR, 'are now back in a neutral position. What they seem to be saying is that they would be quite happy if BTR gains control of Dunlop with a financial package that continues to aid Dunlop in the future.'

The decisive meeting took place on March 8 when Green and fellow director Norman Ireland met with Edwardes. The Dunlop chairman said he wanted 'a six in the offer', meaning 60-plus pence per share. Green obligingly mentioned 26, but swiftly agreed to offer 66 pence per share. Michael Edwardes and his fellow director Roger Holmes agreed that the abandonment of options helped secure the higher price from BTR.

On 13 March Edwardes wrote to shareholders recommending acceptance of the BTR offer. By the end of April 1985 80 per cent of the stockholders had accepted and Dunlop Holdings had ceased to exist as an independent organization.

Sir Michael added a footnote to the company's last annual report. 'When Robin Biggam, Roger Holmes and I came into Dunlop last November [1984] we felt the fortunes of this great company could be restored by 1986, a view shared by our principal bankers. After intensive reorganization, and having drawn up our strategic plan, we were satisfied that Dunlop was starting on the road to recovery.' (In much the same terms, Sir Campbell Fraser had promised shareholders in 1982: 'Benefits from radical changes in the structure of the group ... are beginning to come through'. The rainbow, alas, remained elusive.)

Sir Michael went on :

> In considering BTR's offers we were conscious that we were only two months into the year and that the bulk of our rationalisation programme still had to be implemented. In addition, we were about to have to ask shareholders to put up a very large sum of new money to recapitalise the company, and after this we did not expect there to be significant earnings for shareholders in 1985. Shareholders could not have expected to receive any dividend from their existing ordinary or new shares until 1986 at the earliest.
>
> Against this background we concluded we could not recommend the continued independence of Dunlop in the light of fair and reasonable offers from BTR.

Edwardes concluded by thanking 'all my colleagues at Dunlop for their enthusiasm and determination' and wishing them a successful future 'as part of the enlarged BTR group'.

And what of the victor, Sir Owen Green? In an interview[1] Sir Owen told me he would never have got involved with Dunlop so long as it was involved with tyres. 'We got out of them in '56 and don't want anything to do with them.'

He believes you must be one thing or the other – either a tyre manufacturer, or a diversified group. Not both.

Green's timing was superb. Campbell Fraser always thought he was the man who would pick up the pieces.[2] So BTR, the 'scruffy outsider', inherited much of the mighty Dunlop empire.

The man who describes himself as 'a bad golfer and good reader', took control of the most famous name in golf, having sold off a 'good read' – the Heinemann Publishing Group acquired by BTR when it bought control of the Thomas Tilling conglomerate in 1983.

The down-to-earth Tees-sider is overwhelmingly interested in the bottom line. In the end the shareholders have to be satisfied.

He has little time for non-executive directors who often tend to be too close to the chairman and less likely than is believed to view matters independently. He reckons also that the old Dunlop was too centralized. Managers were not in control; they weren't free to manage and the formalization of trade union representation had further eroded managerial authority.

'Quickness of decision is absolutely vital. We have that at BTR. You must be responsive. You must change to grow.'

BTR has certainly grown: from a turnover of £10 million in the mid-sixties, just before Green became managing director, to £6 *billion* by the late eighties. Profits of more than £800 million were shared among 118,000 shareholders and income by 98,000 workers worldwide. Dunlop, minus the tyres, except in profitable Southern Africa, fits neatly into the BTR frame. The company has been 'turned round' in a spectacular manner, making a profit of £80 million in its first full year under new management.

Dunlop appears prominently in most of BTR's divisions: Dunlopillo and Dunlop Slazenger International in consumer related activities; Dunlop Aviation and Automotive in transportation; Dunlop Oil and Marine in the energy division; Dunlop General Rubber in industrial.

There are both similarities and contrasts between the philosophies of 'old' and 'new' Dunlop. The BTR board report repeats Sir Owen Green's views about non-executive directors – so dear to the old Dunlop:

> The familiar arguments which give increasing prominence to non-executive directors, in our view, depreciate the intelligence, worldliness and integrity of the executive director in large multi-national operations. They also vastly under-estimate and under-value the work of his contribution founded on intimate knowledge of the corporate business scene.

Against that BTR echoes the old Dunlop belief in spreading prosperity as evenly across the country as possible.

> We [BTR] are arguably the most evenly-spread regionally-based employer outside State ownership and utilities. In the UK we have 1500 work centres embracing 43,000 employees. In percentage terms 39 per cent are employed in Scotland and the Northern Region, 38 per cent are in the Central Region and only 23 per cent are employed in the well-endowed South. By sector, 72 per cent of our employees work in manufacturing operations and 28 per cent in distribution and services.

There is a positively Sir Eric Geddes' resonance in Owen Green's declaration:

197

The magnificent results placed before you [the shareholders] represent the commitment of people of many colours, creeds and tongues, each following that most fulfilling of all occupations – work.

But it is not just in such attitudes that there is continuity between the old and new Dunlop.

Take this BTR report :

Dunlop Slazenger International further enhanced its position as one of the leading and more successful sports equipment groups in the world ... Steffi Graf, using the Dunlop Max 200G, became the world's No 1 ladies' player. Jimmy Connors chose to play with the new Slazenger Pro-ceramic ... The Dunlop Max 300i was launched to complement the successful Max 200G. In golf Dunlop scored their highest-ever 19 tournament victories and were used by Curtis Strange, the leading money winner and by Ian Woosnam, Europe's leading golfer.

The story of Dunlop's achievement in producing the world-beating DDH golf ball has been told. It was, of course, developed by the 'old' Dunlop. So was the brilliant 200G tennis racket.

As an example of a superb technical and marketing riposte to the challenge of change, the development of the 200G should be an inspiration and comfort to British industry.[3]

Having been in the forefront of racket manufacture for more than half a century, Dunlop was faced in the mid-seventies with a technological revolution. The oil crisis of 1973–4 had forced people to cut back drastically on consumption, and one of the sports to suffer most severely was skiing. The ski manufacturers decided they would need to diversify and they chose tennis, a summer sport, as their way out. Tennis was growing twice as fast as skiing and so provided a tempting complement.

Rosignol and Fischer, the two largest, began making tennis rackets. They were expert in the use of advanced plastic materials for skis and they applied this expertise to the creation of tennis rackets which were lighter and superior to conventional rackets. They were also a whole lot dearer. In the same year, 1975, Howard Herd, a US aircraft engineer who had invented the metal ski, turned his attention to tennis rackets too. He brought out the Prince racket, 35 per cent larger than the old type, combining largeness with lightness. The bigger hitting area went down well with the tennis public and within three years he had cornered nearly one-third of the US market.

Dunlop now faced a wholly altered scene. They had brought off a major coup by signing up the tempestuous John McEnroe – who, indeed, won Wimbledon in 1981 with a wooden Dunlop Maxply that differed hardly at all from the Maxply used by Rod Laver to achieve the Grand Slam of tennis in 1969. Findlay Picken recalls that McEnroe Jnr and McEnroe Senr, father, lawyer and negotiator, were actually quite reasonable to deal with.

John McEnroe promptly featured in an advertisement which showed him glowering through the strings of a Dunlop Maxply, with the caption: 'The most fearsome sight in tennis' – of which no truer word was spoken.

McEnroe however would not stay with an old-fashioned racket; nor would millions of other tennis enthusiasts. So Dunlop's research and development manager, Bob Haines, set his team to work on a crash programme to produce a composite tennis racket that would reduce labour costs to a level competitive with Taiwan's labour-intensive products. Their choice fell on the injection-moulded process using chopped fibres in a thermo-plastic compound. To quote a case study in design by Jim Whyte:

> The outcome was the 150G, a conventional-sized racket using a modern version of the lost wax process in which a casting made from low melting point alloy of tin and bismuth is melted out of a carbon fibre reinforced nylon moulding and the empty space filled with polyurethane foam.[4]

This racket was launched in November 1980, but the trend to larger size rackets was now in full flood so the Haines' team set about restructuring to produce a 'mid-size' racket, 25 per cent larger than the old-style wooden racket. The result was the Max 200G which received five major UK design awards, including the Queen's Award for technology and export.

The 200G, though thirty times costlier in raw materials than wood, was highly economical in all other respects. 'The racket,' said Haines, 'was designed completely from a production engineering point of view, but we also ended up with a product that performs better than conventional rackets and one with a sympathetic feel.' It had that certainly. To revert to Jim Whyte:

> Some 50 per cent of regular players suffer from tennis elbow at some stage in their careers. Dunlop's ... process absorbs vibrations significantly better than the epoxy composites of the more common compression moulded frames, which are rigid in construction. This not only reduces the risk of injury to wrist, arm and shoulder, but also contributes to greater control of the ball.

Marketing expertise matched engineering brilliance, but what turned the 200G from a fine technical achievement into a world-beater was John McEnroe's enthusiastic adoption of it.

McEnroe was suffering from shoulder trouble during the Tournament of Champions at Dallas in 1983. His brother, Patrick, offered him Dunlop's new 200G. The shoulder strain was eased, control over the ball bettered, and McEnroe went on to win the tournament and regain his Wimbledon championship. Within a year Dunlop's 200G sales leapt tenfold from 20,000 rackets to 200,000. The following year it reached 300,000, three-fifths of the UK quality (£50 plus) market. By 1986 the racket had notched No. 1 in Japan and Germany.

This triumph cost just over half a million pounds in research and development and start-up facilities, an example of cost-effective engineering in which Dunlop Slazenger can take much pride.

Thus with tennis rackets and the DDH golf ball, another Haines product, Dunlop technicians showed how first-class skills can go on operating despite financial nightmares.

In their research the Dunlop sports specialists were backed all the way by management, as were those in the aviation division who clinched a £60 million contract to supply light-weight structural carbon brakes for the Boeing 757 aircraft in face of fierce US competition in 1982, even while the financial blinds were about to be drawn.

Dunlop's abiding strength, its sheer technological skill and inventiveness, remained unimpaired in the non-tyre side of the business which flourishes more strongly than ever under the more sinewy management of BTR.

And what of the tyre side of the business? What of the great Fort Dunlop, the pride of the Du Cros', the symbol of Dunlop, and Birmingham's predominance in the happy heydays of the thirties, forties and fifties?

By 1983 the Fort was but a shadow of itself. The main offices had been abandoned except for the computer department. Everyone else had moved into one-storey sheds on the huge site. Morale was abysmal as, one after another, key people quit.

When Sumitomo officially took over on 1 January 1984, Fort Dunlop was divided into three (the sumptuous head offices in London having been sold off). The tripartite division was BTR, SP Tyres – as the Sumitomo ones were called in tribute to a great former Dunlop tyre – and a third part for potential 'new' development.

Gerry Radford, first chief executive, now chairman and managing director under Sumitomo, says the turn-around started almost immediately: 'The shock of the change in ownership acted as a catalyst for change.... The new owners had the necessary finance to invest in the business, as a mixture of loans and capital.'[5]

While the board was split 50-50 between British and Japanese, all the executives remained British. Commented Toshio Takabayashi, director of SP tyres,[6]

> Our style is to take a low profile and let the British management get on with the job. So far it has been very successful. SP Tyres employs 2,600 people in the UK. We now run our operation from Fort Dunlop and have no regrets. We have not had a single grant from the British Government.

Fortunately for Sumitomo they didn't have to pay out any redundancy money either. Dunlop Holdings had done that work for them, so Sumitomo could start with a clean sheet and a sparkling image. Sumitomo assured its customers and staff that the Dunlop name would be retained (SP was a Dunlop brand too). 'This,' says Radford, 'was a major attraction to Sumitomo in buying the company.'

Respect and admiration for the Dunlop name was expressed in a letter to me from Mr Kyohei Yokose, chairman of the Japanese parent company, Sumitomo Rubber Industries.

> In commemoration of this centenary [the invention of the pneumatic tyre] the 13 Dunlop Group companies who are engaged in the manufacture and sale of Dunlop brand tyres throughout the world have executed many events and programmes celebrating this historical year – centenary symbol marks, press conferences, newspaper advertisements, co-operation in the 24-Hours race at Le Mans....
>
> As one of the events of the centenary celebration Sumitomo Rubber searched for descendants of Mr J.B.Dunlop and after much hard work found them. Japanese Television took a film of them and it was shown in Japan.

A poster which Mr Yokose sent me showed the well-known features of J.B.Dunlop which had once so impressed the Nigerians who mistook him for Jesus Christ.

This enthusiasm for the achievements of the past, for continuity and tradition, undoubtedly helped the Japanese owners to established rapport with those who have served Dunlop for many years and whose fathers, and even grandfathers, worked for the company before them.

Constant communication is the order of the day – along with tidiness and cleanliness. Managers talk to their staff and the method of leadership is closely patterned on that employed by Field Marshal Montgomery.

Just as 'Monty' insisted that every rank must be fully informed of the strategic objectives and the means of achieving them, so do

Dunlop Tyres' new owners require the fullest consultations and encourage a two-way flow of ideas from management to shop-floor and back again. Sales and production are integrated and people from the factories go to meet the customers on their premises.

In this Britain has a long way to go to catch up on the parent in Japan. There they have an average of 200 suggestions a year per employee. The rate in the UK is one per employee per year.

Old-style hierarchical differences have gone. Everyone, managing director included, wears the same outfit and goes to the same canteen (there used to be seven – the other six are now devoted to training).

Much emphasis is placed on personal pride in having shiny, bright machinery and ensuring that top-quality products are made on it. Quality control is the most important element in the Japanese liturgy of efficiency. It has paid off. By the end of 1986 the British company had made a pre-tax profit for the first time in thirteen years. By the end of 1987 it made its first post-tax profit for fourteen years. Output has risen by more than 10 per cent a year.

Yet in this success story continuity has also played its part.

Sales and marketing director Greg Wand pointed out that 'we are becoming a lot more efficient at doing short runs to make what the customer wants.'

That very same objective was pursued by Dunlop management as far back as 1978.

Under the much-criticized board of that era – Sir J. Campbell Fraser in the chair – a most ingenious scheme was launched to revolutionize tyre manufacture by miniaturizing the entire process.

Known as ECS, from the initials of its sponsor, the Engineering Consultancy Service, the project was set up, under great secrecy, in Wigan. The concept of a fully automated process for manufacturing conventional tyres with miniaturized equipment belonged to Eric Holroyd, who had been a Dunlop engineer for thirty years. His ECS was treated as a completely autonomous unit, strongly supported by tyre director Colin Hope and managing director Alan Lord.[7]

Along with fellow Dunlop engineer, Geoffrey Morton, Holroyd produced a system that could enable tyre-makers to manufacture, cost-effectively, as few as 10,000 units per week (about *one-sixth* of the normal output of a tyre plant operating in an economical fashion) with a huge saving in energy, manpower and floor space. The system was tailor-made for giving customers what they wanted in the numbers they wished to buy.

Over-capacity had been the bugbear of the European and North American tyre industries for a generation. Now here was Dunlop, the most plagued, debt-ridden and vulnerable of the world's tyre-makers, on the verge of producing a winning combination. The board even sanctioned a purpose-built facility at Bridgend, Wales. No less than £15 million was poured into the project at a time when Dunlop was desperately short of cash. The scheme would have answered the criticisms of such people as sales manager Peter Soddy, who complained that old Dunlop followed the pattern of 'making tyres and then finding out where to sell them, rather than making them with customers in mind'.

A Dunlop spokesman guardedly explained that the Holroyd-Morton process 'involved a major re-think of the compounding process', with a far more efficient blending of compounds than that achievable by conventional methods and consequently much higher quality. Savings of 50 per cent on capital cost and plant maintenance were well within the system's reach, as was a spectacular saving in man-power, for automation and computerization would eliminate whole segments of the work force (a highly attractive feature in days of skill shortage, though not nearly so attractive in the high unemployment days of the mid-eighties).

Then, just as the moment approached for equipping the Bridgend factory, the roof descended on the old Dunlop management. The semi-bid from the Malaysians, the fall of Fraser, and finally the full take-over by BTR and Sumitomo.

What to do with Engineering Consultancy Service and its magic potion? Sumitomo were not anxious to take on additional and indefinite expense. Chairman Yokose confirmed that the acquisition of ECS would have been 'very expensive'. There is also the likelihood that Sumitomo Rubber was working on similar lines. BTR likewise shied away from a leap into unknowable costs – especially given BTR's reluctance to get drawn into any tyre manufacture.

So ECS was sold to Goodyear, the world's No. 1 tyre manufacturer. Even here there is a huge dilemma. As Colin Hope stated to the *European Rubber Journal*: 'You don't really get a great deal of benefit by integrating the modules concept into existing systems ... [you] have to go the whole hog and put down a whole plant.'

Which means you spend millions investing in a system that will render obsolete all the conventional equipment throughout the world, including your own.

Of course, if the method is valid then nothing will stop its progress. The *Dreadnought* rendered other battleships obsolete, and Britain, with far more battleships than anyone else before 1914, had to go ahead and build them. The steel radial tyre revolutionized the life of a tyre and brought headaches to the entire tyre industry. But those who didn't adapt quickly enough to the new reality – including old-style Dunlop – paid a heavy penalty for tardiness.

Be it Goodyear, Sumitomo or whoever, tyre technology will advance apace.

The point of old Dunlop's involvement at the very frontiers of technology, right up to the moment it ceased to be independent, is evidence that the company never lost its appetite for research and development, even while the financial pillars were crumbling.

Continuity is a virtue much prized by the Japanese. They will unquestionably carry on Dunlop's proud tradition, stretching back to the first pneumatic tyre, of promoting invention and innovation.

Indeed just because Sumitomo has been for so long connected with the Dunlop organization it may well be the catalyst for a quantum leap forward in tyre technology, as that occasioned in John Boyd Dunlop's backyard. Then competitors would be faced by a very formidable new Dunlop. That certainly is the view of Sir Campbell Fraser, as he expressed it in *The Economist* of 3 November 1984: 'There must be a chance that Sumitomo will dominate European tyres within a decade, and the Dunlop brand will be its spearhead – not at all what Mr Michelin intended.'

CHAPTER XVIII

CENTENARY PROLOGUE

In business, as in life, change is constant. The old Dunlop died because it failed to differentiate between wise change – adjusting swiftly to the radical challenge of the steel radial tyre – and unwise change – launching into the Pirelli union because 'Europe' was the popular cause of the moment.

So, Dunlop's present situation, split between Sumitomo's world-wide tyre-making business and BTR's control of the rest, may change again. Both Sumitomo Rubber and BTR are dynamic and successful enterprises. Either, or both, may wish to identify more closely with the Dunlop image. They may do so independently, or jointly. That is in the sphere of speculation.

What is certain is that both groups have high admiration for the name Dunlop. For millions it has a magic ring.

Motor racing enthusiasts recall the famous Dunlop bridges at international tracks and rejoice to see the Dunlop name featuring prominently again at meetings like Le Mans. Dunlop sportswear has a massive following round the globe and there is a deal of affection for the solid, dependable characteristics so well portrayed in the benign features of that solid, dependable Victorian, John Boyd Dunlop.

The Japanese recognize this. So do the Australians. Dunlop Pacific is making great preparations to celebrate the centenary of Dunlop's establishment in the Antipodes in 1892. North America likewise exploits the Dunlop tradition and treasures the memory of a great institution. The same applies to Southern Africa.

Dunlop is held in higher esteem overseas than in its own homeland. This is probably so because, in its later years, old Dunlop became associated in the public mind with stick-in-the-mud policies and too-close association with cosy corporatism and 'establishment' prejudices.

Throughout this book I have constantly emphasized the extraordinary degree to which Dunlop has mirrored the national mood: the gifted Victorian amateur inventor almost accidentally creating a huge new industry; the racy, corner-cutting Edwardian adventuring of the du Cros clan, followed by dedicated war service. The recovery of the twenties and the expansion of the thirties based upon dominance of the market which encouraged, rather than precluded, a spirit of non-competitiveness in tyre manufacture and distribution. The war once more, with Dunlop exactly reflecting the 'right spirit' of national service. Similarly, in the immediate post-World War II period of austerity, the company did its duty by purchasing cotton at the government's request and doing everything required of it 'in the national interest'.

In the sixties and seventies Dunlop tried too hard to keep pace with fashionable nostrums. It was almost as if the old boy was a bit too eager to ape current fashion, from social audits to 'going European'. Finally, in 1979 came a decisive break. For the first time, Dunlop ceased to mirror the national mood as expressed and personified in the new prime minister, Margaret Thatcher.

Some aspects of Dunlop doubtless evoked admiration in the premier. Its family atmosphere, its record of patriotic endeavour, its technical skills and triumphs. But other aspects, the huge and increasing load of debt to the banks, the readiness with which Dunlop acceded to price and wage control, the devotion to corporatism as evidenced by Dunlop executives cutting a dash in the CBI, Neddy and other such establishment platforms, doubtless dismayed her.

In 1977 while Dunlop loyally collaborated with Mr Callaghan's socialist government (a government which was about to extend the State's grip on the economy still further by nationalizing the shipbuilding and aerospace industries), Mrs Thatcher gave a speech to the Zurich Economic Society. In it she vouchsafed her views on what should be done. More significantly perhaps, she articulated the sea-change in public opinion in Britain; a sea-change of which Dunlop appeared to be blissfully unaware.

> Where the State is too powerful, efficiency suffers ... Britain in the last two or three years [the Wilson-Callaghan administrations of 1974–77] provides a case-study of why collectivism will not work ... our ills are creating their own antibodies.... The younger generation produces large numbers of young people for whom the post-war settlement has failed and who are ready to examine our [free enterprise] arguments on their merits.

This was a declaration of war on the consensus politics which had ruled Britain for twenty years, the so-called 'Butskellism' (a combination of Conservative Rab Butler's name and that of Hugh Gaitskell's, the socialist leader) which Margaret Thatcher and the other radical Tories blamed for Britain's remorseless downward spiral.

Mrs Thatcher's economic 'guru' of that period was Sir Keith Joseph. He was later to expand on her attitude towards government-business relations.

> She saw Britain's economic decline partly stemming from successive governments which by increasing money supply kept on rescuing managements from having to become more competitive ... which enabled our competitors to soar past us in competitiveness, in prosperity, in social services, in standard of living and in purchasing power for all their people. She saw financial slackness as infecting management and making it flabby.[1]

These last words are the commonest criticism of the Dunlop management towards the close of its independent life. But the fault certainly does not lie with Dunlop alone, nor was it the only British business which had come to rely excessively on government and passively to accept the corporatism of the era.

Not since Churchill's administration of the early fifties had a Conservative government reversed any of the socialists' nationalisation measures. Not since 1957 had any Tory government tried to reduce the money supply to bring it into line with production increases. 'Consensus' was that the mixed economy – with the 'mix' becoming steadily more statist as industry after industry was nationalized – could best be sustained through controls on prices, established either by self-regulating methods (resale price maintenance), or by direct government command (prices and incomes board and exchange control).

For two generations Dunlop had absorbed this system, and for much of the period had flourished under it. Now the system was about to be blown apart. The old Dunlop succumbed. The new Dunlop(s) are sure to thrive because the more invigorating economic climate of Britain in the eighties and nineties suits the competitive mood of BTR and Sumitomo.

After a decade of the Thatcherite revolution, Dunlop, in its centenary year, can look ahead to a brightening future.

The name lives on. The skill endures. The spirit is quickening.

For Dunlop, the centenary marks not an epilogue, but a prologue.

NOTES

Chapter I

1 Eric Tompkins, *History of the Pneumatic Tyre* (Dunlop Archive Project, 1981)
2 Sir Arthur du Cros, *Wheels of Fortune* (Chapman and Hall, 1938)
3 Letter to the Pneumatic Tyre Company secretary, dated 11 September 1890. The letter was kept secret and not minuted.
4 *Inside Asquith's Cabinet: from the Diaries of Charles Hobhouse* (1893–8, 1904–15), ed. by Edward David (John Murray, 1977)
5 Du Cros, *Wheels of Fortune*

Chapter II

1 Tompkins, *History of the Pneumatic Tyre*

Chapter III

1 The following information on early Australian motoring is taken from Keith Winser, *Dunlop: The First Hundred Years in Australia* and his *Story of Australian Motoring* (both books in preparation).

Chapter IV

1 Others said the name was due to a mishearing of 'Port Dunlop', which bargees called out on nearing the company's Birmingham HQ.

Chapter V

1 Thomas Hancock, *The Origin and Progress of the Caoutchouc or India-Rubber Manufacture in England* (1856, reprinted 1920)
2 Winston Churchill, *The World Crisis, 1911–18* (Macmillan, 1939)
3 A. J. Sylvester *Life with Lloyd George: Diary 1931–45* ed. by C. Cross (1975)
4 Trevor Royle, *The Kitchener Enigma* (Michael Joseph, 1985)
5 David Lloyd George, *War Memoirs*, Vol. IV (1936)
6 Keith Grieves, book on life of Eric Geddes, in preparation.

Chapter VI

1 John Scott, *Legibus: History of Clifford-Turner* (King, Thorne and Stace, 1980)

2 Letter from Sir Harry McGowan to Company Secretary Bergin, 31 July 1919

Chapter VII

1 See Geoffrey Jones, 'Growth Performance of British multinational firms before 1939 ; The case of Dunlop' in *Economic History Review*, 2nd series, p. 984.
2 Charles Tennyson, *Stars and Markets* (Chatto and Windus, 1957)
3 Patrick Hastings, *Cases in Court* (Heinemann, 1949)

Chapter VIII

1 Much of the material in this chapter comes from Sir Ronald Storrs' study *Dunlop in War* (Hutchinson, 1946), the contemporary press and *Tyres and the War* (T.M.P., 1946).
2 A cynical remark common at the time when President Roosevelt was calling on neutral America to give Britain 'all aid short of war' was that Britain was getting 'all aid short of help'.

Chapter IX

1 Eventually *four times* as long, 50,000 miles against the conventional 12,000 miles

Chapter XI

1 See Peter Grosvenor and James McMillan *British Genius* (Dent, 1973)
2 From the author's *American Take Over* (Frewin, 1967)
3 Dunlop Archive Journal
4 Paul Jennings, *Dunlopera* (privately published by Dunlop in 1961)
5 From an interview in the *Birmingham Post*, February 1983

Chapter XII

1 But not for Geddes. In a paper called 'The European Dimension' he dismissed the CAP obstacle : 'The net cost of CAP, spread over a proper transition period, will not be as harmful as the critics claim. A small increase in economic growth would pay for it.'
2 For the following description and much else concerning tyre development I am deeply indebted to Eric Tompkins's *History of the Pneumatic Tyre*.

Chapter XIII

1 In a paper, 'An Approach to the Philosophy of Company Law', March 1967

Chapter XIV

1 Address delivered to the British Institute of Management, July 1968
2 From *Fortune Magazine*, September 1968

3 Christopher Tugendhat, *The Multinationals* (Eyre and Spottiswoode, 1971)
4 Fraser disputes this. He recalls that the first indications of Pirelli's declining fortunes came later.
5 Interview with the author on 7 July 1988
6 Theoretically there was – if one or other country went communist! In the seventies that was not an impossible eventuality in Italy.

Chapter XV

1 Also beyond that of a good many men, including this author.
2 Reproduced in Eric Tompkins, *History of the Pneumatic Tyre*
3 Author's interview, October 1988
4 Author's interviews with Lord and Fraser in September 1988
5 Fraser points out that his planned pay rise had actually fallen due to loss of income from Pirelli. He accepts that, as chairman, he was ultimately responsible for what happened, although he says much had been done to put things right – for which others would reap the benefit.

Chapter XVI

1 Author's interview, October 1988
2 In an article prepared for *The Director* magazine
3 Sir Michael Edwardes, *Back from the Brink: An Apocalyptic Experience* (Collins 1983)

Chapter XVII

1 5 April 1988
2 Conversations in September 1988
3 I am indebted to Findlay Picken, former head of Dunlop Sports, and Mr Jim Whyte, senior lecturer in marketing at Edinburgh University, for this information
4 From an article by J.Whyte in *Plastics and Rubber Processing and Applications* Vol. V, No. 1 (1985)
5 Interview in article by Clutterbuck Associates in *The Director*
6 *The Pony Telegraph*, 20 September 1988
7 As disclosed by Lord and fully explained in a special issue of the *European Rubber Journal* (1986)

Chapter XVIII

1 Radio interview, 19 May 1985

INDEX